Women in the Middle:
Their Parent-Care Years

Elaine M. Brody

SPRINGER PUBLISHING COMPANY
New York

Springer Publishing Company, Inc.
536 Broadway
New York, NY 10012

90 91 92 93 94 / 5 4 3 2 1

ISBN 0-8261-6380-7

Printed in the United States of America

This book is dedicated to
my beloved sister

Corinne J. Weithorn
February 28, 1929–October 16, 1987

One of the best people who ever lived,
her love, generosity, and wit enriched
my life and the lives of all who knew her.

Contents

Acknowledgment

Professor Stanley "Steve" J. Brody, who for 46 years has been my colleague and mentor as well as my husband, is first among the people to whom I am indebted. He patiently read this book chapter by chapter, criticized it (sometimes sharply, but always constructively), and made many helpful suggestions. Parts of the book were also read by my friend Professor Bess Dana, whose perceptive comments are deeply appreciated. The shortcomings and flaws of the book, of course, are mine, not theirs.

Dr. M. Powell Lawton, Director of The Gerontological Research Institute at the Philadelphia Geriatric Center, is the quintessential research gerontologist. With the generosity that is his trademark, he stimulated my interest in research and has inspired and instructed me for a quarter of a century.

Research is always a collaborative enterprise, and I have been remarkably fortunate in my collaborators. Dr. Morton H. Kleban has been my partner in all of the major research studies we conducted. In addition to lending me his superb skills in design and data analysis, he has coauthored many papers and has been my faithful friend. It is impossible to name all of the other colleagues who participated directly in the research endeavor as fellow investigators, project directors and managers, and research associates, or all of the colleagues who engaged in rewarding exchanges of ideas. Among them are Steve Albert, Marc C. Fulcomer, Christine Hoffman, Pauline T. Johnson, Abigail Lang, Sandra Litvin, Miriam Moss, Patricia Parmelee, Rachel Pruchno, Robert Rubinstein, Avalie R. Saperstein, Claire B. Schoonover, Abigail Spector, and Sandra Tannenbaum. Dozens of enthusiastic interviewers collected the quantitative data. Jeanette Putman-Dickerson and Catharine Toso did the sensitive interviewing of the parent-caring women who participated in the qualitative studies. I am grateful, too, to the many gerontologists elsewhere, too numerous to identify, whose work informed my own.

Closest to me in the production of this book has been Anita Roffman.

Apart from being a supersecretary, she has given me friendship, patience, and support that cannot be measured, as well as an intelligent comprehension of what I was trying to say.

Indebtedness of a different order is owed to Arthur Waldman, the first Executive Vice President of the Philadelphia Geriatric Center who initiated research in that service organization; Bernard Liebowitz, the current Executive Vice President; Frank Podietz, Director of Operations; and Lawrence Cohen, Administrator of the York Houses. They created a climate in which research flourished and the knowledge gained was translated into services and facilities for the older people and families for whom the center cares.

The funding that made my research possible came primarily from the National Institute of Mental Health, which financed almost all of the large studies. The understanding and consultation of Dr. Barry Lebowitz (Chief, Center for Studies of Mental Health and the Aging) and his predecessor, Dr. Gene Cohen, before and during the studies was critical to those efforts. Those federally funded surveys were supplemented by grants from The Frederick and Amelia Schimper Foundation of New York, which supported the in-depth interviews from which most of the case studies in the book were developed.

My loving thanks go to members of my immediate family for their steadfast loyalty, support, and encouragement—my husband, of course; my children, Dr. Peter R. and Ms. Debra Brody, and Ms. Laurel A. and Dr. Robert Karpman; and their children, Hannah and Jodi Karpman, and Jocelyn and Rachel Brody.

Finally, my most profound gratitude goes to the women in the middle who candidly and generously shared their experiences and deepest feelings with us. Their names and all other identifying characteristics have been changed, but their words have not. I will have accomplished my goal if this book helps them and their families and others like them.

Introduction

It took me 5 years to get my master's degree to prepare for working when I reached the "empty nest" stage of life. But last year, my mother left the stove on and started a fire. She has been getting more and more forgetful and confused and can't be alone at all. I'm depressed, and I don't sleep well. How can I go to work when she needs constant supervision?

***

Mom moved in with us because she had a bad stroke. Our whole lives are disrupted. She criticizes my 15-year-old son for the way he dresses and makes my 17-year-old daughter and her friends turn off the music. The kids and my husband complain, and I'm caught in the middle. I have to be the peacemaker and keep them all happy.

***

My two brothers and I are attorneys. When our mother, who lives in Florida, fractured a hip, everyone assumed that I would fly down and stay for a while. My brothers are good sons, but my suggestion that we take turns met with surprise. They said they had "to earn a living." And do you know something? I can't figure out why, but I do it. I don't know how long I can keep up this juggling act.

***

I'm divorced and work as a secretary to earn a living. My 90-year-old mother has rheumatoid arthritis and has to be lifted. I had to place her in a nursing home, but I felt terribly guilty. Now I'm in terrible conflict. My son and his wife are pressuring me to move near them, 3,000 miles away. I'm 64, and that's all I have to look forward to. But I can't move my mother now, and I can't leave her here alone. My visits are all she has.

***

I retired after teaching for 30 years, and my husband is tapering off his medical practice. We thought we'd travel a bit at this stage of our lives. Money doesn't seem to solve the problem of my 89-year-old mother-in-law. She has three shifts of nurses, but we can't even get away for a vacation. If a nurse doesn't turn up, I have to fill in and spend hours trying to get another. On top of that, our daughter is getting a divorce and she and her 2-year-old have come back to live with us.

Those are the voices of just a few of the millions of women who are in similar situations. They are daughters and daughters-in-law who come from a range of economic, social, and ethnic backgrounds and have different combinations of personal circumstances. They may be 30 or 50 or 70 years old. Some are married; others are widowed, divorced, or have never married. Some are homemakers, some have worked all of their adult lives, and others are part of the huge number who have recently entered or plan to enter the labor force. Whatever their individual situations, what they in common is that they are taking care of disabled older people in their families, have many other roles and responsibilities, and are feeling the pressure and strains.

My interest in such women began in the 1950s, when my work at the Philadelphia Geriatric Center involved interviewing older people who were applying for admission to the Center's home for the aged. Those who had daughters were almost invariably accompanied by an adult daughter in middle age; those who did not were accompanied by a son and usually by his wife as well. Virtually all of the adult children were deeply, painfully disturbed by the need to place a parent in an institution. Most of them had been caring for the elderly person devotedly for long periods of time, and most had been doing so with enormous difficulty. Some had taken the parent into their own homes with all the disruption that entails. In many instances, the event that finally precipitated the application to our institution was something that happened in the caregiver's family, such as her own or her husband's illness, her husband's death, or problems with one of her own children.

Despite the loyalty to their parents and parents-in-law that these women had amply demonstrated, despite the reality factors that made it impossible for them to go on doing the day-to-day hands-on tasks of parent caring, they felt guilty, conflicted, and even ashamed. Deeply ingrained values—personal and societal—emphasize that taking care of a parent is a daughter's responsibility. When the women could no longer do so, they felt that somehow they had failed to fulfill that responsibility and had failed the parent. They suffered intensely and felt that they were doing something wrong. After all, the widespread myth tells us, "Nowadays families don't take care of their elderly parents as they used to in the good old days," and women see themselves as the ones in the family whose job it is to provide the care. That myth has not died, but it certainly did not check out with my own experience.

I was, of course, seeing the women when they had reached the point of no return after enduring many hard years of parent care. It was obvious that their experiences had taken a toll on their emotional and physical well-being and that their families had been affected as well. I had many concerns and questions. What had those years been like? What roads had the women travelled along the way to our nursing home? How had their lives been affected? What were the compelling forces at work that had made them wait so long before considering placement? How could they be helped?

My conversations with those women changed the course of my own life. They set in motion the research studies I then carried out that focused on the problems and dilemmas being experienced by women who had not yet reached the doors of nursing homes. That preoccupation has never left me and is the reason for this book.

I have characterized such women as "women in the middle." They are the adult daughters and daughters-in-law who become the primary providers of care when their parents and parents-in-law become old and need someone on whom to rely. Daughters predominate as the ones in the family who provide dependent older people with emotional support and with assistance in tasks ranging from shopping and transportation to personal care such as bathing and dressing. Not all older people have daughters or have daughters who live close by, however. It is then that daughters-in-law often fill that caregiving gap. Some of the women have many long parent-care years that include care to several older people in their families simultaneously or sequentially.

These middle generation women are in the middle because, in addition to parent care, many of them have multiple roles and responsibilities that compete for their time and energy. Some are also in the middle in being pulled by the claims of potentially conflicting values. On the one hand, they subscribe strongly to the powerful traditional value that care of the elderly is *their* responsibility. On the other, they feel the pressure of the new value: that it is permissible, even desirable (and often necessary), for women to work outside of the home. And they are in the middle from an emotional standpoint when interpersonal problems erupt between elderly parents and other family members.

The leaders of the Women's Movement have expressed deep concern about what they call the "fallout" of the movement on young women who try to be Superwomen and "have it all." There has been an outpouring of articles in the professional literature and the media about the young women who are suffering from what sociologists call "role overload"—stress that derives from the difficulties of juggling a career, marriage, and raising young children. According to professionals, such demands often leave young women guilty, exhausted, and without free time; confused about self-identity and self-esteem; and unable to coordinate career and family timetables. Abundant newspaper and magazine articles describe the strains, conflict, confusion, and ambivalence of women who are under constant pressure in trying to manage home, family, and job.

The predicament of such young women is deserving of all the concern and attention it receives. But if young women are not "Superwomen," neither are middle-aged and aging women. They too suffer from "overload" and guilt about not being able to do it all. And many of them have additional problems associated with those stages of life. In the main, however, the situation of parent-caring women only recently has begun to claim a share of attention.

People nowadays are much more aware of parent care and its problems, for reasons that will be described in this book. More women are taking care of more parents and parents-in-law, and more are in the middle than ever before in history. Their reluctance to place a disabled elderly family member in a nursing home has not diminished. And the strains and even suffering they increasingly experience during the caregiving process have not been alleviated. Since most people nowadays are confronted with the need to help a parent or parent-in-law at some time in the course of their lives, the topic of parent care ultimately concerns almost all of us who have had, now have, or may in the future have an elderly parent, and all of us who have children and hope to grow old ourselves.

This book focuses directly on the women themselves and tells about parent care from their perspective. It is not a "self-help" book; it does not instruct daughters and daughters-in-law about methods and techniques of providing care for older people. Rather, the feelings, experiences, and problems of parent-caring women themselves will be described, as will the effects upon their mental and physical well-being, lifestyles, and family relationships. The subject is important not only to the women themselves, but to all members of their families. It is for that reason that I want to share my experiences with other workers in the field. Professionals, educators, researchers, and policy-makers must understand the problems so that a situation that has been unrecognized and unattended too long can be alleviated.

Much of the book draws heavily on my own work, with the content deriving from several sources. First, as a social worker, during the first two decades of my 35 working years, I interviewed upwards of 2,000 older people and their families; as Director of the Department of Human Services at the Philadelphia Geriatric Center, I read countless additional case records written by my staff. Second, seven of my large research studies focused directly on issues relevant to this book, with the data collected by means of interviews with approximately 1,500 women, 300 of their husbands, and 150 of their siblings. Five of those projects were funded by the National Institute of Mental Health (NIMH) and two by the Administration on Aging. Those studies explored women's changing roles as they affect care of the elderly and the women-in-the-middle themselves, the effects on the well-being of daughter caregivers when they are in the labor force, the effects on the husbands of the caregiving daughters, adult sibling relationships during the parent care years, and the effects on family members of having a depressed older person in a nursing home. A demonstration project of respite services for family care-givers of patients with Alzheimer's disease was funded by the John A. Hartford Foundation of New York. Two additional NIMH-financed studies now underway are examining parent-care issues that relate to women's various marital statuses and the effects on adult children of having a parent in a nursing home. The third source of information was made possible by grants from the Frederick and Amelia Schimper Foundation of New York that allowed tape-recorded, in-depth interviews to be conducted with 62 caregiving daughters and daughters-in-law. All of the case studies and case excerpts throughout the book were developed by means of the Schimper grants and the preliminary phases of the NIMH marital status study.

The four chapters in Part I present data relevant to the widespread women-in-the-middle phenomenon. Chapter 1 describes the powerful demographic and socioeconomic trends that account for millions of women being in that position. Chapter 2 answers other questions: How many older people need help? What is the nature of the assistance they need? Who provides that help? Chapter 3 contains information derived from quantitative research about the effects of parent care on women and the particular "external" or objective factors that produce or mitigate their strains. Chapter 4 examines one of the explanations for the caregiving behavior of women and the stress they experience—specifically, the tension between the different values they hold. Some of those values compete and therefore are part of the emotional soil from which the women's problems spring.

Part II (Chapters 5–12) looks closely at the women who appeared as statistics in Part I. It explores the "internals" of caregiving—the inner experiences of daughters and daughters-in-law, and the effects on their lives and family relationships.

Chapter 5 introduces the subject of the major inner themes caregiving women experience and presents data that are the rationale for grouping the women in accordance with their marital and family status in subsequent chapters. The most fundamental and pervasive themes are explored in Chapters 6 and 7. Those themes speak to daughters' feelings of being responsible for providing parent care and their experiences in doing so. Chapter 8 focuses on the reasons (especially the psychological reasons) why a particular adult child in the family becomes the one to be the main caregiver to a parent and remains in that role. In that chapter, the other adult siblings appear as well, including their perceptions of the care situations and the effects they experience during the caregiving years.

Subsequent chapters in Part II discuss additional themes that relate to daughters' and daughters-in-laws' subjective caregiving experiences. These chapters include 24 case studies. Because their own family status is so central to the ways in which caregiving affects their lives, this group of chapters is organized in accordance with the women's family status. There are chapters about married daughters and their husbands and children (Chapter 9), and those who are not married but are widowed, divorced, or have never married (Chapter 10). We meet daughters who have rich family networks and those who are relatively alone in caregiving either because they are only children or their sibling(s) have died. There are daughters who are completely alone because they are only children and have no husbands or children.

Though many aspects of caring for older people are similar for daughters and daughters-in-law, there are also striking differences in their subjective experiences. Chapter 11, therefore, is about daughters-in-law who become caregivers. Part II ends with Chapter 12, a commentary on the case studies.

Part III is about two matters that are of major importance to filial caregivers. Chapter 13 provides information about the effects of parent care on women who are employed and on those who do not work outside the home. The interplay between responsibilities to jobs and parents is examined. Since the business world is now aware of the predicament of many of its employees, its relevant activities are described.

Chapter 14 concerns the most painful decision of all—the decision some children must make to place the parent in a nursing home. Information will be presented about the conditions that lead to such placement, the special needs and characteristics of the elderly people concerned, and the effects on their family caregivers during and after nursing home placement.

The book concludes with Chapter 15, which summarizes the major issues that were discussed and identifies some of the unfinished agendas with regard to women in the middle. Policy-makers, professionals, researchers, women in the middle themselves, and men have unfinished business about parent care.

Through the years, I have been acutely aware of the older people for whom their children and children-in-law are providing care. They are the other side of the caregiving equation. The voices of older people are not heard in this book. Their feelings and experiences are not described, but the reader is asked to keep them in mind. The disabled aged undergo painful losses of independence and function, they often lose their homes and possessions, and, most poignant of all, they lose people they love. What are *their* inner experiences when they need to depend on others, when they are aware of the disruptions their dependency occasions in the lives of their families, when they become "guests" (welcome or unwelcome) in the homes of their children or residents in nursing homes? Having worked with such older people for 35 years at the Philadelphia Geriatric Center, I know that their well-being is interlocked with the well-being of their family members. I hope very much that the book will be of some value in helping not only present and future women in the middle but that it ultimately will help the aged themselves (some of them, in their time, have been women in the middle), the men in the family whose lives also are profoundly affected, and society as a whole.

Part I

Background

Chapter 1

Women in the Middle:
How it Happened

In a situation unprecedented in history, millions of women in this country and in other nations are confronted with the need to help their disabled elderly parents, parents-in-law, and other elderly relatives. These filial caregivers are often under severe strain because of their multiple responsibilities. In addition to their traditional family roles as wives, homemakers, mothers, and grandmothers, many women nowadays assume the role of caregiver to the vastly increased number of older people who need help. Yet still another role has been added for those women who have entered or reentered the labor force.

Whether or not they work outside of their homes, the dilemma of these women lies in trying to fulfill all of their roles—to respond to the competing demands and to sort out their priorities. Some of them suffer intensely and are bewildered by the situations in which they find themselves. The pressures they experience come not only from the multiple claims on their time and energy, but from the emotional aspects of their situations. There is a negative impact on the health and financial status of some of these women, but the most severe and pervasive effects are emotional strains such as anxiety, depression, frustration, conflict, anger, feelings of guilt about not being able to "do it all," and stress from trying to do so. (These effects are discussed in detail in Chapter 3.)

Such women have been characterized as "women-in-the-middle" (Brody, 1981):

- They are most often in their middle years, though they range in age from their twenties to their seventies.
- They are, in the main, a middle generation in three- or four-generation families.

- They are caught in the middle of the requirements of their various roles.
- Many are in the middle between conflicting values: the powerful, deeply rooted traditional value that care of older people in the family is *their* responsibility, and the newer value that it is all right—even desirable—for women to work or to pursue other interests outside the home.
- Some are in the middle emotionally when the elderly people they are helping become rivals for their attention with their husbands and children.

The phrase "woman in the middle" is, of course, a metaphor for all family members who find themselves in that position—the husbands and wives of the disabled elderly, their sons and daughters, children-in-law, grandchildren, and, at times, even other relatives. And, because problems affecting one family member inevitably affect the others, the entire family is often in the middle. Research evidence shows clearly, however, that the vast majority of care-givers to the old are women—primarily wives and daughters, but also daughters-in-law and other female relatives. Daughters are the largest group of women-in-the-middle; they provide even more of the needed long-term care services than do elderly people's spouses (U.S. Department of Labor, 1986).

The predicament of those who care for the elderly is a salient personal issue. It is also an issue of major importance for older people themselves, for the entire family, and for society as a whole. The capacity of close family members, called the "informal" support system, to provide the required assistance determines what services and supports should be provided or financed by what is called the "formal" support system of government and social agencies. As this book is being written, government's role in long-term care is being hotly debated. Bills are being introduced in the Congress, and many major proposals concern the question of what kinds of care should be provided and how it is to be financed.

Women in the middle are extremely diverse not only in age but also in their stages of life, ranging from those with young children to those who are old themselves. They vary in their economic situations, social, and ethnic backgrounds, and in marital and family status. They have different personalities, adaptive capacities, and combinations of personal circumstances. The quality of their relationships with their parents varies widely. The nature and amount of assistance they provide varies in accordance with the older people's functional capacities and cognitive status. Some of the women have lived "traditional" lives as homemakers. Most are in the labor force, and many do volunteer work. Some women worked when they were young and gave up their jobs for marriage and motherhood, whereas others have worked all of their adult lives. Some move in and out of the work force as their own and their families' needs dictate. Still others are part of the huge number who have recently entered or reentered the labor force or wish to do so. Many women work because they and their families need the money for day-to-day expenses or to send children to college, for example. Others work because of commitment to careers, and still others because their jobs give them various kinds of satisfaction. Most work because of combinations of such reasons.

The problems of parent caring women have been virtually ignored until very recently:

- Publicity about women who work usually focuses on young women—their achievement of advanced educational levels, their entry into occupations formerly considered the domain of men, and their rise up the corporate ladder. Both the professional literature and the media reflect concern with the effects of women's working on their marital relationships, on the emotional development of their young children, and on the young women themselves.
- Social policy has tended to take the position that caring for the aged should be solely a family responsibility. In that context, since "family" is a euphemism for women, women are expected to be the caregivers, and services to help them to do the caregiving are grossly underdeveloped.
- The Women's Movement, preoccupied largely with the problems of younger women, has devoted its efforts to matters such as eliminating sex discrimination in educational institutions and in the work place, the abortion issue, and the provision of services such as day care for children. In general, it has not given a high priority to the problems of the elder-caring middle generations.
- The helping professions—medicine, psychiatry, social work, and psychology—have been moving rapidly in recent years to develop information about the elderly and the processes of aging. A growing number of professionals are focusing their interests and efforts on the aged. This is a highly desirable trend, of course. But the family caregivers are too often ignored or viewed as people to be instructed in how to implement professional recommendations for the older people and trained in their care. The caregivers' strains, if attended to at all, are regarded as deriving only from their personal, intrapsychic, or interpersonal problems.

The pressures experienced by women in the middle are exacerbated by misconceptions concerning the behavior of the modern family with respect to caring for its dependent older members. A persistent myth adds to these

women's problems—specifically, the widespread misconception that, nowadays, adult children do not take care of their elderly parents the way they
used to in the "good old days." Despite a massive and consistent body of
evidence to the contrary, that myth stubbornly refuses to be dispelled in
popular belief. It is ironic that many of the parent caring women themselves
believe that myth of the "good old days" even though they do much more
parent care than their counterparts in the past.

Whatever their individual situations, what parent-caring* women have
in common is that they are feeling the stunning impact of massive demographic and socioeconomic trends that have converged to place them in
the middle. Those trends have made "nowadays" very different from the
so-called good old days. Two of the trends are demographic—the vast
increase in the aging population and the falling birth rate. A third trend is
the increasing need for older people to have help in their daily lives. A
fourth is socioeconomic—the large-scale entry of women into the work
place. Still other influential trends are the changing patterns of marriage and
childbearing. Those trends will be described in order to explain how the
situations of women in the middle came about and are being affected.

DEMOGRAPHIC TRENDS

In the current climate in which care of old people has become a major focus
of interest for researchers and professionals as well as an important social
issue, it is well to remember that prior to the 1960s there was virtually no
interest at all in that subject. A major factor stimulating interest in the
families of older people was, of course, the emergence and growing visibility
of a large aging population.

The rise in the number and proportion of older people in our population
has been one of the most dramatic and influential developments of the 20th
century. The number of people 65 years of age and over has grown rapidly
and steadily in proportion to the number who are under the age of 65. (For
excellent descriptions of demographic developments, see Taeuber, 1983,
and U.S. Bureau of the Census, 1984.) At the turn of the century, there were
3.1 million older people, representing 4% of the population. In a fivefold
increase, by 1960 there were 16.6 million older people (9.2% of the population), and by 1985 there were 28.6 million. By 1987, there were more than
30 million older people—12.4% of the population, or nearly one in eight of
all citizens of the United States.

That demographic revolution was brought about by public health measures, improved welfare programs, better nutrition, antibiotics, and dis-

*In this book, the phrase "parent care" often refers to parent-in-law care as well.

coveries of ways to prevent the great epidemic diseases such as cholera, smallpox, diphtheria, and poliomyelitis. As a result, more people have been able to survive because such illnesses used to prevent them from ever reaching old age. It gives one perspective to realize that in ancient Greece, life expectancy at birth was only 21 years; it took 2,000 years to increase life expectancy to 49 years by 1900. Only 80 years later, a new baby could expect to live to 74 years of age—a jump of 25 years—and more than three-fourths of those newborns could expect to reach that age. The trend will continue. The number of elderly is projected to increase to 39.2 million (13% of the total U.S. population) by the year 2010, to 64.6 million by 2030 (21%), and to 67.4 million in 2050 (22%).

Another aspect of the demographic revolution affected the issue of filial care even more directly. In the past 20 years, the number and proportion of *very* old people has increased more rapidly than the older population in general. This came about because of hi-tech medicine, coupled with Medicare (1965), which made such medical care available to older people. Together, hi-tech medicine and Medicare account for the fact that the number and proportion of people 75 and over, particularly those 85 and over, have grown and will continue to grow more rapidly than the older population as a whole. At present, approximately 40% of all people 65 years of age or over, are 75 and over, and that proportion will increase. Men and women who reach the age of 65 can expect to live 14.6 and 18.6 more years, respectively. Because of the differences in life expectancy and because men tend to marry women younger than they are, wives are more likely than husbands to care for disabled spouses. (The ratio of men to women rises from 83 to 100 at age 65–69, and 40 to 100 at age 85 and over.)

In the future, most of the growth in the older population will occur among those who are 80 years of age and older. By the year 2010, the 80-plus group will increase by 5.9 million, whereas the 65–79 group will increase by 4.7 million. (Tables 1.1 and 1.2 display the projections of the increases in the elderly population.) As for the very, very old, it is startling to realize that in 1980, there were 13,000 centenarians, but by the year 2000 there will be 100,000 such people and before the middle of the next century there will be a million people 100 years of age or older!

The result of these radical changes will be a continuing increase in the need for filial care, since it is the very old who are the ones most vulnerable to the chronic illnesses that lead to disability and dependence on others for care (see Chapter 2.) In addition, rates of widowhood soar as people move toward advanced old age, so that fewer of the very old have a surviving spouse on whom to depend. When a spouse is present, he or she is also likely to be in advanced old age, to have health problems and be less able to provide care, and, therefore, to be more dependent on adult children for help in doing so.

TABLE 1.1. Projected distribution of the elderly population by age (1985–2050)[a]

Numbers show percent distribution

Age group	Year			
	1985	2010	2035	2050
66 to 69	32.2	29.9	24.0	24.6
70 to 74	26.6	21.8	24.3	20.0
75 to 79	19.6	17.4	21.0	17.1
80 to 84	12.2	14.0	14.8	14.5
85 and over	9.4	16.9	16.0	23.7
Total	100.0	100.0	100.0[a]	100.0[a]

[a]Total does not add to 100 due to rounding.
Source: Computed from Bureau of the Census Publication Series P-25, No. 952, 1984.

TABLE 1.2. Projected increases in the elderly population by age (1985–2050)[a]

In millions of people

Age group	Year		
	1985-2010	2010-2035	2035-2050
65 to 69	2.5	4.3	0.6
70 to 74	1.0	7.6	−2.7
75 to 79	1.2	7.2	−2.5
80 to 84	2.0	4.4	−0.1
85 and over	3.9	4.1	5.3
Total elderly	10.6	27.6	0.6

Source: Computed from Bureau of the Census Publication Series P-25, No. 952, 1984.

Thus, demographic trends that have been called the "greying of America" have had and will continue to have a direct impact on the demand for parent care.

While that powerful trend was occurring, another major and influential demographic trend was also taking place. As the aging population increased, fertility rates declined. The falling birth rate (a trend that also is continuing) made even more pronounced the alteration in the ratio between the old and the younger generations.

Birth rates fell steadily between the year 1800 and the late 1930s, when a new low was reached (Uhlenberg, 1974); the average number of children born to a mother surviving to at least the age of 40 declined from eight children to fewer than three. This decline accounts in part for the *proportionate* growth of older people in the population. In just 50 years, between 1931 and 1981, the percentage of women who had borne four or more children dropped from 47.1% to 25.5% (Heuser, 1976). Between 1967 and 1979, lifetime birth expectations for married women in the main childbearing years of ages 18 to 34 decreased from 3.1 births to 2.2 births (U.S. Department of Commerce, 1982). In other words, a woman who is now very old—that is, 80 years old or more—has many fewer children than her mother did when the latter was old. A shorter period of parent care was needed then since the mother was more likely to die at a younger age and as a result of an acute, short-term illness.

The net result is that older people nowadays have many fewer adult children who can share the responsibilities of parent care. That is, the pool of children on whom they can rely is much smaller now than used to be the case. Fewer children means fewer daughters. And since many women are daughters-in-law as well as daughters, the chances of being called upon for parent or parent-in-law care, or both, increase greatly. It is sobering to realize that in 1975 only 60% of older people had at least one daughter, but only two-thirds of those people—that is, 40% of all older people—had a frequently seen or nearby daughter (Soldo, 1982a).

Those trends—the increase in the elderly population and low fertility rates—have radically altered the structure of the family and the conformation of the family tree. The four-generation family has become commonplace rather than a rare phenomenon, a change that affects all generations. As recently as 25 years ago, a major scientific conference was called to consider the implications of the fact that the *three*-generation family had become so common (Shanas & Streib, 1965). At the very time that the social scientists were deliberating, however, Shanas and her colleagues were conducting a major cross-national study that would show that 40% of older people with children had great-grandchildren (Shanas et al., 1968)! By the 1980s, the four-generation family had become even more commonplace; approximately half of all people 65 and older have great-grandchildren (National Institute on Aging, 1982), and five-generation families are no longer rare!

It is instructive to look at the new family tree from the perspective of the younger generations. At every age beginning with birth, people have more parents, grandparents, and great-grandparents than used to be the case. Between 1900 and 1976, for example, the number of people who experienced the death of a parent before they reached age 15 dropped from one in four to one in twenty (Uhlenberg, 1980). Thus, more children now can expect to have both of their parents survive until they reach maturity.

The pattern of having more parents and grandparents alive continues through young adulthood and into middle age. During that same time-span (1900 to 1976), the number of middle-aged couples with two or more living parents increased from 10% to 47% (Uhlenberg, 1980). In the early 1960s, approximately 25% of people over the age of 45 had at least one surviving parent, but only a decade later, 25% of people in their late 50s had a surviving parent (Murray, 1973). By 1980, the data were even more startling: 40% of people in their late 50s had a surviving parent, as did 20% of those in their early 60s, 10% of those in their late 60s, and even 3% of those in their 70s (NRTA-AARP, 1981). Because of differences in life expectancy between men and women, most very old parents are women. In 1980, 65% of 50-year-old women had surviving mothers, compared with 37% in 1940.

At present, therefore, many families contain at least two generations of older people, the old and the very old (Brody, 1978). Of all people 65 or over, 10% have at least one adult child who is also over the age of 65. The U.S. Bureau of the Census, in making projections for the 21st century, points out that more people will find themselves caring for very old persons after they themselves have reached retirement age. Assuming that generations are separated by 25 years, people who are 85 years old are likely to have children who are 60 years of age. In 1980, there were approximately nine persons 85 and over per 100 persons of 60–74 years of age. That ratio is predicted to double by 2010 and reach 33 per 100 when the people in the baby boom reach 85 and over, in the year 2050. By 2050, every third person 60–74 years old could have a surviving parent! (U.S. Bureau of the Census, 1986). Tables 1.3 and 1.4 show the changing age structure of our population and the support ratios of children and the elderly.

From the standpoint of filial care, then, since it is the very old who most often need help, they are more likely to have adult children who also are old or are approaching old age, a phenomenon that will be even more widespread in the future. At the same time, the growing proportion of births to women in their 30s (U.S. Bureau of the Census, 1988) means that more women in the future will be providing care while they still have young children at home.

The situation is much more complex, however, than even those data indicate. Some people in the parent-care years have both parents alive, and, since many of those aging children are married, a roughly comparable proportion of their spouses would also have a surviving parent. Twenty years ago, it was predicted that the emphasis might shift from the problem of which of the children looks after a widowed parent to the problem of how a middle-aged couple can reconcile dependent relationships with *both* sets of parents (Townsend, 1968). When there are two generations in the aging phase of life, adult grandchildren may find themselves helping both their parents and grandparents. Some such situations arise even now, but there are no data available on how frequently they occur.

One must be careful in looking to the future, however. Biomedical

TABLE 1.3. Age Structure of the U.S. Population: 1980–2050.

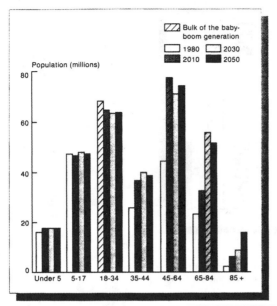

Average Annual Rate of Growth
(In percent)

	1980-2010	2010-2030		1980-2010	2010-2030
Total, all ages	+0.8	+0.4	Adult (35-44)	+1.4	+0.5
Preschool (under 5)	+0.3	*	Empty nest (45-64)	+2.5	-0.4
School age (5-17)	*	+0.1	Young old (65-74)	+1.0	+3.5
Young adult (18-34)	-0.2	-0.1	Aged (75+)	+2.9	+3.0

*Less than 0.1%

*a*Less than 0.1%.
From U.S. Department of Commerce, Bureau of the Census, Statistical Brief, SB1-86, December 1986. Washington, DC: U.S. GPO.

breakthroughs could occur, for example, that would reduce dependency among the aged by preventing or ameliorating age-related and disability-causing chronic ailments such as Alzheimer's disease and arthritis. If that should happen, the needs of very old people for help in their daily lives would decrease. At the same time, it is impossible to foresee population changes and the new groups of disabled people that conceivably could occur if new diseases [such as acquired immune deficiency syndromes (AIDS)] arise and spread. In addition, economic as well as social conditions may change, making extrapolation of needs and resources a high-risk enterprise.

TABLE 1.4. Support Ratios of Children and the Elderly: 1980–2050

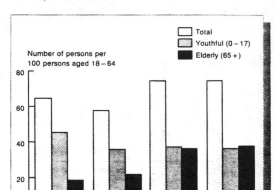

From U.S. Department of Commerce, Bureau of the Census. Statistical Brief, SB1-86, December 1986. Washington, DC: U.S. GPO.

CHANGING NEEDS OF OLDER PEOPLE

The increased needs for help by older people began to make themselves felt in the 1960s, a development that occurred in the context of changes in the socioeconomic environment. During that decade, Social Security (enacted in 1935) was beginning to take hold in improving the income position of those who were covered. The income floor was low and incomplete, however, and there was no social insurance against the costs of catastrophic disability in old age. Medicare would not come into being until 1965. Most states still had legislation holding adult children responsible for the financial support of their parents in the form of the harsh Legally Responsible Relatives' provisions of public assistance programs. These persisted until they were eliminated first by Medicaid (1965) and later by Supplemental Security Income (SSI) (1972), which was the successor program to Old Age Assistance. There were, in the early 1960s, virtually no specialized housing or long-term care services for the elderly.

Against that background, the 1960s witnessed the growth of long waiting lists for institutional facilities, and community agencies experienced increasing pressure for services such as homemaker service, which traditionally had been geared towards helping young families. What was happening was that the increased numbers of older people, particularly very old people, were experiencing the chronic illnesses that are associated with age—Alzheimer's disease and related disorders, cardiovascular diseases, and arthritis, for example. The demand for health care was shifting radically from acute care to chronic care.

The phrase "long-term care" emerged to describe the system of government and private agencies and facilities that are needed to provide the variety of continuous, sustained services required by people with chronic disabilities. Attempts to define long-term care were not made until the late 1970s (Brody, 1977; U.S. National Committee on Vital and Health Statistics, 1978). Such care has been defined as one or more services provided on a sustained basis to enable individuals whose functional capacities are chronically impaired to be maintained at their maximum levels of health and well-being. Attempts began to develop the components of the continuum of long-term care—in-home services, semiindependent living facilities, different types and levels of institutional care, and linkages of one to the other so that care plans could change as the older people's capacities changed. (See Figure 1.1 for components of a model long-term care system.)

Community and government agencies were slow to respond to the new needs, though attention to them is now increasing. But the family did respond by inventing long-term care well before the phrase was articulated by professionals. In making the shift from episodic, short-term acute care to long-term care, the family proved to be more flexible, willing, and effective than professionals and policy-makers. While the family was struggling to meet the vastly increased needs of the old, however, its capacities to do so were being exceeded.

If we are to understand the predicament of parent-caring women, it is important to recognize that elder care has become a "normative" experience—an experience with which most people will be confronted at some time during their lives. Taken together, the increased number and proportion of very old people in the population, the rise in chronic ailments and the disabilities that result, and the falling birth rate mean that *contemporary adult children provide more care and more difficult care to more parents and parents-in-law over much longer periods of time than ever has been the case before* (Brody, 1985b). And, as Chapter 2 shows, adult children translates mainly to daughters and daughters-in-law.

WOMEN'S CHANGING LIFE-STYLES

While the demography and the kinds of help needed by older people were changing, so too were the life-styles of the women who are the main caregivers to the old. The life patterns of women were becoming in-

FIGURE 1.1 Inventory of recommended available services, appropriate to a long-term care support system.

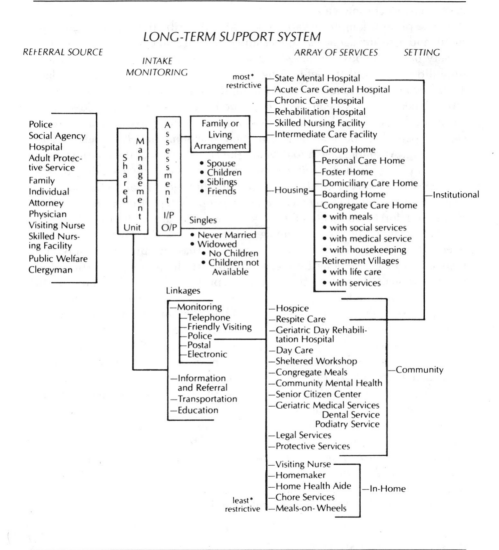

*The classification of from most to least restrictive is a general view of services and may vary within each service. (From *AJPH*, November 1980, vol. 70, no. 11.) Developed by S. J. Brody, School of Medicine, University of Pennsylvania.

creasingly heterogeneous, and a "decrystallization" of rigid life patterns was occurring (Lopata & Norr, 1980). To a greater extent than ever before in history, women now are following divergent paths in the pursuit of personal life-styles.

One of the most visible change in women's life-styles has been the vastly increased number of women who are employed or who do volunteer work. Among the factors that have contributed to that trend are the smaller number of children to keep women at home, economic pressures, the high divorce rate that sends many women to work, delayed ages at which marriages and motherhood occur, and, of course, the Women's Movement and changes in attitudes about gender-appropriate roles. Not only do contemporary women have fewer children to keep them at home than did women in previous generations, but they have more time for out-of-home activities such as employment and volunteer work because so many labor-saving devices for the home have been invented—washing machines, dishwashers, packaged goods, and throwaway paper products such as napkins and diapers, for example. Increased educational levels have stimulated career interests. Not least among reasons, by any means, changes in the economy—inflation and the rising cost of living—compel many women to seek paid work.

Reinforced by the culture, work satisfaction and economic need form a powerful combination that motivates women to do paid work. Moreover, people have higher expectations for their children to have longer periods of education that require more money, and many couples enjoy and want to continue the higher standard of living that becomes accessible to the double-income family.

The proportion of women of all ages who work outside the home has quadrupled in the past half century. In 1930, for example, 10 million women or 24% of all working-age women were in the labor force, and they represented 22% of the total work force. By 1979, the participation rate rose to 51% and women workers represented 41% of the total work force (U.S. DHHS, 7/21/80). By 1985, seven of every 10 women 25–54 years old were in the labor force, and women workers represented 44% of the total work force (U.S. Department of Labor, Bureau of Labor Statistics, 1986). Projections indicate that the growth will continue. By 1995, the proportion of women who work will rise to eight of 10 women—nearly 60 million strong—and they will be 46% of the work force (U.S. Department of Labor, Bureau of Labor Statistics, 1986). Three-fourths of employed women work full time. This situation is not unique to the United States, but is similar to that in the United Kingdom and Denmark, for example (United Kingdom Statistical Service, 1979).

A large proportion of the increase in women's labor force participation is attributable to the entry of *middle-aged women* into the work force, and those are the women who are most likely to be in the parent-care years.

Between 1920 and 1974, for example, the number of women workers between the ages of 18 and 34 increased 115%, but increased by 143% for those
35–44, by 266% for those 45–54, and by 352% for those 55–64 (Lingg, 1975).
Between 1950 and 1970, the proportion of women workers between 45 and
54 rose from 37.9% to 54.4%, whereas that of women between 55 and 64
increased from 27.0% to 43.0%. These represented increases of 43.5% and
59.3%, respectively. By 1979, 56% of married women in the 45–54 age
group were in the work force (U.S. Department of Labor, Oct. 1979), as
compared with 60% of all women in that age group (U.S. Department of
Labor, 1980). Whereas young and single women used to predominate in the
work force, now the most frequent (or modal) category of working women is
middle-aged married women (Bengtson & De Terre, 1980).

CHANGING PATTERNS OF MARRIAGE AND CHILDBEARING

The changes described thus far—demographic change, changes in the nature of older people's health problems, and the large-scale entry of middle
generation women into the labor force—are the broad trends that have
combined to produce the women-in-the-middle phenomenon. (The problems of parent-caring women who work and the effects they experience are
discussed in detail in Chapter 13.)

But those trends do not tell the whole story. Women's life-styles have
been taking increasingly diverse paths in ways other than their labor force
participation. Patterns of marriage, divorce, and remarriage, and childbearing have been changing rapidly. The U.S. Long-Term Care Survey of 1982
found that 44% of daughter caregivers were not married. These not-married
women either had never married (13.4%), were widowed (14.2%), or were
divorced or separated (16.2%) (Stone et al., 1987). This is in marked contrast
from data reported only two decades previously, when almost three-fourths
of people (other than spouses) to whom older people turned for help in a
health crisis were middle-generation married women (Shanas, 1961). The
data from the Long-Term Care Survey suggest that not-married daughters
may be overrepresented as filial caregivers; although they represent 44% of
daughter-caregivers, only 39% of all women between the ages of 40 and 64
are not married.

A selection process appears to go on in many families so that an elderly
parent tends to rely on the child with fewest competing responsibilities
(Ikels, 1983; Shanas et al., 1968; Stoller, 1983). The high rates of widowhood
among middle-aged women (the principal caregivers to the old), the soaring
rates of divorce, and the increase in the proportion of women who do not
marry probably account for the increase that has occurred in the proportion

of women doing parent care who are not married during those years of parent care.

Though the divorce rate in the United States has been rising almost continuously since the early 1900s, the rise has accelerated recently, with divorce almost tripling in the years between 1962 and 1981 (Nation Center for Health Statistics, 1985). According to Weed (1981), "The recent rise in the American divorce rate, to heretofore unprecedented levels, must be counted among the major demographic changes in the United States since World War II" (p. 1). By 1980, approximately one marriage in four had ended in divorce for women born between 1908 and 1912. However, one-third of the first marriages of women born between 1923 and 1927 had ended in divorce by that year, and 42% of the marriages of females born between 1948 and 1950 will do so (Schoen, 1985). It is estimated that approximately one-half of all marriages entered into today will eventually end in divorce (Weed, 1981); for both men and women born after 1947, more marriages will end in divorce than in either death or widowhood (Schoen, 1985).

Although statistics on divorce have frequently been cited as evidence of the seeming unpopularity of marriage and family life, data on remarriage tend to refute this assertion. Remarriages have always been common in the United States, but until the 1900s almost all remarriages were after the death of a spouse. Since then, remarriage after divorce has increased and, in the last few decades, has become the predominant form of remarriage (Cherlin, 1983). In fact, 1983 data reveal higher marriage rates for divorced people than for those who are single, with an increase between 1982 and 1983 in remarriage rates for divorced women in their middle years (National Center for Health Statistics, 1986).

Remarriage after divorce implies a complexity of family life unknown to other types of families. Unique and compounded problems of kinship, family authority and responsibility, and legal relationships represent added opportunities for disagreement, strain, and divisions among family members. Family relations in remarriage after divorce appear to be precarious, as evidenced by a higher divorce rate for such families than for first-family marriages (Weed, 1981). The fragility of these "blended" families may be due to the fact that the institution of the family offers no standardized norms or solutions for problems faced by the remarried—that the institution of "family" developed primarily in response to the needs of first families. Consequently, the institutionalized patterns of family behavior are not in place for families of remarriage (Cherlin, 1983). There is no information about the patterns of parent care that obtain in such situations. Nor is there information about those patterns when the parents now in need of help had remarried. To which parent or set of elderly parents do the filial loyalties go?

It is likely that widowed daughters will constitute an increasing proportion of caregiving daughters. The disabled elderly come primarily from the
ranks of the rising number and proportion of *very* old people whose children
are older and, therefore, more likely to be widowed. Rates of widowhood
soar beginning in middle age. At age 45–54, approximately 7.6% of women
are widowed, a proportion that rises to 18.8% at age 55–64 and to 41.2% at
age 65–74 (Brotman, 1980).

More women are remaining unmarried. The marriage rate for all unmarried women aged 15 and over fell from 77.9 per 1,000 in 1972 to 59.9 in
1983, the lowest it has been since such data were first recorded in 1940. The
marriage rate for never-married women aged 15 and over has also declined
(National Center for Health Statistics, 1986).

If those trends continue, in the future there will be even more daughter
caregivers without husbands during their parent care years. Expectations
about parent care that are placed upon not-married daughters may be
greater than for their married peers (see Chapter 4). In addition, not-
married women experience strains specific to their marital status that are
unrelated to parent care, but that may complicate the picture when they are
helping a parent. Those strains are described in Chapter 10 and are apparent
in the case studies in that chapter.

MYTH AND THE EVIDENCE

Despite all those trends that have increased the needs for parent care and
increased women's responsibilities, and no matter how much evidence is
assembled about the women's reliability, the myth of the "good old days"
persists. It is so stubborn that Ethel Shanas has called it a "Hydra-headed
monster" (Shanas, 1979a). (The Hydra monster of Greek mythology had nine
heads and could not be killed because it grew two new heads in place of each
one that was cut off.)

It is very likely that the myth has multiple determinants. Undoubtedly,
it was reinforced by the sociological theory of the "isolated nuclear family."
That widely accepted theory held that the nuclear family (parents and
growing children) was the main and most effective family form in modern
industrialized society, having replaced the extended family of the United
States of an earlier time (Parsons & Bales, 1955). Freudian approaches, in
concentrating on the nuclear family, also reinforced that focus. As a result,
the aged were believed to be isolated from and even rejected by their
families.

Research on these questions began slowly with studies that examined
the relationships of older people in general with their families. The findings
of those studies challenged a variety of assumptions related to the myth of
family alienation from the aged. It was generally thought, for example, that

the elderly rarely saw their families, that intergenerational bonds had become weaker, and even that families "dumped" disabled old people into institutions. In the early 1960s, broad surveys of noninstitutionalized older people across the nation began to assemble facts. These surveys, notably those conducted by Ethel Shanas and her colleagues (Reid, 1966; Rosow, 1965; Shanas, 1960, 1961, 1979b; Shanas & Streib, 1965; Streib, 1958; Shanas et al., 1968), found the following facts:

- Virtually all older people do have some family members, with only a tiny proportion having absolutely no kin. Approximately four-fifths of all people 65 and over have at least one adult child. Of those, 90% have at least one grandchild and 40% have at least one great-grandchild.
- Ties between the generations are strong and viable. Adult children do not abdicate their responsibilities, and continuing contacts are the rule rather than the exception.
- Most older people live within an hour's distance of at least one adult child. They and their children prefer to live near but not with each other, a preference that has been described as a wish for "intimacy at a distance" (Rosenmayhr & Kockeis, 1963). Most of the elderly not only live close to a child but see those children (and grandchildren) frequently.
- Intergenerational exchanges of services are the rule rather than the exception. Those exchanges are reciprocal, with the aged giving as well as receiving the garden-variety of help that family members give each other on a day-to-day basis.
- When families are unable to care for their disabled elderly, a constellation of personal, social, and economic factors are at work. In the main, institutionalization of older people is the last resort of families after all possible alternatives have been explored (Brody, 1966a, 1977a; Brody & Gummer, 1967; GAP Report, 1965; Goldfarb, 1965; Townsend, 1965). (Institutionalization is discussed in detail in Chapter 14.)

There are no indications at all that the situation is any different today. Of the 26.3 million older people living in the community (that is, not in institutions), 8 million live alone, 80% of whom are women (Kovar, 1986). Such people have frequent contacts with relatives. If they have children, they live near them, and see and talk with them on the phone frequently. In the 1984 government survey, two-thirds of the elderly saw an adult child at least once a week (Kovar, 1986).

When, in 1963, The Gerontological Society of America and Duke University sponsored the symposium mentioned above in order to examine the facts about the family relationships of older people (Shanas & Streib,

1965), the conveners felt that the *three*-generation family required consideration because it had become so common. They agreed that many programs for older people were based on social myths that had persisted because the assumptions on which they were founded had not been scrutinized by scholars.

That symposium was a significant watershed in the study of intergenerational relations. There was such consensus among the social scientists that one of them called the conference a "bench mark of the final respects paid to the isolated nuclear family before its interment" (Rosow, 1965, p. 341). A consistent theme was the responsible behavior of adult children in helping their parents. Important for the concerns of this book, however, was the conferees' acknowledgment that the effects on those caregivers were hardly touched upon during the conference (Streib & Shanas, 1965).

The scholars who participated in the conference were so certain that discovery of the facts would put an end to the notion of the isolated nuclear family that one of them stated flatly, "The isolated nuclear family is a myth. This has already been conclusively demonstrated. It does not merit any further attention from the field, and I, for one, refuse to waste any more time even discussing it" (Sussman, 1965). Unfortunately, however, the notion of the isolated nuclear family is still so firmly entrenched that it continues to perpetuate the myth of abandonment of the elderly.

Another reason for the persistence of the myth may relate to nursing homes. The number of elderly people placed in nursing homes was increasing rapidly during the 1960s and 1970s because of the increase of the very old who were disabled. Such facilities became highly visible on the American scene. Though this did not represent family abandonment (see Chapter 14), it was often interpreted in that way. Moreover, institutions were (and often still are) viewed negatively in reaction to abuses both in institutions of an earlier day (such as poorhouses and mental hospitals) and in those of today about which periodic scandals erupt.

More subtle psychological forces are also at work in keeping the myth alive. The many role losses and interpersonal losses of aging and aged people may be experienced psychologically as abandonment. Perhaps this accounts for Shanas's (1963) finding that among those most likely to blame adult children for neglect of the aged were old people themselves, particularly childless old people. The elderly may be expressing an unconscious fear of additional losses or a wish for more attention and care than their children are able to provide. In the Shanas (1963) study, another group that perpetuated the myth was comprised of professional workers who, because of the very nature of their work, saw mainly those old people who were without children or who were alienated from their families.

The myth may also be an expression of the guilt of a youth-oriented society in need of a scapegoat for the general social neglect of its old. Certainly, it represents a lag in social expectations that have not changed to keep pace with the changing socioeconomic and demographic developments described above. The "etiquette of filial behavior"—that is, the outmoded conventions and stereotyped attitudes of an earlier phase of history—have persisted rather than responded to current realities (Brody, 1970). Value-laden words like "abandonment" and "dumping" are used to describe a situation in which older people do not always receive the services they need or wish for from adult children because the latter are unable—*not unwilling*—to provide them.

The myth is also consonant with the strength of the values of "home" and "family." Phrases such as, "There's no place like home" and "Home is where the heart is," reflect those deeply entrenched values and feelings. In psychological terms, then, the myth may be translated as the fear of losing one's own home, life-style, and independence. The myth also may persist because of certain inner feelings that exist in adult daughters, which are elaborated in Part II.

Finally, there is always a tendency to romanticize and idealize the past. A good example of that tendency is the notion that in the past three-generational living was preferred, whereas nowadays older people long wistfully to be taken into their children's home but are rejected. This is epitomized in the bitter saying, "One mother had room for all her children, but none of them has room for her." Yet available information shows that "the three-generation family to which contemporary commentators often point with nostalgia, in some cases, may have been forced on poor families for lack of any palatable substitute" (Rosenheim, 1965). Kent (1965) characterized as the illusion of the "Golden Past" the fact that "the three-generation family pictured as a farm idyll is common, yet all evidence indicates that at no time in any society was a three-generation family ever the common mode, and even less evidence that it was idyllic." In the same vein, when Laslett (1976) studied historical documents such as legal records, household census data, and parish registries, he referred to the "world-we-have-lost syndrome." He pointed to the rarity of three-generation families in the past, the instances of bitter family conflict, and the impoverished neglect suffered by some old people.

Where multigeneration households did exist in the past, it was likely that young couples, on marrying, lived in the homes of their parents. Such arrangements were considerably more feasible in the rural communities of the old days than in the crowded quarters of our urbanized, industrialized society. They also reflected the economic inability of young marrieds to live on their own. The modern pattern is for a young couple to set up a separate home.

Bengtson and Treas (1980) point out the influence of social, economic, and demographic considerations in shaping intergenerational relations in the past. Not only were multigeneration households uncommon, but when they did exist they were of short duration. Economics played a major role, since older people often could not afford to live separately. Moreover, an older person with income was an asset to poor families, and grandparents (particularly grandmothers) could provide much assistance with child care and housekeeping. Prosperous old people could exercise much control over the lives of adult children. Parental power was formidable when day-to-day subsistance and even the chance to marry depended on parents' willingness to provide dowries to daughters and to turn over the family farm or business to sons. Many historical accounts show that considerable, even bitter conflicts occurred at times between elderly parents and their adult children.

As noted above, by their own account, the elderly prefer to live *near* but not *with* their children. Financial problems limit choices about living arrangements, however. With the improved levels of income older people have nowadays, more of them are able to live the way they prefer, separately from their children, but they remain close by (Shanas, 1979a). Yet the social expectation is that a middle-aged or aging child should introduce a disabled old parent into her home, sometimes after half a century of separate living.

It is interesting that, as the generations were freed in the main from financial obligations to each other, emotional bonds rose in relative importance and apparently are stronger, rather than weaker than they were in the past (Nye & Berardo, 1973). In a study of three generations of women, for example, it was found that today's middle-generation women were giving more emotional support to their elderly mothers than the latter had given to *their* mothers when at the same ages (Brody et al., 1982b). Those elderly mothers, however, had given more financial help to their mothers than they were receiving from their daughters. At the same time, the younger women had more competing responsibilities than did their mothers at comparable ages and had helped their own adult children longer both financially and emotionally. More of the middle-aged women studied were in the labor force or were more involved in volunteer work than their mothers had been at comparable ages.

To summarize: the trends that brought about the phenomenon of women in the middle have been the development of a large population of chronically disabled older people, the falling birth rate, and the changing life-styles of women (including labor-force participation and changing patterns of marriage). Other relevant trends such as increasing geographic distance between parents and children and the longer lives of the developmentally disabled will become apparent later in this book.

The next chapter looks at the scope of the need for parent care at present—how many older people need help, the kinds of assistance they need, and the role of adult daughters and daughters-in-law in providing it—that is, the role of women in the middle who nowadays have more competing responsibilities than ever before in history.

Chapter 2

Scope of Parent Care

Basic information relevant to the scope of parent care includes the following:

1. the number and proportion of older people who need help to function in their daily lives and the various kinds of help they need
2. the distribution of helping services between the family or informal system of care and the formal system of government, agencies, and paid workers
3. the identity of the particular members of the family who actually provide the needed care, with special reference to the role of adult daughters and daughters-in-law

OLDER PEOPLE'S NEEDS FOR CARE

Chapter 1 notes that the needs of the increasing population of old and very old people have changed because chronic ailments have replaced acute diseases as their major health problems. By definition, chronic diseases cannot be cured and often last for many years. In contrast to acute ailments, those diseases result in disabilities that require ongoing dependency on others. As acute diseases such as pneumonia, tuberculosis, poliomyelitis, childbed fever, and smallpox were brought under control by advances in public health and by the development of antibiotics and vaccines, a dramatic drop occurred in the proportions of deaths due to such illnesses. Between 1900 and 1980, the percentage of deaths due to infectious diseases dropped from 40% to 6%!

When so many people were enabled to surmount the barriers that previously had caused deaths at earlier ages, there was a rise in the incidence and prevalence of chronic, age-related disorders such as Alzheimer's disease and related disorders, rheumatoid arthritis, diabetes, osteoporosis, and cardiovascular and cerebrovascular disease. The postponement of death by medical interventions has been called the "Failures of Success" (Gruenberg, 1977). That is, disabled people's lives are prolonged by hi-tech medicine into more years of dependency that in turn mean more years during which there must be someone on whom to depend. The net result has been a radical change in the nature of the health services needed by elderly people. Our health systems are struggling to make a major shift in emphasis from acute (i.e., temporary) to chronic (i.e., sustained) care.

The rise of chronic disease and resultant disability gave impetus to the development of ways of assessing people's capacities to function in their daily lives. Such assessment has been defined as any systematic attempt to measure objectively the level at which an individual is functioning in a variety of areas (Lawton, 1971). The phrase "functional assessment," so commonly used today, has its roots in the field of rehabilitation. The orientation to *function* rather than to *diagnosis* recognizes that diagnosis (although of vital importance to medical treatment) does not indicate the nature of the day-to-day services required. People with the same diagnosis—arthritis, for example—may require vastly different kinds of help. One person with some arthritis in a shoulder or hand may be completely independent, whereas another may be so disabled as to be in a wheelchair and require help with toileting, getting in and out of bed, and other personal activities.

Functional assessment serves many purposes. Originally, it was seen as the basis for setting treatment goals to improve an individual's level of functioning. It can also indicate the amount and nature of the help an individual needs from others and make it possible to estimate the numbers of people who have various levels of disability. When assessment data on many individuals is aggregated, the information can be used to plan programs and indicate what social policy should be.

First came ways of measuring people's capacities for what are called "activities of daily living" (ADL)—that is, basic functions such as bathing, dressing, eating, toileting, transferring, and ambulating (Katz et al., 1963). Then came assessment of higher order capabilities that are called "instrumental activities of daily living" (IADL): the ability to use a telephone, shopping, food preparation, housekeeping, laundry, transportation, medications, and the ability to handle finances (Lawton & Brody, 1969). If the ADL and IADL capacities of older people are assessed and the people who help with the various tasks are identified, it becomes possible to identify not only the numbers of the elderly who are in need of help, but also the sources of the assistance they receive. (Readers interested in assessment methodology are referred to Lawton et al., 1982, and Kane and Kane, 1981.)

FUNCTIONAL STATUS OF OLDER PEOPLE

Assessment instruments have been used in many studies to estimate the dependencies in the elderly population. When looking at the proportions of old people who need various levels of help, it is extremely important to remember that the data are cross-sectional. That is, the data tell us about how many individuals need help *at any given time*—the time at which the particular survey was done. But people's capacities change over time. An older person who needs help only with transportation and shopping today may need help with those tasks plus housekeeping and cooking tomorrow. Still further in the future, she may need all of those forms of help plus assistance with bathing and dressing. Still later, help with feeding and toileting may be needed as well.

Not all people develop increasing disabilities gradually, of course. Some may make a rapid transition from total independence to considerable dependency if they experience a sudden catastrophic illness such as a massive stroke. That is not to say that the direction of change is invariably downward, though it often is. Functioning levels may be improved as people recover from acute episodes of disease or with good care and rehabilitative measures, and often do so (Brody, S., in press; Manton, 1988). Careful evaluation is always important, therefore, so that the older person can be enabled reach his or her maximum level of functioning. When an older person is helped to go from an inability to walk to being able to walk with a walker, or from being unable to get in and out of bed to being able to do so independently, it makes a tremendous difference to the caregiver as well as to the disabled individual.

The most recent data on the functioning levels of older people come from two national surveys conducted by the government. One was the National Health Interview Survey by the National Center for Health Statistics. It found that almost 60% of all people 65 and over and even 40% of those 85 years and over had no limitations on their activities. Slightly more than 15% were limited in outside activities only, 13.6% in the kind or amount of activity, and 11.4% were unable to perform their usual activities. However, there were large decreases in functioning with increasing age. For example, among those who were 65–74 62% had no limitation, whereas only 40% of those 85 and over had no limitations. It must be noted, however, that this information is about noninstitutionalized older people. As shown in Chapter 14, with advancing age, larger proportions of people are in nursing homes and their functional capacities are very poor compared with the noninstitutionalized population as a whole.

The second source of information is the nationwide 1982 Long-Term Care Survey conducted by the U.S. Department of Health and Human Services. Nearly one-quarter (22.9%) of all people 65 years of age and older were found to be functionally disabled (Doty, 1986). That is, approximately one in four of the elderly requires assistance from another person with ADL or with IADL, or both. The six ADL activities used in the survey were bathing, dressing, eating, toileting, getting out of bed, and getting around indoors. The seven IADL activities were managing money, moving about outdoors, shopping, doing heavy housework, meal preparation, making phone calls, and taking medication. In addition, older people may require more technical health-related care such as bandage changing, injections, and tube-feeding.

The one in four figure includes both noninstitutionalized older people and those in nursing homes. Only one in five of those disabled elderly (or approximately 4.5% of all older people) are cared for in nursing homes. The remaining four-fifths of the disabled elderly who live in the community are cared for primarily by family and friends.

To put the matter in perspective, it is emphasized that *at any given time, more than three-quarters of older people do not need help to function in their daily lives*. Although 18% of the total 65+ population or 4.6 million elderly in the 1982 survey were not institutionalized but had some disability, the levels of help they needed varied greatly. Two-thirds of them had IADL limitations only or had one or two ADL limitations. At the other extreme, there were approximately 850,000 elderly people (19% of all disabled old people) with severe limitations (five or six ADL deficits), who were residing in the community (Liu, Manton, & Liu, 1985). Table 2.1 shows the proportions of older people who had various levels of disability in the 1982 Long-Term Care Survey. From the viewpoint of caregivers, helping an old person with IADL tasks such as shopping, money management, and transportation is very different from helping with ADL activities such as bathing, dressing, and eating, and with nursing tasks.

KINDS OF HELP NEEDED

Though day-to-day functional assistance is a vital and major form of caregiving, it is not the only kind of help needed by older people. Horowitz (1985a) conceptualized family caregiving behavior as falling into four broad categories: the direct services described above, emotional support, mediation with formal organizations and providers (government and social and health agencies), and financial assistance. She points out that sharing one's home with a disabled old person is a special form of caregiving that may encompass and facilitate the other kinds of help.

To that categorization of helping services should be added other forms of assistance that do not occur on a day-to-day basis and almost invariably are provided by the family—response and dependability in emergencies, at

TABLE 2.1 Percent of persons with limitations in activity, by source of assistance and limitation level: United States, 1982[a]

Limitation level	Number of persons in thousands	Source of assistance (percent)		
		Paid helpers	Nonpaid helpers	Both paid and nonpaid helpers
Total	4,405	5.5	73.9	20.6
IADL only	1,368	6.8	81.1	12.1
ADL, 1–2	1,506	6.6	74.9	18.5
ADL, 3–4	683	4.0	68.6	27.4
ADL, 5–6	849	2.5	64.7	32.9

[a]Note: Total does not equal 4.6 million total disabled elderly because of unknowns.
From *Health Care Financing Review*, Winter 1985, Vol. 7, p. 52.

times of temporary illness, or special need, and when convalescent or rehabilitative care is necessary. These other kinds of help make special demands on caregivers. If such assistance were to be included in counting the numbers of caregivers and care-recipients, estimates of the proportion of elderly receiving help and the amounts of help they receive would be larger.

Certainly, older people who are essentially capable and do not need day-to-day functional assistance may need such special help from time to time. But the disabled elderly undoubtedly have such needs more frequently. They are hospitalized more often, for example, more often need convalescent or rehabilitative care, and more often move from one residence to another. They may move into specialized housing for the elderly, into an adult child's home, or into a nursing home. Such occasions often constitute a major upheaval with much effort and time demanded of the helping relatives.

The provision of emotional support and service mediation are probably underestimated with respect to the time and effort consumed and the amount of strain they can cause.

Emotional support is the most universal form of family caregiving, the one most wanted by older people from their children and the one the adult children themselves feel is the most important service they can given their disabled parent(s). It is also the kind of help for which no government or paid worker can substitute. Emotional support includes being the confidant, or the one with whom problems can be talked over; providing social contacts such as phoning, visiting, or taking the elderly person out to family events; and help with decision-making. Most of all, such support means giving the older person the sense of having someone on whom he or she can rely— someone who is interested and concerned, and who cares. The role of adult daughters in providing this form of support was shown in one study by the responses of elderly women when they were asked to name their main confidant. When the women were married, they most often named their husbands, but widowed women most often named a daughter (Brody et al., 1982a). Becoming a widowed parent's main source of emotional support can be the first as well as an ongoing and important filial service.

The effort and difficulties involved in providing emotional support to a parent should not be underestimated. Some older people need so much support that it can consume many hours a week and be stressful as well. When there have been interpersonal problems between parent and daughter, the increased time spent with each other and opportunities for differences can exacerbate the problems. Although most adult children want to visit and to take the older person on outings, activities of that kind may be difficult to fit into a busy schedule. Or, the notions of the older person and the daughter may not mesh with regard to how frequently such contacts should take place. This in itself may be a strain for the caregiver—that is, the realization that her parent feels that what she is doing is not enough (see Chapter 6).

Mediation with organizations is a service that is now being called "service management" or "case management" when it is done by professionals. The real case managers, however, are family members who far outdo professionals in performing that function. Such mediation or management involves knowing what entitlements the older person has—for Social Security and Medicare benefits, for example. It involves identifying what services are needed and knowing whether they are available in the community— homemaker, meals on wheels, and in-home nursing, to name just a few. It involves gaining access to those services—getting in touch with the particular organization, establishing eligibility, and following through to see that services are actually received. Such activities are not only time-consuming but are often frustrating as well, as step after step must be taken to unravel the red tape involved.

The need to do those things may be new to both the older person and the adult child, neither of whom may have had any previous need to use services from the formal system. Nor is service management a one-time effort. The conditions and needs of older people and their families change over time, requiring constant monitoring. Services require rearrangement and access to new ones gained. The most careful arrangements break down from time to time. An in-home paid worker may fail to show up on time or to arrive at all, for example, making a flurry of unexpected activity necessary (see Chapter 15 for further discussion of case management).

Nowadays, *financial support* for day-to-day living expenses and to pay the costs of medical care for those living at home has become a much less important pattern than was true in the early part of the century. As many studies have shown, it is now generally accepted that securing an income floor for the elderly should be a government responsibility. Through Social Security (1935) and SSI (1974), that income floor has been established, though it is low. Taking money from one's children is the form of help least wanted by older people and is undoubtedly part of their overarching wish not to be a burden.

The dramatic change in patterns of financial help is shown by the fact that the proportion of older people who were wholly dependent on their children for economic support dropped from approximately half in 1937 to 1.5% in 1979 (Upp, 1982). (Pensions and savings have also helped, of course.) Similarly, before Medicare came into being in 1965, an aged person's catastrophic illness could wipe out his or her own savings and impose a severe financial burden on adult children.

Total economic dependency is different, however, from not receiving any financial help at all. Some adult children do indeed help out with money or by purchasing things needed by the parent. The contributions may be for necessities or for the amenities that make life more comfortable. Estimates of the proportion of adult children who provide financial help to elderly parents range widely from 10% to half (for a review, see Horowitz, 1985a).

Although information about the dollar amounts that children contribute for actual care of the disabled elderly is not complete, recent census data show that approximately 900,000 older people received regular financial support from their adult children in 1985, with the average payment being approximately $1,484 per year. Almost two-thirds of parents receiving such help but living apart from their children received it from their sons (U.S. Department of Commerce, 1988). It may be that gender differences in filial contributions relate to the fact that almost two-fifths of adult daughters of the dependent aged are not in the labor force. Having no earned income of their own, such daughters might be reluctant or unable to ask their husbands to contribute financially. (It is interesting to note that in the census data approximately 500,000 adult children received regular help from aged parents, with the average amount being $3,755 per year, not including college costs.) Averages tell us little, of course, since many people spend little on such care and others spend considerably higher amounts. In a New York study, for example, approximately half of the adult children provided some financial aid to the parent, with the amounts ranging from a few dollars to several thousand dollars a year (Horowitz & Dobrof, 1982). It was more likely that the children gave in-kind help (paying for clothing, food, or household items), though some gave money on a regular basis.

There are costs other than out-of-pocket outlays, however. Preliminary data from the 1982 Long-Term Care Survey indicate that adult children (most of them daughters, of course) spend an average number of 26 hours weekly on providing long-term care services to their elderly parents. Costing those services out on the basis of the minimum wage, this would have an imputed market value of $4,529 annually (Doty, 1986). Costs that have been invisible until very recently are the opportunity costs incurred when adult children or other relatives quit their jobs, reduce the number of their working hours, or refuse job promotions in order to take care of elderly relatives (see Chapter 13).

In any case, the complete picture of financial contributions by adult children, whether for amenities or for the purchase of actual care of their disabled parents, has yet to be filled in.

SHARED HOUSEHOLDS

Both elderly parents and adult children agree overwhelmingly that it is not desirable for them to share a household, opinions that are supported by the strains reported by caregivers in such arrangements. In the main, shared households are formed when the older person is too disabled to live alone or cannot afford to do so. In a small proportion of families, however, the adult child lives in the parent's home rather than the reverse; the child may be developmentally disabled, or may never have married and left the parental home, for example.

Contrary to popular beliefs about the past, the prevalence of households shared by older people and their adult children was low in the late 19th century, as it is now. In 1975, only 3.9% of elderly men and 13.4% of elderly women lived with an adult child. Widowed older people are much more likely than their married peers to live with a child, particularly in advanced old age when disability precludes independent living (for review, see Mindel, 1979). The effect of disability has a significant effect only on the odds of living with children, particularly with daughters (but not other family members) relative to living alone (Shanas et al., 1968; Wolf & Soldo, 1986). Daughters outnumber sons in a ratio of four to one in sharing their households. Again, a caution is in order about cross-sectional data. That is, although approximately 18% of old people share a household with a child at any given time, a significantly higher proportion (perhaps twice as many) will do so at some time in their lives.

Most shared households contain two generations. The proportion of older people living in *three*-generation families is very small at any given time. The analysis of Soldo (1980) of a national data set indicates, for example, that 2.16% of all people aged 65 and over live in the homes of daughters between the ages of 40 and 59 who have both a parent and a child under 18 in those households. Since those figures do not include three-generation households of sons, those in which the daughter is under 40 or over 60, or those containing children over 18, a conservative estimate is that 4% of older people or approximately one million of them, live in three-generation households at any given time.

Again, however, cross-sectional data obscure the picture to some extent. Over time, some older people become unable to live alone any longer and move to the homes of adult children, some of whom still have their own children living at home, and others go to nursing facilities. In the 1982 Long-Term Care Survey, 36% of the extremely disabled elderly lived with an adult child, most of them with a daughter; 60% of the caregiving daughters shared their homes with the parent, and one-third of those (20% of the total) had both the disabled elderly parent and at least one child under 18 in their households (Stone et al., 1987). Calculations based on those data indicate that there are approximately 250,000 households of filial caregivers (sons and daughters) containing both a severely disabled older person (i.e., in need of ADL help) and at least one of the caregiver's children. (Chapter 9 discusses the effects of shared households on caregivers and the differential effects of one-, two-, and three-generation households.)

PARENT ABUSE

In recent years, much attention has been drawn to the problem of abuse of older people. Congressional hearings held on this serious and deplorable situation estimated that approximately 4% of the elderly are victims of some form of abuse (U.S. Select Committee on Aging, 1981). In the context of this book it is important to note, however, that most abuse is not by family members, and parent abuse is not a widespread pattern. In the best research to date, a large careful study of a random sample of elderly people, less than 1% were found to have been victimized by their adult children (with the definition of abuse including physical abuse, psychological abuse, and neglect) (Pillemar and Finkelhor, 1988). [A review of the literature on elder abuse is found in Callahan (1988). Quinn and Tomita (1986) offers a detailed treatment of the subject including some of the dynamics involved.]

WHO HELPS THE DISABLED ELDERLY?

A major issue that has preoccupied gerontologists, government, and all of society is the role that should be played by the "informal system" of family and friends vis-à-vis the role of the "formal system" of government and agencies in helping the disabled aged. The factual evidence about what actually happens is vitally important because, depending on that evidence, different paths may be indicated for social policy and practice approaches. If, for example, the evidence shows that the family has both the capacity and the willingness to meet all the needs of the disabled aged, then little would be needed in the way of formal services, except to encourage the family by providing back-up services. If the family has the capacity, but not the willingness, then efforts should be directed to encouraging the family's efforts—telling it to shape up, rather than burdening the taxpayer with the cost of the services needed. But if the family is willing, but does not have the capacity to provide all the help needed by the elderly, a responsible society should develop the programs needed to supplement and buttress the family's efforts.

The notion that family values about care of the aged have weakened and that the formal system provides most of the helping services is another expression of the myth of isolation and abandonment. Study after study has found that the vast majority of helping services received by older people come from family members. That statement deserves emphasis. *The family, not professionals and the bureaucracy, is the main source of assistance to the disabled elderly; only a very small proportion of assistance is provided by the formal system.*

Since the reliability of the family was first documented by research in the 1960s, evidence has continued to accumulate confirming that the family has been steadfast in that respect despite the vastly increased needs for care and the reduction in potentially available family caregivers. The family provides 80% of the medically related services (such as bandage changing and injections) needed by older people living in the community (U.S. Department of HEW, 1972). That the family provides an even larger proportion of household maintenance and other instrumental services (80–90%) was a major finding of the classic study of the Cleveland area carried out by the U.S. General Accounting Office (U.S. GAO, 1977; Laurie, 1978). (Remember, those estimates do not include emotional support, dependability in emergencies, negotiations with the formal system, and the mobilization and monitoring of nonfamily services.) The family often provides those kinds of services for long periods of time. And, when older people are bedfast, are housebound, or can no longer live on their own, their families often bring them into their own households (Brody, Poulshock, & Masciocchi, 1978).

Again, the 1982 Long-Term Care Survey offers the most recent and extensive source of data about this subject. It found that nearly three-quarters of disabled elderly people who live in the community rely solely on family and friends for the assistance they require; most of the remainder depend on a combination of family care and paid help (Doty, 1986). Only

15% of all "helper days" of care received by the disabled elderly came from nonfamily sources, and only a very small minority received all their care from paid providers.

WHO IN THE FAMILY PROVIDES HELP

Families, of course, include many people, male and female, and of all ages and relationships to the older person. Having established the reliability of the family, a next stage of investigation asked "Who in the family provides various kinds of care?" A long series of studies has found that there is generally one person in the family who is the main provider, an individual who is usually characterized as the principal or primary caregiver (e.g., Brody & Schoonover, 1986; Cantor, 1983; Frankfather, Smith, & Caro, 1981; Johnson, 1982; Noelker & Poulshock, 1982; Stoller & Earl, 1983). Other family members may help out on a regular basis or from time to time, but they play a much smaller role in terms of the amount and intensity of the help they give (see Chapter 8). Equal sharing of responsibility by two or more family members does occur in a small proportion of families in which there are only two adult children and both are daughters, but this is the exception rather than the rule (Matthews, 1987).

There is a hierarchy in the relationship of caregiver to care recipient. When a married older person is disabled, the spouse almost invariably becomes the principal caregiver. Elderly spouses are enormously loyal to each other. They provide the most comprehensive care and go on doing so even when the disabled husband or wife is very severely disabled. Because of the discrepancy in life expectancy between men and women and because men usually marry women younger than they are, most caregiving spouses are women. Those elderly wives are likely to have limited capacities, however, and therefore are often helped in their caregiving efforts by their adult children. Daughters provide more than three times as much help as sons to elderly caregivers with disabled spouses (Pruchno, 1988).

Adult children are next in the hierarchy of those in the family who are most likely to become the primary caregivers. Recognition of the multiple responsibilities assumed by these adult children for the old and the young (their own children) led to their characterization as the "patron" (Hill et al., 1970), "keystone" (Fogarty, 1975), "caught" (Vincent, 1972), or "sandwich" (Schwartz, 1979) generation.

It soon became clear that just as family almost invariably means spouses or adult children, adult children most often means adult daughters. It is adult daughters who help elderly parents care for each other and who are the principal caregivers for those among the 10 million widowed older widowed persons who need help (Brody, 1978, 1981, 1984b; Myllyluoma & Soldo,

1980; Shanas, 1967, 1979; Stehouwer, 1968; Troll, 1971; Tobin & Kulys, 1980; Townsend, 1968). It is those middle-generation women—the women in the middle (Brody, 1981)—who are the reliable "significant others" who shop, do household tasks, give personal care, fill in when an arranged care program breaks down, and provide a home when necessary.

Sons love their parents, do not neglect them, and have feelings of responsibility. In general, however, sons tend to do certain tasks reflecting the cultural assignment of gender-appropriate roles such as money management and home repairs, and often are major participants in making important decisions. But direct hands-on care of the elderly, like care of young children, is generally viewed as a woman's role (see Chapter 6). Sons assume the role of principal caregiver when they have no sisters or none close by. When they do so, however, they are helped by their wives (the daughters-in-law), do less than daughters, and experience less strain (Horowitz, 1985b). (Chapter 8 and 9 will describe the help provided by the caregivers' siblings and husbands.)

The power of gender in determining who in the family becomes the caregiver extends to other relatives as well. When disabled older people do not have a spouse or an adult child, female relatives—sisters and nieces, for example—predominate over their male counterparts (Horowitz & Dobrof, 1982).

Two other factors are straightforward as determinants of being the principal caregiving adult child—geographic proximity and being an only child. Because older people nowadays have fewer adult children and mobility has increased, there often simply are fewer choices when there is only one child, or one female child, or only one child close at hand. There also are psychological factors at work that will be discussed in detail in Chapter 8. Whatever situational or psychodynamic factors are at work, the particular daughter who becomes the primary caregiver almost invariably provides the bulk of care, with or without help from others in the family.

Relatively little is known about other family caregivers who fill the caregiving gap when there are no spouses or adult children available—elderly siblings, for example. Nor is much known about caregiving by grandchildren when there is no one available in generation two because the elderly parent has outlived her own children. (A sad statistic is that an elderly woman with a son has a one in four chance of outliving that son.) Chapter 9 will discuss the roles of grandchildren in helping their grandparents or helping their mothers care for grandparents.

Friends and neighbors of the elderly provide considerable help, but that help is by no means as intensive as that provided by the family. They do not substitute for family when the older people concerned are significantly disabled (in need of help with ADL), nor does the help they give approach family help in level or duration (Cantor, 1978).

Once again, the 1982 Long-Term Care Survey provides the most recent and complete information about family sources of help (see Stone, Cafferata, & Sangl, 1987 for details). It must be kept in mind, however, that the following statistics are about caregivers to the most disabled segment of the population of older people, those who required assistance with ADL, not those who provide care to older people who had only IADL deficits.

The survey found that 72% of all caregivers (including secondary caregivers) providing ADL help were women—29% were adult daughters, 23% were wives, and 20% were other female relatives and nonrelatives. Husbands constituted 13% of the caregiving population, sons 8.5%, and other male relatives and nonrelatives 7.2%.

Of all the daughter caregivers in the survey, most (more than 70%) were the primary caregivers to the disabled parent. One-third of this group were not only the primary caregivers, but were the *only* caregivers in that they were receiving no assistance at all from other family members or from the formal system. The 30% who were identified as secondary caregivers were probably the ones who were helping a parent care for his or her disabled spouse or a sibling or sibling-in-law.

Although there are different patterns of filial care, the care of mothers by adult daughters is by far the most prevalent. In half of the parent-care situations, daughters were helping their elderly mothers, and in one-third, daughters were helping their fathers. Of the remainder, sons were helping their mothers in 10% of the situations, and 7% of sons were helping their fathers. (Data calculated from Tables 1 and 2 in Stone et al., 1987.)

Overall, the survey confirmed previous research to the effect that *daughters outnumber sons in a ratio of approximately four to one as primary caregivers to severely disabled parents and are about four times as likely to share their homes with a parent when the latter can no longer manage alone.* The sons in the survey who were caregivers were more likely than not to be secondary rather than primary caregivers. Moreover, we do not know how many of the 20% of caregivers who were "other female relatives or non-relatives" were daughters-in-law. It is safe to conjecture, however, that many daughters-in-law provided most of the day-to-day help or were secondary caregivers when sons were named as the primary caregivers.

DAUGHTERS' CHARACTERISTICS

The 1982 Long-Term Care Survey identified some of the characteristics of caregiving daughters. Their average age was approximately 52.5 years. They came from many different backgrounds and varied in socioeconomic status. Almost two-thirds of them were in middle age—that is, between the ages of 45 and 64. But one-fourth of the daughters were under 45, and 13% were 65 years of age or over! The daughters, then, ranged widely not only in age but also in the *stage* of life at which parent care was necessary. Some (almost one-fourth) still had children under 18 living at home, whereas others undoubtedly had reached the theoretical "empty nest" stage. The 13% who were over the age of 65 exemplify the growing number of situations in which one generation of older people takes care of members of a still older generation.

No matter the caregivers' ages or stages of life, caring for this segment of the population of older people is no easy task in view of the fact that they are the most disabled, with all of them having deficiencies in ADL. The levels of disability undoubtedly account for the fact that three out of five of the daughters actually shared the same household with the parent, a form of living associated with considerable strains.

As noted in Chapter 1, almost half (44%) of these caregiving daughters in the survey were not married, being widowed, divorced or separated, or never-married. (The differences in the problems experienced by married and not married women are described in Chapters 9 and 10.) Another marked change from the situation a few decades ago is that 43.5% of the caregiving daughters were in the labor force. That percentage is deceptive, however, since an additional 11.6% had been working but had quit their jobs because of caregiving. Moreover, caregiving had caused almost 30% of the working women to reduce the number of their working hours, rearrange their work schedules, or take time off from their jobs without pay. (These problems are discussed in detail in Chapter 13.)

Daughters' marital status and work status has some impact on the patterns of help to their elderly parents. There is a tendency for the role of filial caregiver to fall to the daughter with fewer competing roles—to not-married (divorced, widowed, or never-married) daughters, for example (Stoller, 1983). When married and not-married daughters are in comparable positions as primary caregivers, the former provide somewhat less help (Lang & Brody, 1983). Similarly, working daughters tend to provide slightly less care than nonworking daughters; the elderly parents of the workers receive as much overall care as parents of nonworkers, with the difference being offset by services purchased by the family (Brody & Schoonover, 1986).

WHAT KINDS OF HELP DO DAUGHTERS GET FROM OTHER FAMILY MEMBERS?

It has already been noted that caregivers receive very little help from nonfamily sources and that the primary caregiver most often provides most of the care the elderly person needs. How much help does the daughter actually get from other family members—her husband, her own children, and her sibling(s)? A good deal depends, of course, on the size of the family network, the geographic proximity of various family members, whether other family members are male or female, and the kinds of help the older person needs. Although information is not complete about the contributions of other family members, a few studies cast some light on the subject.

In one study (Brody & Schoonover, 1986) in which daughters were the primary caregivers to widowed elderly mothers, the daughters provided approximately two-thirds of the help with ADL (personal care) and IADL (such as housework, laundry, shopping, and transportation) as determined by the number of hours each kind of help was received by the mothers. They provided a higher proportion, approximately three-fourths, of meal preparation and help to the mother in using the telephone. They also gave the mother more than half of the emotional support she received and 60% of the help with money management and service arrangement.

As for other family members, the daughters' husbands (the sons-in-law) provided approximately 4–6% of most of those forms of help and 11% of the help with money management, shopping, and transportation. When the caregivers' children still lived at home, they provided just about as much help as the sons-in-law. Other family members (primarily the caregivers' siblings) also provided little help with most tasks except for money management and emotional support, in both instances providing approximately one-fifth of the assistance.

A clue to the helping role of daughters-in-law was provided in a study by Horowitz (1985b). When sons were the primary caregivers, they expected and depended upon both emotional and concrete support from their wives. More than three-fourths of the married sons, but less than half of married daughters who were primary caregivers reported the involvement of their spouses in care of the elderly parent. (Chapters 8 and 9 elaborate the nature of help husbands provide to caregiving daughters and daughters-in-law.)

CARE REQUIRED: HOW LONG AND HOW MUCH?

Because disabled older people have chronic ailments, caregiving activities must be sustained from day to day, week to week, and year to year. The amount of time spent in caregiving, like the nature of the tasks involved, changes over time if and when the older person becomes more disabled.

The Long-Term Care Survey found that three-fourths of the daughter-caregivers provided help to their parents every single day. As might be expected, they were outdone by spouse-caregivers of whom almost all gave daily care. On the average, the daughters devoted slightly more than 4 hours daily to helping their parents. Some were investing an hour or so a day, whereas others were virtually on full-time duty. Almost half of the daughters (45%) had been providing care for 1–4 years and one out of five had been doing so for more than 5 years. Those averages should not obscure the wide variations that occur, however. Some caregivers were newcomers to the parent-care scene, whereas others had been involved for several decades. (Some women report that they have been spending more years in parent care than they had spent in caring for their own children.)

During those hours in which they were caring for a parent, most daughters in the survey (69%) helped the parent with personal care such as feeding, dressing, bathing, and toileting. More than two out of five helped the parent to get in and out of bed or to get around the home, and more than half administered the parent's medication. The vast majority (87%) helped with household tasks such as meal preparation, house cleaning, and laundry. Three out of five handled financial matters for the parents, and almost all (91%) did the shopping and transportation.

Again, it is underlined that the family study of the 1982 survey describes caregivers to the most disabled segment of the impaired elderly population—those in need of ADL assistance. The characteristics of caregivers vary from study to study, as do their activities depending on the characteristics of the older people for whom they are caring. Thus, in a Philadelphia Geriatric Center (PGC) study that included daughters who were helping only with IADL and also those who, in addition, were helping with ADL, the daughters had a median age of approximately 50 (2.5 years younger than those in the LTC survey). They averaged fewer hours a day in care-provision (three versus four as in the survey).

CAREGIVING CAREERS

Parent care is not a one-time episode in a caregiver's life. Many women have *caregiving careers*. Almost half of married daughters caring for widowed mothers in a PGC study, for example, had helped their elderly fathers before they died, and one-third of the women had helped other elderly relatives in the past (Brody, 1985b). Moreover, 22% of those daughters who were currently helping their disabled mothers were helping another elderly family member at the same time. That help was being given to parents-in-law, grandparents, aunts, cousins, and even to more distant relations. Two-thirds of the women had their own children living at home. Given the discrepancy in life expectancy between men and women, it is inevitable that many of the same women will care for dependent husbands later in their lives.

Apart from the sheer demands on such women's time and energy, it is evident that many women in the middle occupy that position more than once. Not only do they do so at different ages and stages, but one woman can have the experience at more than one of her age periods or life stages. And each time, psychological issues arise and with different variations on the emotional themes (see Chapter 7).

The effects on women of their caregiving activities are described in the next chapter.

Chapter 3

Effects of Caregiving on the Caregivers

As the first two chapters have shown, families have reacted responsibly—even heroically—to the vastly increased demand for parent and parent-in-law care. It is the women in the family—wives, daughters, and daughters-in-law—who provide the vast majority of services needed by dependent older people, with daughters predominating in helping those elderly who are the most severely disabled. The needs of disabled older people have exceeded the capacities of many caregiving women. In addition, societal values about women's roles have been changing so that the different values they hold may pull them in opposite directions. This chapter examines the effects of caregiving on parent-caring women and the objective factors in their situations that cause those effects.

As professionals and social scientists were becoming aware of the role of the family in caring for older people, so too did the realization grow that caregiving affected the caregivers themselves and the entire family. For a long time, the focus of attention had been solely on the elderly themselves and their needs. When the caregivers were considered at all, it was as the sources of care—as people in the background who might or might not be available to provide services for the disabled aged. In the 1960s, there was some beginning exploration of the experiences of the caregiver and the family (Brody & Spark, 1966; Posner, 1961), and the forerunner of large-scale studies was taking place in the United Kingdom (Grad & Sainsbury, 1966; Sainsbury & Grad, 1966). In general, however, caregiving family members received relatively little attention until the mid-1970s. In a review of the literature on the subject (Horowitz, 1985a), for example, three-fifths of all the articles in the reference list had been published between 1980 and 1984 and another 27% between 1975 and 1979. Such studies have proliferated in the past decade, resulting in the assembly of a large and remarkably consistent body of information.

To put the matter in perspective, it is emphasized that the vast majority of women *want* to care for elderly parents and *do so willingly*. They derive many positive benefits from parent care such as satisfaction from fulfilling what they see as their responsibilities, adhering to religious and cultural values, expressing their feelings of affection, seeing to it that the parent is well cared for, reciprocating help the parent had given them in the past, and feeling that they are serving as a good model for their own children to follow. At the same time, it is undeniable that many caregivers do indeed experience significant stress effects, though the nature and levels of strains they report vary widely.

EFFECTS OF PARENT CARE

Parent care often affects women's emotional well-being, physical health, life-style, and financial status.

Emotional strains are by far the most pervasive and severe negative effects reported by caregivers (Archbold, 1978; Brody et al., 1987; Cantor, 1983; Danis, 1978; Frankfather et al., 1981; George, 1984; Gurland et al., 1978; Hoenig & Hamilton, 1966; Horowitz, 1982; Noelker & Poulshock, 1982; Robinson & Thurnher, 1979; Sainsbury & Grad de Alercon, 1970). The litany of symptoms identified includes the following:

- Depression
- Anger
- Anxiety
- Frustration
- Guilt
- Sleeplessness
- Demoralization
- Feelings of helplessness
- Irritability
- Lowered morale
- Emotional exhaustion

Related to those effects are restrictions on the caregivers' time and freedom, relationship problems, isolation from being confined to the home, conflict from the competing demands of various responsibilities, and difficulties in setting priorities. Complicating the picture are constraints on life-style such as interference with social and recreational activities, disruption of vocational life (see Chapter 13), and loss of privacy and space when the older person is introduced into the household.

The proportion of caregivers who experience moderate to severe negative effects varies from study to study but generally hovers at approximately half. Data from the 1982 national Long-Term Care Survey about the strains of providing help to severely disabled older people (those with ADL deficits) confirmed the findings of many smaller studies in that 40–50% of respondents reported emotional strain, interrupted sleep, and limitations on their social lives; 30% said the older person required constant attention, and 24% reported interferences with privacy (Stone, R., personal communication, 1986).

The caregiver's immediate family is also affected by interference with its life-style, privacy, patterns of socialization, plans for vacations, and even plans for the future such as retirement or moving away. The caregiver's time and energy may be diverted from family members to the older person. Preexisting relationship problems can be exacerbated, and interpersonal conflicts may be stimulated among family members—the older person, the caregiver, and the latter's husband, children, and siblings. All of these reactions will be discussed and illustrated by case studies in Part II of this book.

The older person's disabilities and decline are often worrisome to those who care for and about her. It is difficult to witness the discomfort, pain, and unhappiness of someone about whom one cares. It is inevitable that the thought comes to mind, "Will this happen to me?" That question, spoken or unspoken, is particularly distressing when a parent suffers from Alzheimer's disease or a related disorder.

Though the emotional strains are the most frequent and severe consequences for caregivers, significant minorities experience physical and financial strains as well. Though information is not precise, various studies estimate that between 15% and 33% adult children experience detrimental effects on their physical health (e.g., Brody et al., 1987a; Horowitz & Dobrof, 1982). (In the 1982 Long-Term Care Survey, the proportion was 16%.) Some speak of back problems from lifting and turning helpless older people and of stress-related ailments such as ulcers. Approximately 15–20% have financial problems due to the expenses of the older person's care (17% in the Long-Term Care Survey).

Financial concerns appear to cause relatively less strain than emotional factors (see Horowitz, 1985a for review). Within that broad generalization, however, some caregivers do indeed have severe economic pressures. They may need to purchase in-home services when all the care needed cannot be provided by the family (particularly for the severely disabled) or to contribute to nursing home costs when Medicaid beds are unavailable or unacceptable.

Among other effects on family income are the "opportunity costs" incurred by those who either quit their jobs because they cannot manage both parent care and employment and by those who work fewer hours, rearrange their work schedules, or take time off without pay because of parent care. (The conflicts and problems of daughters who take such actions are described in detail in Chapter 13.) Information is virtually nonexistent about other hidden costs such as that for health care of the caregiver. It is not known how many caregivers need or seek health care as a direct or indirect result of their caregiving activities.

As with much of the information concerning the aged and their families, there is a caveat about cross-sectional data. Caregivers who report few negative effects or none at all at a particular time may experience increasing strains over time as their caregiving continues—as the older people decline and need more arduous care, as the caregivers themselves and other members of their families encounter health problems, and as their situations change in other ways.

CAUSES OF STRAIN

Identifying the factors that predict or are associated with the strains on those who provide parent care is an enormously complex undertaking. Not only do different caregivers experience different amounts and kinds of strains, but the various factors that produce strain interact with each other in intricate ways. Some are relatively straightforward and objective, such as the type of care needed by the elderly person that may be physically demanding, time-consuming, uncomfortable, or even embarrassing. Other factors are more subtle—the personalities and interactions of the parent and daughter, for example, and the inner, psychological meaning and implications of the need to help a parent. The mosaic of information that depicts the extraordinarily complicated picture is being filled in, however. The "objective" causes of strain will be described here; women's "inner" or psychological experiences appear in Part II.

AMOUNT AND TYPE OF CARE

In general, the older elderly people are, the more vulnerable they are to disability; the heavier the care that is needed, the greater is the strain on the caregivers. The latter may begin by giving the little care that is needed at first, but increase their efforts as the older people become more disabled. As disability becomes severe, the older person is more likely to need help not only with IADL activities such as transportation and shopping but also with ADL such as bathing, dressing and toileting. At that point, independent living is no longer possible and the older person is likely to be introduced into the household of an adult child. More time is consumed in providing an increasing amount of care. Some older people reach a point at which they are incontinent and bedfast. Providing help with such intimate tasks is not only difficult physically for daughters and daughters-in-law, but has distressing emotional overtones.

CHARACTERISTICS OF THE ELDERLY PERSON

Although the functional and physical disabilities of the older person are important in producing strains, *mental disabilities—whether functional or organic—are especially stressful and difficult to deal with.*

The forerunner of studies calling attention to the burden of caring for mentally ill older people was carried out by Sainsbury and Grad (1966, 1970) in England. They studied caregiving to mentally ill people of all ages, but found that the burdens on caregivers were much greater when the recipients of care were over the age of 65. Nearly half of the older people demanded excessive attention and companionship. Almost two-thirds of family caregivers ascribed their own emotional symptoms to worrying about the patient, half found their social and leisure activities restricted, and more than one-third described upset in their domestic routines. Three-fifths reported effects on their physical health, whereas smaller proportions said their income was reduced (14%) or that their employment was affected (12%).

Approximately one-third of the caregivers studied by Sainsbury and Grad (1970) attributed their insomnia, headaches, and irritability to the patient's behavior. The investigators spoke of the patient being a danger to herself or himself, "odd" behavior, being restless or overtalkative, being troublesome at night, being uncooperative or contrary, and having hypochondriacal complaints. Those early findings are interesting in the light of subsequent research showing that *disruptive behavior* associated with Alzheimer's disease is more distressing than the diagnosis *per se*.

Older people's mental problems have emerged as predictors of caregiver strain in much other research. In one study, for example, two-thirds of those caring for the mentally impaired aged reported adverse effects on their households, with the most burdensome problems being heavy physical or nursing care and excessive demands of the patient for companionship (Hoenig & Hamilton, 1966). In another study, behavioral patterns such as nocturnal disturbances were among the most troublesome problems for more than half of caregivers who reported anxiety, depression, and restrictions on their social activities (Sanford, 1975).

Still other investigations identified mental abnormality, incontinence, immobility, excessive demands, and irritability as particularly bothersome

(Isaacs, 1971). Gurland and his colleagues (1978) found a higher incidence of depression in family members whose household included a depressed older person; they characterized this as the "contagion of depression." A similar phenomenon occurred in family members of depressed older people who were living in a nursing home and senior housing (Brody et al., 1987c). The presence of a mentally impaired older person in the home is more damaging to family relationships than the presence of a physically impaired older person (Cicirelli, 1980; Noelker & Poulshock, 1982; Robinson & Thurnher, 1979).

The problems of caring for older people with mental disturbances are particularly important because of the increase in the number of elderly with Alzheimer's disease or a related disorder. People with such diagnoses may present extraordinary management difficulties. Not only do they inevitably require personal care during the later stages of the disease, but they exhibit many distressing behavioral symptoms—forgetfulness, incontinence, wandering, sleep disturbances, and combativeness, for example. It is those problematic and disruptive behaviors and the impaired social functioning results from dementia that are stressful for caregivers (Deimling & Bass, 1986; Gwyther & Blazer, 1984). Family members providing home care to Alzheimer's patients were found to report three times as many stress symptoms as the general population, to take more prescription psychotropic drugs, and to participate in fewer social and recreational activities; women fared worse than men in experiencing such effects (George, 1984). In a similar vein, 42% of the caregivers in an experimental respite project for caregivers of Alzheimer's patients were found to be more depressed than a national sample of adults (Lawton, 1989).

There are other aspects of the care of demented older people that add to the strains experienced by caregivers. They often speak of the distress they feel when the patient is unable to communicate with them or to provide feedback by expressing appreciation for the help and attention they receive. And, of course, many caregivers (particularly adult children who have a genetic stake in the matter) are frightened and anxious. They wonder, Will this happen to me? Perhaps most poignant is the feeling that they have "lost" the older person. Many caregivers report that nursing home placement will take place only when the elderly person no longer recognizes them.

The personality of the older person is probably more important in producing strain than has been emphasized. It is particularly upsetting, for example, when the elderly recipient of care is critical of the caregiver and other family members (Robinson & Thurnher, 1979). This is especially likely to be an issue when the older person lives in the caregiver's household and the latter also has a husband and/or children who live at home (Brody et al., 1988).

CAREGIVER CHARACTERISTICS

Certain characteristics of the caregiver are also associated with the amount and type of strain experienced.

Being a daughter rather than a son is associated with strain. Studies of caregiving invariably find that women experience more stress than men (Cantor, 1983; Cicirelli, 1981; Horowitz, 1985b; Johnson, 1983; Noelker & Poulshock, 1982; Robinson & Thurnher, 1979). This is not surprising since daughters who are the main caregivers provide more help and more help of the kind that requires hands-on care than do sons. But a variety of other suggestions have been made as to why filial care is more stressful to daughters than to sons.

A study by Horowitz (1985b) comparing caregiving daughters and sons illuminates some of the differences between them that hold potential for daughters finding parent care more stressful. She confirmed the findings of others that the men tended to take on the role of main caregiver only in the absence of a female sibling and that daughters were more likely than sons to help with personal care, meal preparation, household chores, and transportation. The lesser commitment of the sons was also shown by the more limited time they devoted to parent care. Sons did talk with the parent regularly, however, and did not differ from daughters in the extent to which they helped to manage the older person's money, provided actual financial help, assisted with dealing with bureaucratic organizations, and gave the parent emotional support.

Sons were more likely than daughters to involve their spouses—the daughters-in-law—in the caregiving situation and to depend on them for help with parent care. They also perceived their spouses to have more supportive attitudes towards their caregiving activities than did the daughters. For their part, the daughters were appreciative when *their* spouses—the sons-in-law—were neutral toward their involvement in parent care. More than three-fourths of married sons, but half of married daughters, reported involvement of their spouses in care. In short, the sons expected and depended upon both emotional and instrumental support from their wives.

The sons in Horowitz' (1985b) research were less negatively affected emotionally than the daughters. They were more likely than the women to respond "no problems" (34% versus 11%) in relation to parent care. Compared with daughters, sons were less likely to believe they had to give up anything (32% versus 60%), that they had neglected other family responsibilities (9% versus 31%), that their leisure activities were affected (22% versus 56%), that their emotional states had changed for the worse (31% versus 59%), or that their plans for the future had been negatively affected (16% versus 43%).

The vulnerability of daughters to strain also extends to those adult children who are not the primary caregiver. In a study of the local and geographically distant siblings of daughters who were the main caregivers, local daughters reported more strain than local sons (Brody, Hoffman, Kleban, & Schoonover, 1989), and geographically distant daughters reported more strain than geographically distant sons (Schoonover et al., 1989) (see Chapter 8 for details). Even when older people are in nursing homes, their daughters experience more stress than their sons (Brody, Pruchno, & Dempsey, 1989) (see Chapter 14).

(Part II of this book explores in detail the psychological reasons daughters experience more strain from parent care than sons.)

Though caregiving daughters-in-law experience many stress effects similar to those of daughters, their relationships with the older people are different qualitatively and have different historical roots. Townsend (1965) found that when there were poor relationships with a member of the household in which an older person lived, the problem appeared to have been greater with daughters-in-law than with sons-in-law. Similarly, in research by Noelker and Poulshock (1982), when a disabled older person lived in the caregiver's household, it was found that daughters-in-law had more severe stress effects than any other category of relatives. By no means do all daughters-in-law have relationship problems with their parents-in-law, of course, but existing problems may be aggravated when the daughter-in-law must provide care. (Qualitative interviews with the daughters-in-law described in Chapter 11 illuminate some of their subjective feelings and experiences that lead to their strains).

Being a woman, then, whether one is a daughter or a daughter-in-law, means experiencing more strain from caring for a disabled older person. As Chapter 1 pointed out, many women are daughters-in-law as well as daughters and, therefore, may need to help both their parent(s) *and* parent(s)-in-law. The number of women who are at risk of both parent and parent-in-law care will increase in the future due to the falling birth rate. Fewer children means fewer daughters, increasing the odds of a woman being the parent carer in the family and the one to take care of parents-in-law.

In addition to gender, there are other demographic and health characteristics of caregivers that relate to the strains they experience. Those characteristics do not stand alone in producing strain, but are interrelated with other of their own and their parents' characteristics. Being an older caregiver, for example, is related to having an older and more disabled parent who needs more difficult care and who has needed that help for a longer period of time. Older caregivers are likely to have more health problems of their own and to be experiencing some age-related decrements such as lower energy levels and problems with vision and hearing. Despite their own health problems, however, caregivers tend to go on providing care as long as they possibly can.

Socioeconomic status is important in determining the kind of care provided. Whether they are rich or poor, caregivers are reliable in seeing to it that older people receive the care they need, but those who can afford to do so are more likely to purchase some services. Conversely, those with low socioeconomic status more often find it necessary to provide the hands-on care themselves and to share a household with the disabled older person. The socioemotional costs are greater for those who provide the direct, hands-on care themselves than for those who manage or arrange the care (Archbold, 1983).

Certainly, hands-on heavy care and sharing a household are stressful. But that is not to say that more stress is invariably associated with lower socioeconomic status. It is possible that some daughters who are in better economic circumstances and some of their less affluent peers experience equal amounts of stress, but that their strains derive from different factors in their situations. Horowitz (1985a) suggests, for example, that offspring with high socioeconomic status may have high expectations of leisure time and retirement opportunities; this may create strains when the needs of the elderly relative keep them from realizing those expectations.

Recently, research has begun to address the effects on women of their employment status when parent care is necessary. The subject is of major importance because so many women now work outside of the home and, therefore, is elaborated in Chapter 13. It is noted here, however, that the parents of caregiving working daughters do not receive less care than parents of nonworking women (Brody & Schoonover, 1986). The indications are that working and nonworking daughters experience many strains that are similar, but also some that are different. The pressures of fulfilling both the work and parent care roles lead some women to leave the work force, reduce work hours, or rearrange their work schedules; those who continue to work are subject to a variety of work disruptions (Brody et al., 1987). Values play a role in the decisions women make. For example, some employed daughters who hold higher level jobs are conflicted and worried about the increasing care needs of their parents that may interfere with their vocational goals; others may work because they and their families need the money they earn.

The effects on a daughter of her marital status during the parent-care years is an important issue in view of the dramatic changes now occurring in patterns of marriage and divorce. A large survey is now underway to determine what the differential effects may be (Brody, 1988). Chapters 9 and 10 present some preliminary information based on in-depth interviews with women in different marital status groups.

LIVING ARRANGEMENTS

Contrary to popular notions, the vast majority of older people do not wish to live with their adult children and do so mainly when they become disabled and cannot live alone (see Chapter 2 for data on shared households). When that happens, the older people are approximately four times more likely to live with a daughter than with a son.

Every study of caregiving has found that the strains on the caregiver are much greater when the disabled older person lives in the caregiver's household than when the older person lives separately (Horowitz, 1982; Lang & Brody, 1983; Reece et al., 1983; Sainsbury & Grad de Alercon, 1970). In research in which disabled older people and their caregivers shared households, for example, 22% of caregivers suffered severe multiple stress effects, 50% suffered moderate multiple stress effects, and 28% suffered mild multiple stress effects (Noelker & Poulshock, 1982). (Note that none reported a total absence of stress effects.)

It should not be assumed that simply living under the same roof is stressful in itself, however. It is undeniable that shared households widen the arena for potential interpersonal conflicts; the participants are in enforced contact with each other, and the negative effects on family members stand out in bold relief. But the sharing of a home must be disentangled from other factors. Such living arrangements occur primarily when the older person is severely disabled and can no longer manage independently. It may be the heavy care that produces strain, and problems may be exacerbated if the home is small or ill-equipped for care, resulting in crowding or loss of privacy.

Intrahousehold caregiving not only is associated with "heavier" care and more caregiver strain, but deters labor-force participation for some people (Soldo & Myllyluoma, 1983), is related to women quitting their jobs for parent care or experiencing negative effects on their occupational activities (Brody et al., 1987), and is implicated in strains reported by husbands of caregiving daughters (Kleban et al., 1989) (see Chapter 9).

Although shared households clearly are more stressful than separate households, there are also differences depending on whether the household contains two or three generations. When three different household configurations were compared (Brody et al., 1988) to determine the differential strains on the caregivers, daughters whose elderly mothers lived in separate households again fared the best. Their elderly mothers were the most capable functionally and cognitively, and fewer of the daughters experienced caregiving strain, limitations on their privacy or life-style, or interference with time and relationships with their immediate families and friends. In fact, there was not one strain variable on which caregivers providing interhousehold help exceeded the strains of daughters in two-generation households (elderly mother, caregiving daughter, and the latter's spouse) or three-generation households (when caregivers' children are present).

In the two-generation households, both mothers and daughters were older than their counterparts in the other two living arrangements. Being in advanced old age was associated with the greater sensory and cognitive impairment of the older women and with their receiving the most help. This undoubtedly accounts, to a great extent, for the finding that more of their caregiving daughters reported strain than did those living separately. Theoretically, these daughters and their husbands were at the "empty nest" phase of life, but they exemplify the concept of the "empty nest refilled" (Brody, 1978).

When the "nests" of the caregivers and their husbands contained both their own children and the disabled elderly parent, the daughters had significantly poorer mental health, and more of them reported symptoms of depression, restlessness, and feelings of isolation and missing out on something as effects of care. In addition, compared to the daughters in two-generation households, these daughters were more likely to view their mothers as critical of the sons-in-law and grandchildren, and as more likely to complain. Similar findings about the vulnerability of caregivers in three-generation households have been reported by Noelker and Poulshock (1982).

It is obvious that three-generation households not only hold the potential for problems of space and privacy, but widen the arena for interpersonal conflicts. Such multigenerational living can exacerbate the role strain of the daughter or daughter-in-law in meeting the needs of husband, child(ren), and disabled parent, particularly if the elderly parent complains and is critical of family members.

Living at a geographic distance from a disabled parent may cause different kinds of strain. Because increasing mobility means that more adult children now live at a distance from elderly parents, this has become a significant problem. No matter how concerned and responsible one is, day-to-day care cannot be provided when a parent is far away. In some ways, the strains experienced by such children are similar to those of local children—worry about the parent's decline, for example, and various emotional symptoms. Some strains are specific to the distance between parent and child, however, such as the need to make frequent trips to visit and the feeling that there is no one close at hand on whom the parent can rely. Chapter 8 describes the findings from a PGC study of geographically distant children.

SUPPORT FROM OTHER FAMILY MEMBERS

Virtually all available information indicates that the adult daughter who becomes the principal caregiver provides the bulk of the help needed by the parent, with very little given by the latter's other adult children or other family members. When assistance is forthcoming, it supplements rather than reduces the helping activities of the caregiver (Horowitz, & Dobraff 1982; Noelker & Poulshock, 1982). When the parent lives in the daughter's household, the distribution of services becomes even more unbalanced, with that daughter providing an even greater proportion of the help than when the parent lives separately (Brody & Schoonover, 1986).

There is little evidence to support the contention that increasing the caregiving activities of siblings would relieve the main caregiver's strains. In fact, existing data suggest that the actual amount of help the latter receives does not affect her strains. What does seem to result in less burden is her feeling that she has the emotional support of other family members—that they have supportive attitudes and can be depended on at times of need, for example (Horowitz, 1982; Noelker & Poulshock, 1982; Zarit et al., 1980). Such findings were strongly confirmed in a study of caregivers' relationships with their siblings (Brody et al., 1989; Schoonover et al., 1988) (see Chapter 8).

QUALITY OF RELATIONSHIPS

Any caregiving situation takes place in the context of the qualitative relationships of the family members, relationships that have a long history. Research confirms the logical supposition that it is somewhat less of a strain to help a parent to whom one has always felt close and for whom one has considerable love and affection. Although the presence of good relationships does indeed result in more care being given, adult children feel responsible and provide needed care even when relationships are poor (Horowitz, 1982). In fact, as the case material in Chapters 9 and 10 shows, daughters often go on giving high levels of care in stormy situations, with severe conflict among various members of the family.

NONFAMILY SERVICES

The effects on caregivers when "formal" (i.e., nonfamily) services are provided or when they are lacking is an issue that had been receiving considerable attention in recent years. There is consensus among professionals and researchers that community services are grossly underdeveloped, and that those that are available are uneven regionally, in short supply, fragmented, and are not funded consistently. Apart from the strains induced by the absence of services, caregivers are often confused and frustrated in their attempts to access existing services that are delivered by different organizations each of which has different eligibility criteria (see Chapter 15).

Various misconceptions about the effects of formal services have been refuted:

- Formal services do not encourage family caregivers to reduce the amount of care they provide (Horowitz et al., 1983; Lawton et al., 1989); nonfamily services supplement and complement rather than substitute for family services (Gibson, 1984).
- Families do not greedily overuse services that are made available to them but are often reluctant to use them and are extremely modest in whatever requests they do make (Brody et al., in press b; Zimmer & Sainor, 1978).

The system of long-term care services that are needed is discussed in Chapter 15. Professionals agree that such services should have a family focus—that is, they should address the needs of the caregiving families as well as the needs of the older people themselves. Thus, high on the list of service priorities is respite care—services such as day care, in-home care, and temporary institutional care—that provide caregivers with opportunities to have some relief and time away from the disabled older person.

Determining the actual effects of community services in reducing caregiver stress is an extraordinarily difficult research task. Controlled studies have been scarce, but a few have been carried out (for a review, see Kane and Kane, 1981). In a controlled study of respite service for caregivers of Alzheimer's patients, the service group caregivers kept the older people out of a nursing home for a slightly longer time than did the control group caregivers (Lawton et al., 1989). In the large-scale Channelling experiment, the caregivers showed improvements in well-being as measured by the effects on their privacy and social limitations, but did not show reductions in emotional, physical or financial strains (Corson et al., 1986; Kemper and Associates, 1986; Lawton et al., 1989).

The lack of improvement in caregivers' mental health when formal services are introduced may be due to various factors: the service intervention may be very small as compared with the severity of the strains; the service may not be directed to the most stressful tasks; not all caregivers need the particular service being offered; improvement in one sphere of well-being does not necessarily spill over into another sphere; and some caregivers who may be under severe strain do not avail themselves of enough service, or it may be inadequate to their needs, or they may be too far along in the trajectory of stress (see Horowitz, 1985a; Lawton et al., 1989).

Another way of assessing the effects of a service in reducing caregivers' burdens is to ask for the caregivers' own evaluations. In all reports about respite programs, caregivers are emphatically positive. In the large PGC respite program for caregivers of Alzheimer's patients, for example, the service was given a resounding endorsement: the caregivers said they had received relief, were satisfied with the program, and wished for respite more than for any other service in the coming year (Brody et al., in press b; Lawton et al., 1989; Saperstein & Brody, in press)

INSTITUTIONALIZATION

It is generally assumed that placement of a disabled older person in a nursing home or other institution signals relief for the caregiver. Professionals who work in such facilities have known for many years that this is not so (e.g., Brody, 1977). Recent research that has been examining the question shows that caregiver strains continue after placement (Brody, Hoffman, & Winter, 1987; George, 1984a). Chapter 14 describes in detail the pressures and stress experienced by caregivers when nursing home placement is being considered and after it has taken place.

SUMMARY

There is no question but that the most prevalent and severe strains of caregiving are emotional, though significant minorities of caregivers report physical and financial strains as well. Among the "external" or objective factors that produce strain are characteristics of the older person such as severe disability, mental problems with disruptive behavioral symptoms, and certain personality traits. Caregiver characteristics that relate to strain are gender (being female), being older, work status, role overload, sharing a household with the parent or parent-in-law (particularly if one's own children still live at home), the socioemotional support received from other family members, the quality of past relationships, and help from community services. Having a parent in a nursing home leads to special kinds of strain.

It bears repetition that women experience more strain than men from parent care. The chapters in Part II will look closely at dynamic factors that relate to caregivers' strains—the "inner" or psychological aspects of being a caregiving daughter or daughter-in-law.

Chapter 4

Values About Women's Roles
and Care of the Aged

Among the qualitative aspects of parent care are intangibles such as values, feelings, and the quality of the relationships among those involved. Some values may be remaining constant, whereas others may be changing. The resulting tension between different values may contribute to the strains women experience during the parent care years. More specifically, the question to be explored is whether values about family care of the aged compete with changing values about women's roles.

Values—the "normative expectations [that] serve as guidelines for behavior" (George, 1980)—arise in the context of a particular social environment at a particular time. Though mutable in that they are responsive to changes in the environment, values generally change slowly. Lags may occur, therefore, between conditions that have changed and value changes that respond to the new conditions.

What are often called "traditional" values hold that the provision of help to the disabled elderly is a family responsibility and, in particular, is the role of the women in the family. Those values developed before the massive demographic trends described in Chapter 1—before the radical change in the number and proportion of older people in the population who lived to advanced old age, before the shift in the nature of their ailments dictated prolonged care, and before the fall in the birth rate. All of those trends combined to increase the demand for parent care while reducing the capacity of adult children to provide that care. Those developments occurred in the context of broad socioenvironmental changes such as the phenomena of urbanization, industrialization, mobility, increasing educational levels, public economic support for the elderly, and inflation. At the same time, values about women's roles have been changing. The "new" values hold that it is acceptable, even desirable, for women to have more egalitarian roles with men. The most visible expression of the change has been women's greatly increased participation in the work force.

Parent-caring women, therefore, are living in a window of time—a difficult transitional period in which two sets of values have potential for competition, for placing women in the middle.

Women have always been responsive to social values regarding the roles they should play. Indeed, they not only accept, even endorse, the responsibilities assigned to them by society, but often accept the blame when things go wrong. Consider the prime example of parent-caring women who are now in late middle age and early old age. Through accidents of historical timing, they have been buffeted and blamed by a succession of changing values and psychological theories.

When these women were in their teens and twenties, the goal instilled in them by society and their families was to marry young, and then to stay at home and perform well (and often exclusively) as wife, homemaker, and mother. The pressures to keep them in those roles have been well described by the leaders of the Women's Movement (Friedan, 1963).

Then, when the women had patterned their lives on the model designed by society, along came the newest pronouncements about childhood development. Mothers were held almost solely responsible for any problems evidenced by their children. Little Johnny's "bad" behavior and little Mary's emotional problems were traced directly to mother's doorstep. Moms were told they had "failed"—they were not being perfect (or even adequate) mothers.

As their children grew, those very same women heard the new message being sent by the Women's Movement: they had consented to being unfulfilled by limiting themselves to the wife/mother role: they should have had careers in order to realize their full potential. Some responded by resuming their education, some entered the work force for the first time, and still others returned to careers that had been interrupted by marriage and motherhood. Some of those who did not have felt inadequate—as though somehow they've missed out or have been out of step with the culture of their times.

Then, in response to the new demography, the efforts of those women in providing parent care increased exponentially. Yet again they are blamed, this time by the stubborn myth of filial neglect of the old. They are urged by some policy-makers and social attitudes to redouble their efforts as an expression of the "old" family values. And again, women have an uneasy feeling that they should be doing more and accept blame for not doing so. This was pointed up sharply by a study of parent-caring women in which women were the principal caregivers to their dependent mothers, were in the middle of competing demands on their time and energy, and were experiencing many strains as a result of parent care (Brody, 1985b). Those who had "empty nests" had those nests refilled with elderly disabled mothers—some quite literally, and all in terms of increased responsibilities. For many of the women, care of their mothers was but one episode in time-extended "caregiving careers" to more than one older relative. Some of the women had quit their jobs to care for their mothers, and others were considering doing so or had cut back on the number of hours they worked, and many were experiencing problems on the job because of parent care.

Yet three-fifths of those very same women said that "somehow" they felt guilty about not doing enough for their mothers, and three-fourths of them agreed that nowadays children do not take care of their elderly parents as was the case in the "good old days."

Ironically, as some of these very women are approaching or entering the aging phase of life and some are becoming disabled themselves, the blame is starting a new cycle. Their daughters are being accused by the very same myth of not fulfilling *their* parent-caring obligations.

Are women's values about family care of the elderly changing in response to the enormous pressure exerted by the demographic and socioeconomic trends? More specifically, are there value changes among those who are feeling that pressure the most—the women themselves? Are their "old" values concerning care of the aged being driven out by the "new" values?

The old value is very old indeed. It has been said that "The Fifth Commandment—'Honor your father and mother'—is terse, unambiguous, and powerful in its simplicity. So, too, a parallel form in the Holiness Code 'A man, his father and mother, must revere'." (Greenberg, 1984, p. 17).

Though it is clear that for thousands of years, adult children have been enjoined to honor, respect, and care for their parents, there is also ambiguity about how "to honor" should be translated into actual filial behavior. In Schorr's (1960) words, "Though there are old and honorable antecedents for the precept to render 'offices of tenderness' to one's parents . . . the *content* of this precept changes with social change" (p. 2).

"Offices of tenderness" may mean intangibles such as respect, affection, and emotional support. The phrase may also be interpreted to mean financial support for day-to-day expenses, payment of medical bills, sharing one's home, and the provision of instrumental and personal care services when one's parents are disabled. Part of the problem in discussions of values about filial responsibility is that such distinctions are not always made. That is, the components of that global concept are blurred rather than sorted out and anchored to particular kinds of tasks or responsibilities.

Some values have changed regarding the respective roles of the family and the formal support system in providing help of various types to the elderly. S. Brody (1987) has described societal responses to the aged and their families in this century as having been shaped by the value of avoidance of economic catastrophy. The Social Security Act and its subsequent amendments responded to the catastrophe of widespread poverty. Medicare responded to older people's lack of resources with which to purchase acute medical care. Both responses accepted the new value of societal rather than filial responsibility to meet those economic catastrophes. What S. Brody (1987) calls the third catastrophe—the need for continuity of long-term care—has received only limited response from society, with families still being expected (even exhorted) to meet day-to-day needs for help with personal care and instrumental activities that have gone beyond their capacities to provide.

Caregiving daughters are feeling the impact of that long-term care catastrophe and are a clear expression of the value dilemma. The fundamental question here is whether women's values have changed and, if so, whether their new lifestyles that responded to the value changes will affect the care of their elderly parents and parents-in-law.

Studies of women's values about their changing roles have not usually focused on care of the elderly. There has been confirmation of the popular belief that changes in women's sex role attitudes occurred after the mid-1960s (Mason et al., 1976), and "tremendous shifts" have been reported toward more egalitarian sex roles among married women who were interviewed in 1962 and again 15 years later in 1977 (Thorton & Freedman, 1979). Despite such changing attitudes and the enormous publicity given to the pressures on young women who are employed, they do not enjoy substantially increased assistance from their husbands in domestic tasks (e.g., Abrecht et al., 1979; Stafford et al., 1977; Walker, 1970).

Because there was virtually no information that focused specifically on the intersection of women's changing roles and the increased need for parent care, a PGC study approached the issue by surveying three generations of Philadelphia-area women in 1977–1978.* The women were members of families that included three generations of women—a grandmother, a middle-aged daughter, and a young adult granddaughter. Three generations were studied in order to identify change and continuity in values that bear on caring for disabled older people, particularly values about family care of the aged and about gender appropriate roles. Women were chosen as respondents because they not only are the main caregivers to the old but because the old who are in need of parent care are primarily women.

The relevant issues were studied from several vantage points in order to define and measure the elusive concept of values. Values were operationalized as the women's attitudes, opinions, and preferences that might predict future caregiving. That is, the aims were to discover whether there are differences across the generations; to detect any trends in those differences; and, based on those trends, to determine what they might imply for the future in relation to care of the elderly. Though not identical with behavior, and susceptible to shifts over time, values were seen as significant

*Data on the PGC study of three generations of women were derived from studies funded by the Administration on Aging (grants number 90-A-1277 and 90-A-2174). See Brody et al., 1983, 1984; Campbell & Brody, 1985; Lang & Brody, 1983.

indicators of the directions that actual behavior might take. In addition, the lives of the middle generation women were compared with the lives of the elderly women when the latter were in their middle years. Finally, some information was collected about actual behavior—that is, the family care that was being given to those of the older women in the families who needed it.

Overall, the findings illustrated first, that there has been continuity in some values and change in other values, but that changes that occurred had taken hold unevenly. Second, the global value that favors "filial responsibility" takes on different meanings when linked to specific and different kinds of behavior. Third, the study showed as other studies had shown (see Deutscher, 1966) that the values people express are not always translated into their actual behavior. Finally, differences in the filial and parental behavior of the elderly women and the middle generation daughters illustrated the influence of values and environmental change one upon the other.

ATTITUDES

The PGC study found that *there had been changes across the generations about the respective roles that should be played by women and men*. The women's attitudes with respect to gender-appropriate roles revealed significant trends across the three generations, with progressively more egalitarian attitudes among women of each successively younger generations. Despite these trends—that is, the generational differences—large majorities of all generations endorsed propositions that are consistent with views attributed to the Women's Movement. They favored the sharing of roles by men and women in, for example, traditionally female roles such as child care and parent care. This implies that the attitudes of even the oldest women had changed (though not to the same extent as those of the daughters and granddaughters), as they too had been exposed to the social climate that was encouraging changes in women's roles. The differences among the three generations were greater, however, when the women were asked if sons and daughters should do the same kinds of helping tasks for their elderly parents. The middle generation women were in the middle in that their attitudes about gender-appropriate roles generally were between those of the granddaughters and grandmothers.

Parenthetically, in a brief telephone survey of the husbands of the middle generation women, the men generally agreed with their wives' views about egalitarian roles for men and women. The husbands, however, were more likely than their wives to believe that sons should be given more encouragement to go to college and to feel that a working father should not have to spend as much time bringing up children as a mother does.

Another set of trends was revealed regarding the receptivity of the women to formal (nonfamily) services for the elderly. Surprisingly, the oldest generation was the most receptive to formal services, whereas the youngest was the least in favor of such services. At the same time, the youngest generation of women was the one most in favor of grandchildren helping the elderly. (That attitude was characterized as "grandfilial responsibility.") Here, the oldest women undoubtedly were expressing the well-documented desire of older people not to "be a burden" to their children. The granddaughters may have been responding with the optimism and idealism of their stage of life to hypothetical circumstances which they had not yet experienced. The middle generation women, on the other hand, again were in the middle; they were deeply divided among themselves about receptivity to formal services. A majority of all generations agreed on one item related to formal versus informal services: that it is better for a working woman to pay someone to care for her elderly mother than to leave her job to do it herself.

It is of particular interest that the granddaughters, who are the potential caregivers of the future, felt more strongly than the middle generation women (their mothers) and much more strongly than their grandmothers about "grandfilial responsibility" (that older people should expect help from their grandchildren). More than three-fourths of the granddaughters favored such help, in contrast to only approximately one-fifth of the grandmothers; the middle generation women (again) were in the middle in that they were evenly divided on the question.

One can only speculate on the meaning of such strong generational differences about the role of grandchildren. Although the young women's attitudes may reflect their inexperience and life stage, at the least they indicate the vigorous survival of feelings of family responsibility. We do not know why the middle generation women lacked consensus on that issue. Those who did not expect grandchildren to provide care to their grandparents may not define the responsibilities of grandchildren as including such help, or they may wish to protect their daughters from the excessive responsibilities and strains they themselves were experiencing or were seeing other women experiencing. Those who were in favor of grandfilial responsibility may have been expressing values reflecting strong family cohesion.

Side by side with the trends—that is, the generational differences noted—was continuity. *Values about family care of the aged had not changed from generation to generation.* That is, there were no generational differences in values relating to family responsibility toward the elderly. Regardless of the generation to which they belonged, large majorities of all the women expressed positive attitudes toward family help for the aged and toward intergenerational solidarity and dependability.

It is significant that the traditional value about family care of the old held its ground among the middle generation women even though three-fifths of them were in the labor force (a proportion identical to national data at the time). Moreover, the attitudes of employed women and those who did not work outside the home did not differ. And those attitudes held firm regardless of the amount or type of help needed by their elderly mothers.

Surprisingly, their own endorsement of family help to the elderly did not prevent the women from indicting other families for filial negligence. Nearly four out of five women in each generation believed that adult children nowadays do not take as good care of elderly parents as they did in the past. The vitality of that myth was demonstrated once again.

Continuity as well as change were expressed in other responses the women made. Majorities of all three generations were in agreement about what adult children should and should not do to behave responsibly toward a dependent parent. In this, they took into consideration the individual circumstances and competing responsibilities of adult children. They agreed that adult children *should* adjust their family schedules and help to pay for professional care for a disabled widowed mother if need be, but that they *should not* be expected to adjust their work schedules or share households with the parent. The three generations also paralleled one another in expecting less financial help but more adjustments in family schedule from a nonworking daughter than a working daughter.

It is important to note that traditional and new values often existed side by side. Despite their general endorsement of egalitarian attitudes toward gender roles, the women also revealed vestiges of the "old" views. For example, all generations were more likely to expect working daughters than working sons to adjust their work schedules to help their mothers. The lack of consistency obtained in areas other than care of the elderly. Even the youngest women—those most in favor of egalitarian roles for men and women—were divided on the question of whether or not a woman who earns as much as her date should pay her own way when they go out together. Approximately half thought she should do so, one-third thought she should not, and one-fifth were undecided.

PERSONAL PREFERENCES FOR SERVICE PROVIDERS

Another set of questions asked the three generations of women about their personal preferences for the sources of help they preferred (or would prefer) in their own old age. These questions were specific to the women themselves rather than asking what people in general should do.

The preferences expressed also showed both continuity and changes in values. There was continuity in that large majorities of each generation preferred adult children for the intimate functions of confidant (someone to help with problems) and management of their financial affairs in their own old age. But the middle generation women once again were in the middle in that they were least likely to prefer an adult child as provider of housework and personal care services. And they were very much less likely to choose a child for financial help even though they felt that in principle it is all right for old people to get such help from children.

The preferences of the middle generation women for formal (nonfamily) sources of instrumental help and financial support should be noted, for they will be the next cohorts of older women. (Since the study was done in 1977–1978, many of them have now entered the aging phase of life.) The preferences they expressed may mean that they were feeling the pressure of their multiple responsibilities (or were observing such experiences of other family members or friends) and wished to spare their own children similar burdens. They may also have been more sophisticated about government income supports and community services than the elderly women. Their responses are striking indications of their dilemma in wanting to be filially responsible as daughters but not wanting to become dependent on their children in their own old age.

The findings showed too that the meaning of needing help may differ with the specific kind of help that is needed (such as housework, emotional support, financial support, personal care), with the source that one turns to (such as formal programs, friends and neighbors, family, even different members of the family), with the stage in one's life when help is needed, and with a variety of other situational factors.

BEHAVIOR

The *behavior* of the women and their families produced even more evidence for continuity, demonstrating once again that attitudes and opinions are not always reflected in actions. Despite their attitudinal acceptance of formal services for many instrumental helping activities, the vast majority of services to the elderly women who needed help was provided by family members. And though there was overall consensus about egalitarian roles for men and women, *the adult daughters were the major source of help for parents who needed it*. Thus, they behaved in accordance with "traditional" values about women's roles.

The middle-aged daughter's age, her provision of larger amounts of help, and her sharing a household were interrelated—that is, older daughters were more likely to share households with their mothers and to provide more hours of help, illustrating what has been characterized as the peaking of responsibilities and the refilling of the empty nest (Brody, 1978). The elderly women who needed more types of care (including personal care) were more likely to be receiving more hours of help, more likely to be living in a daughter's household, and more likely to be older. Daughters who shared household with their mothers provided eight times more help on the average than those who did not, and daughters who were 50 or older provided five times more help than those who were younger.

When faced with competing demands on their time, what these women gave up was their own free time and opportunities for recreation and socialization.

Such findings are consistent with the conclusion of Troll and Bengtson (1979), that while the rapid pace of social change encourages new ways of expressing old values, it is largely old values that are expressed. But although the data provide behavioral confirmation for the continuity of family values, they also speak strongly to potential burden on aging caregivers and their families and to possible conflict deriving from competing values.

MIDDLE-GENERATION WOMEN THEN AND NOW

Continuity and change again were apparent when the lives of the oldest and middle generation women were compared when each group was between the ages of 30 and 54.

The middle generation women had more responsibilities than their mothers had during those ages, particularly with respect to helping their own adult children financially and with emotional support. They also were doing more paid work and more volunteer work. These women in the middle also were giving more emotional support to their elderly parents than the latter had given to *their* parents. An area in which the current middle generation women provided less help to parents than their mothers had provided to their parents at comparable ages was financial assistance. This of course, reflects the improved income position of older people nowadays.

The middle generation women seemed to be trying to "do it all." For example, they had already worked many more years than they had expected to as young women and had more responsibilities than did their mothers in *their* middle years.

There was also evidence of the continuity of the quality of family relationships within each family down through the generations—particularly as evidenced in the giving and receiving of emotional support. Those women who had received more emotional support from their parents reciprocated by giving more emotional support *to* those parents. Similarly, those who provided more emotional support *to* parents received more *from* their parents. This reciprocity continued down through the generations. That is, those women who gave and received more emotional support to and from their now elderly parents also provided more emotional support *to* their own adult children and received more *from* them.

It appears that family qualitative relationships, whatever their level, continue upward or downward across generations. This finding is consistent with the research and clinical evidence concerning the continuity of individual personality over time (for reviews of this literature, see Neugarten, 1968, 1973) and lends support to the hypothesis that families, too, have "personalities" that are continuous over time (Brody, 1974).

WOMEN IN THE MIDDLE: NOW AND IN THE FUTURE

The counterpoint, even tension, in the operation of different values—both between and within generations—is apparent if the findings are reviewed from the perspective of the current and future generations of middle generation women.

The middle generation women who were in the situation of being both an adult child to an elderly parent and a parent to an adult child best illustrated the potential conflict of the values they held. The ambiguities associated with that situation undoubtedly account for the lack of unanimity among them on some issues. That is, these women may have reacted to the survey questions in their dual roles of adult child and parent. They were the generation least in favor of expecting financial help from children and the least in favor of an impaired parent moving into a child's home. Their multiple roles may account for views that often seem incompatible. For example, though they held egalitarian values, they were the least in favor of married sons adjusting their work schedules or arranging to share a household with their mother. In this, they probably reflected the fact that an elderly woman's son is likely to be a middle-aged woman's husband; that is, the women may have been thinking in their roles as daughters-in-law as well as daughters when they replied to the questions.

The pressures on these middle generation women are suggested by the data indicating that they had already worked many more years than they had expected to as young women and had more children and more responsibilities than did their mothers in their middle years. And, of course, "more responsibilities" includes more parent care.

The granddaughters provided us with a glimpse of what the future may bring. The potential for conflict in values that was most visible in their mothers was also at work with these young women. At an average age of 23, they were the ones most in favor of equal sharing of roles by men and women, but they were also the generation most in favor of the value of family care of the aged. They were expecting to spend more of their lives in the work force than did their mothers and grandmothers at that age, but they also expected to marry and have as many children as did their mothers and grandmothers. These young women, even more than their mothers, were expecting in advance to be able to "do it all." In the effort to live up to their own expectations, they may well become the women in the middle of the future.

The findings of the PGC study, of course, cannot be generalized to the total population, and it took place some years ago. Nevertheless, the research did shed some light on women's present and future caregiving:

- All three generations expressed strong feelings of family and filial responsibility and willingness to be depended on by the elderly parent.
- The finding that attitudes toward gender roles were more egalitarian in each successively younger generation is consistent with popular notions about the impact of women's changing roles and the Women's Movement. The agreement of all three generations that a working daughter need not quit work to care for her elderly mother indicates widespread acceptance of women working. Many young women nowadays appear to be suiting action to the words of the granddaughters in the PGC study. For the first time, more than half of new mothers are remaining in the job market; that percentage has risen from approximately 30% in 1976 (the first year in which the Census Bureau calculated the statistic) to half in 1987.
- Egalitarian attitudes were diluted by items that specified the sharing of household chores. This suggests that, although women expect more sharing with men, some of them still accept certain tasks as gender appropriate.
- The middle generation women were more consistently middling and divided in their attitudes toward formal and informal services. Their lack of consensus may be due to the fact that, being the middle generation, they were thinking in their roles as mothers as well as daughters. Anticipating their own dependency needs in old age, they may have been reacting from the perspective of a care recipient as well as that of a caregiver. Their divergent responses also may derive from the predicament of many of this generation of women in the middle (Brody, 1979b).

The new values about women's roles apparently have not displaced old values such as those associated with family care of the elderly. For example, though a majority of the middle generation women were in the labor force (a figure that corresponds to the national average), the strength of their attitudes toward filial responsibility is compelling evidence that the old value (of family care of elderly parents) remains strong despite the new phenomenon of a majority of middle-aged women working. This suggests that most women who work also will continue to be filially responsible and may be particularly vulnerable to the stress and conflicts of role overload.

The new values seem likely to stimulate changes that have the potential for "role strain" and burden. The information about the lives of elderly mothers and their middle-aged daughters, for example, provided evidence that nowadays the latter have more competing responsibilities.

The women of the youngest generation strongly favored shared roles, but at the same time they were even more emphatic than the mothers or the grandmothers about filial responsibility. The emphasis of the youngest women on "grandfilial responsibility" will need to be monitored as the dependent, very old population continues to increase and as their caregiving daughters also age. It is impossible to predict the extent to which the attitudes of these young women will be translated into willingness and/or capacity to help two generations of older people (i.e., parents and grandparents) or the extent to which the responsibilities of caregiving will be shared by their brothers and husbands. In the future, they may face a dilemma even greater than that of their mothers.

Overall, it is clear—contrary to popular misconceptions—that values connected with family care of elderly parents have not eroded, even among women who are overwhelmingly in support of nontraditional roles for both genders.

The increased help by the middle generation women to their own children is due to the increased educational levels, which prolong the time during which young people are dependent on their parents. Nowadays, financial assistance generally flows from parents to children rather than the reverse (Kingson, Hirshorn, & Cornman, 1986), continuing through the early years of the adult child's marriage—i.e., until the young couple "gets on their feet." The *amount* of financial help varies (with socioeconomic class), but the *direction* is the same. Less financial help to elderly parents nowadays undoubtedly is the result of the better economic position of today's older people who have the benefit of Social Security, SSI, higher life-time earnings, more pensions and savings, and Medicare. Together, the improved income status of the current generations of older people and the increased emotional support they receive from their adult children confirms the contention of Bengtson and Treas (1980) that affective norms have replaced norms of economic dependence of the elderly on their children.

For some families, the direction of the services and financial help may change when the parent is disabled and in advanced old age. In the main, however, older people are clear about certain of their values: most of them do not want financial help from their children, overwhelmingly expressing the wish not to be a burden. The expectation developed in the United States in this century—the new value—is that basic income for older people should come from government programs. In 1935, the Social Security Act was the first major legislative marker expressing this value. Other western developed nations had made the same commitments 50 years earlier. Subsequently, Schorr's (1980) classic monograph documented the grave negative impact of policies that attempted to compel financial support of old people by their adult children. Medicare, Medicaid, and SSI together and cumulatively signed the death warrant of the destructive and inappropriate Legally Responsible Relatives' provisions that compelled adult children to support their parents. The effect of those pieces of legislation was a precipitous drop in the proportion of old people financially dependent on family (see Chapter 2).

The wish for emotional support and the wish not to need or receive financial help from children exist side by side. *Family feeling is not equated with the giving of money*. Adult children are preferred as providers of emotional support and confidants, but not for day-to-day financial help. It is necessary, therefore, to discriminate between responsibility and emotional bonds on the one hand, and the specific ways in which they are expressed on the other. Financial support is not equivalent to affectional ties, and the data in the PGC study confirmed that distinction.

The PGC research reaffirmed the need to assess the quality of past family relationships in setting goals for behavior toward elderly family members. Family styles, whether close or distant, often persist over time. Though relatively poor previous relationships do not necessarily preclude the provision of a basic level of caregiving, the quality of the affective relationships has been found to determine those who "go beyond the call of duty" for a frail elderly relative (Horowitz & Shindelman, 1981).

Perhaps the most striking implication of the PGC study was that despite egalitarian attitudes of the women in the middle about men's and women's roles in parent care, despite the fact that so many of them were in the labor force, and despite their endorsement in principle that formal services are acceptable for many instrumental helping tasks, those women were providing virtually all the parent care needed.

Moreover, the unevenness with which the "new" values about women's roles take hold implies that the process of sharing between men and women is also likely to be uneven and very slow in developing. Consider the results of a *New York Times* nationwide survey in late 1987 (Burros, Feb. 24, 1988). It found that women ". . . have not made much headway in having their husbands share the household chores . . ." and that ". . . even though more women are in the work force and have less time at home, they are still the primary caregivers . . ." (pp. A1, C10).

Taken together, the findings suggest that in the future, families will provide their elderly with various instrumental services to the extent that they have the capacity to do so and in response to situational needs. The fear that current and future generations will become cold, unfeeling, and stop doing what they can to help their old appears to be unfounded. At the same time, the indications are that the pressures on parent-caring women will increase.

How can families reconcile the vastly increased need for chronic care for the elderly with belief in family obligations and women's changing roles? What *should* adult children and daughters in particular do to help their parents?

There are extraordinary difficulties involved in setting values about what constitutes responsible filial behavior. By what yardstick do we measure "normal" (i.e., "healthy" or "good") filial behavior? Do we apply the same yardstick to all families? There are as yet no "normative" standards of behavior for families with aged members as there are for young families in relation to young children, and perhaps there never can be such standards. Setting normative standards with respect to aging families is much more complex. It is compounded by the enormous variability in the extent to which older people need services, the nature of the supports they need and their ability to utilize them; and the ages and life stages at which their dependencies occur. In addition, there are variations in family constellations; in the ages, life stages, health, economic situations, and other responsibilities of the adult children who are depended on; in situational factors such as living arrangements, geographic distance; in the quality of past relationships; and in individual and family tolerance for stress.

There is no simple answer to that question of what adult children *should* do, and it is inappropriate to rely on values developed in earlier periods of time when conditions were vastly different. What is possible now is different because of demography, mobility, women's work force participation, and the much longer overlap in people's obligations to their parents and to their children. (For an excellent discussion of ethical issues about what children "owe" their parents simply because they *are* their parents, see Daniels, 1988.)

Finally, values underlie the judgment of society as to how much and what kind of formal help should be offered through public policy. What should the balance be between individuals' filial responsibility and our collective filial responsibility? The implicit value questions are: How much burden should families be expected to accept before remedies are developed in the form of formal services and facilities? What should the content of filial responsibility be, and what are its limits? How, in fact, do we measure the social and economic cost—to individual, family, and society—of failure to relieve such burdens? And, ultimately, is it not a value judgment as to which type of cost should be the paramount measure?

When values do not accommodate to changing conditions, the lag can add to the strains of caregiving. The case studies in Part II of the book, in which the "internals" of caregiving are explored, show how the value conflicts experienced by women in the middle affect their well-being and the decisions they make about parent care. The intersection of parent care and employment as it affects women in the middle and care of the elderly is examined in detail in Chapter 13.

Part **II**

Inner Experiences*

*Data in this Section derive primarily from studies funded by the National Institute of Mental Health (grants number MH35252, number MH35252-04, number MH40380, and number MH4337). The case studies were developed with funding assistance from The Frederick and Amelia Schimper Foundation of New York and also as part of MH43371.

Chapter 5

Subjective Experiences:
Introduction

Part I of this book summarized the broad demographic and socioeconomic trends that produced the women-in-the-middle phenomenon. It presented quantitative data about some of the consequences of those trends—older people's needs for help, the sources from which that help comes, and the effects of parent care on the daughters and daughters-in-law who provide most of the required assistance. Part I also explored the potential effects of tension between the women's values about family care of the aged and about women's changing roles. Values and trends such as those described interact with inner processes to influence behavior. With that information as background, Part II looks more closely at the subjective experiences—the "internals" of parent care—of some of the real people who appeared earlier as statistics.

We now will hear from the women (in their own words) about their parent-care years. Some of the main issues apparent in their stories will be identified—their inner experiences about caregiving and their interpersonal relationships with their elderly parents and parents-in-law, their siblings, and their husbands and children. The various themes and dynamic processes will be illustrated by many brief case excerpts and by 24 longer case studies. To the extent that available information allows, the perspectives and perceptions of the other family members will be described. Though the main emphasis is on women as caregivers to the elderly mothers and mothers-in-law who constitute the bulk of care recipients, some fathers and fathers-in-law will appear as well. The goal is to advance our understanding of the qualitative aspects of women's parent-care years—the intangible, internal forces that are at work when they assume and continue the caregiving role.

It is, of course, impossible to capture the full range and depth of the internals of care. Since parent care has become a virtually universal experience, the women come from all walks of life, are rich and poor, highly educated and uneducated. They vary in age and stage of life, in ethnic background, in personality, and in adaptive capacities. The quality of their previous relationships with their parents differs. Their families vary in structure and composition. They are in different stages of their caregiving careers. For some women, those careers may be just beginning as the older people's capacities have begun to decline gradually or were abruptly reduced by a catastrophic illness. Other women have been caring for many years for parents who now are in need of total care. Some of the caregivers share their homes with the older people, whereas in other situations the elderly parents or in-laws live in their own homes. And many women help more than one older person simultaneously or sequentially. All of those factors affect the ways in which the parent-care years are experienced.

Despite the heterogeneity of women in the middle, many of them share certain major recurrent themes and issues that relate to parent care. Chapter 6 describes some fundamental and prominent inner experiences that focus mainly on the parent/daughter relationship: the reasons parent care is seen by women as *their* role, and the issues that arise when the older person's disability necessitates a shift in the balance of dependence and independence between parent and daughter. Chapter 7 discusses still another major concern of both daughters and daughters-in-law—their stage of life during the parent-care years. The themes in Chapters 6 and 7 are not the only ones that are experienced, of course, and others will become apparent in the chapters that follow.

The experiences of women do not take place in a vacuum unrelated to the experiences of other close family members—their husbands and children, and their sisters and brothers. Succeeding chapters, therefore, shift the focus to the women's interactions with those close members of their families who constitute a major part of their "social support system."

Chapter 8 concerns the daughter's relationships with other members of her first family (the family of origin)—her parent and her siblings, who are often characterized as "secondary caregivers." The approach is first to examine some of the factors that determine how it happens that one member of a sibling set—a particular daughter, usually—becomes and continues to be the primary caregiver. There has been little exploration of the perceptions of her siblings about the caregiving situations, the effects they experience as a result of parent care, or about their relationships with the primary caregiver. Therefore, the chapter also examines the roles the siblings play and compares the ways in which caregiving differentially affects the primary caregiver and her sisters and brothers. Some of the problems and rewards in the sibling interactions will be described as they relate to the caregiving situations.

Daughters mature, of course, and form or do not form families of their own. To follow daughters developmentally, we then turn to parent-care themes that derive from the structure of their own nuclear families. When they have husbands and children, women may enjoy considerable emotional and instrumental support, or there may be conflict and competition that make the situation more difficult. Other daughters are alone and lonely during their parent-care years because they do not have husbands. Some of these are even more alone because they are childless or are only children.

Since family support is so central to the parent-care experience, the next two chapters are organized in accordance with the daughters' marital status. Although the brief excerpts in Chapters 6, 7, and 8 illustrate common themes in the lives of parent caring women, longer case studies in Chapters 9 and 10 will permit us to see their parent-care years in the context of the family as a whole. The case studies also offer a longitudinal perspective—a view of how the women's situations change over time. The themes many women share will be apparent in the cases, but each chapter will highlight experiences shared by women who are members of a particular marital status subgroup.

The rationale for organizing the chapters in accordance with the women's marital status derives not only from the centrality of women's family status during their parent care years, but also because women's lives have been taking increasingly diverse paths. Changing patterns of marriage, divorce, remarriage, and childbearing have resulted in more women being without husbands and more women being childless during the parent care years (see Chapter 1 for detailed data).

In that context, Chapter 9 focuses on married daughters and parent-care issues that relate directly to that status—in particular, concerns that pertain to their husbands and children (when the latter are present). There will be information about the perceptions and experiences of those husbands and the roles of children when their wives/mothers are involved in parent caring. Six of the eight married women in this chapter have children, and two are childless.

Not-married daughters—that is, those who are widowed, divorced, or separated, or who had never married—claim our attention in Chapter 10. Two of these nine women are widowed, three are divorced, and one is separated. Some of these have children, and some do not. There are also three daughters who had never married. Two of them are "only" and alone; they have no husbands, children, or siblings, and have some unique inner experiences not shared by their caregiving peers who do have close family members.

Chapter 11, which includes seven case studies, is about caregiving daughters-in-law. In some ways, their salient subjective experiences are quite different from those of daughters.

Chapter 12's commentaries summarize the major themes illustrated by the case studies and concludes Part II of the book.

In reading Part II, the effects on all family members and on their relationships with each other should be kept in mind. Whatever the quality of those relationships, they are intricately layered and interwoven with each other in an extraordinarily complex manner. The feelings and behavior of the caregiver and the other actors on the family scene inevitably affect each other in reciprocal fashion. The impact on each individual and on the family as a whole can only be understood if there is an awareness of those interlocking relationships.

The interrelationship of the well-being of family members was not always fully understood. A major philosophical thrust of this century has been recognition of that interdependence; the homeostasis of the family as a whole is affected by a disturbance in any of its parts.

Consideration of family relationships in the later phases of the family life cycle is an even more recent development. One of the reasons why later life relationships suffered neglect is that the aged were not much in evidence when psychodynamic formulations about human behavior began and emphasis was placed on the young nuclear family. Simultaneously, social theorists, impressed with the impact of industrialization, mobility, and urbanization, postulated the isolated nuclear family as the modal, optimal family type in modern society (see Chapter 1). As Townsend (1968) pointed out the last stages in the development of the family were systematically disregarded and only pessimistic predictions of the dissolution of family relationships were made. Stereotypes persisted about the isolation of the aged and their abandonment by families. When, after considerable research, responsible family *behavior* had been thoroughly documented, Rosow (1965) emphasized that it was time to turn to the study of the *quality* and *meaning* of intergenerational relations.

During the family life cycle, there is a constant balancing and rebalancing of dependent relationships. The family that functions well has the capacity to be flexible, with the family homeostasis shifting over time to meet the changing needs of family members. Each change in the capability of each family member necessarily affects every other family member.

Change is a constant process in individuals and families in the later stages of the family life cycle as well as in early phases. The chances of the healthy, married 65- or 70-year-old woman or man of today to become disabled, widowed, and dependent on adult children increases with every added year of life, for example. The factor of change applies to the other family members as well. Over time, 40-year-old children become 65- or 70-year-old children. They may retire, develop health problems, and experience losses during the lifetimes of their very old parent(s). The family constellation is constantly being modified by an ebb and flow in family membership as new members are added through marriage and birth while others are lost. Thus, every family experiences continuing processes of change and "Periods of Adjustment" that never really cease.

When an older person needs care, reverberations are set up that affect every member of the family. Though the concepts of interdependence and rebalancing stand out in bold relief when an elderly family member becomes disabled, theoretical understanding of the impact on the entire family has not been fully operationalized in studies of family caregiving. Most of the research and clinical literature documents the mental and emotional strains experienced by the individual characterized as the primary caregiver.

At every stage of life, the individual's and family's psychological capacities and relationship patterns are important determinants of how the family manages the various transitions and crises it experiences. Depending on their life experiences and personalities, individuals vary in their capacities to be appropriately dependent and in the extent to which they have the capacity to be depended on by others.

Individual and family behavior at the later phases of the individual and family life cycle is no more uniform than at the early phases. Older families are not exempt from variability along the spectrum from close, warm bonds at one extreme to severe conflict or emotional distance at the other. Any model of ideal behavior at the parent-care stage of life, then, like all models, must be modified by the complexities of each situation. People are diverse in personality, emotional maturity, and stability, and there is wide variability from family to family in the quality of their relationships. Since there are no perfect people or perfect families, it can be expected that residual problems, whether small or large, will be carried forward in time. Similarly, the strengths in the family may come to the fore and facilitate the situation for all concerned.

The relationship between an elderly mother and her caregiving daughter has a long history and is, of course, a central and salient factor. Some ambivalence is virtually omnipresent. Cartoonist Cathy Guisewite captured this concept in her "Cathy" strip in which two middle generation women are chatting. The first woman says to the second, "I'm in this horrible phase with my mother, Charlene." Charlene replies, "Yeah, me too Cathy." Cathy goes on, "I love her. I need her . . . I think about her all the time . . . But when I'm finally with her, I'm defensive, cranky, and impossible to be with." "Yeah, me too," Charlene agrees. "When did your phase start?" asks Cathy. "Birth" is Charlene's terse answer. "Me too," Cathy says. "No wonder we're so good at it," Charlene concludes.

Whatever the quality of previous family relationships, the need for parent care involves increased amounts of interaction in new and unanticipated forms—between parent and adult children, and among the siblings and other relatives involved. What is important here is that parent care does not *cause* problems in family relationships. Rather, the pressures are such that relationship problems that may have been quiescent are reactivated or exacerbated. The quality of the relationships between caregivers and their parents and parents-in-law, with husbands and children, and among the adult siblings ranges from being close and mutually supportive to being emotionally distant or openly hostile.

The dependency of the parent exerts pressures that compel a rebalancing of roles and relationships, however. The rebalancing may be stimulated by the parent's slow decline that permits a gradual transition. Or, the family may be thrust precipitously into a major upheaval by a parent's catastrophic illness. Whatever the pace of the readjustment, the caregiver's husband or children may compete with the old person for time and attention. New battles may be fought in the old wars among the siblings; old loyalties and alliances as well as old rivalries operate. Even when the family is dispersed geographically, the emotional currents continue to flow and to affect the caring situation. Given the interpersonal and intrapsychic tensions, it is not surprising that the emotional strains of caregiving have been such a consistent theme in research reports.

Though this part of the book is designed to help in understanding the "internals" of care, the "external" factors that relate to the strains of caregiving (see Chapter 3) should be kept in mind as well. Among the objective or external factors that are interwoven with subjective issues are the level and type of the older person's mental and physical disability and the kind of care needed, the living arrangement of the older person (that is, living separately from the adult child or in the latter's household), and the other roles the daughter plays.

The family situation also interacts with the socioeconomic, physical, and social environment in which caregiving occurs, a context that plays a major role in determining how care is provided and what the effects on all family members may be. Economic status is among those more objective and vitally important factors. The ability to purchase help in caregiving or the availability of services through third-party payors can be of major importance in making the situation more bearable, allowing the caregiver to have some respite and life of her own. Hand in hand with the importance of money is the availability or lack of availability of community services. Caregivers often are unaware of even those services and entitlements that do exist. Even when they are aware of such resources, the difficulties of actually obtaining them can be time consuming, frustrating, and exasperating (see Chapter 15). In short, caregiving activities take place in and are affected by the social context—the existence and accessibility of services, facilities, and entitlements that could help them or that may be unavailable to those who need them.

Values, too, though intangible, exert a powerful influence on the daughters and daughters-in-law (see Chapter 4). Religious, cultural, and social values become visible through the ways in which the women describe and enact the caregiving role.

There are caveats to be kept in mind as the following chapters are read.

First, themes that are shared by many caregivers (Chapters 6 and 7) vary in intensity; they may be barely discernible or exist in exaggerated form.

Second, some of the patterns described are by no means shared by all caregivers, parents, and other family members, or even by large proportions of them. Some of the themes are major in that they are articulated by many daughters. Others are minor because they are experienced by smaller groups of women. Even the minor themes are major, however, in the sense that they are prominent in the subjective experiences of those in whom they exist.

Third, many of the themes and processes coexist. The admixtures of the various themes and the contrapuntal interplay among them is complex and infinitely varied.

Fourth, and finally (and perhaps most important), no judgments are made about the point at which caregivers' behavior goes beyond the range of "normality"—that is, when the line is crossed so that therapeutic help for them appears to be indicated. For one thing, different professionals might make different judgments, and no standards have been developed that identify the parameters of "normality." In addition, the interviews on which the observations are based were not designed to identify "pathology" or to delve deeply into the historical relationship patterns and psychodynamic processes that are at work. Those processes may be subtle or stand out in bold relief. The illustrative case excerpts and longer case studies were deliberately chosen because they make certain patterns clear. The purpose of identifying the themes and patterns is to stimulate professionals to a more complete understanding of the various processes, to think about some of the solutions to any problems that may exist, and to explore relatively un-explored frontiers in order to point the way to helping approaches that could alleviate much suffering.

Nevertheless, it is inescapable that some women will be seen as doing well, whereas the severe strains others experience will be obvious. Some families mobilize their own and their families' resources and community resources that may exist in a relatively orderly fashion; the various family members help each other along the way. Other family scenes are chaotic and characterized by conflict.

It will be apparent that some daughters and daughters-in-law are able to set limits on what they do, whereas others are not able to do so. Some of the latter provide arduous care for many long years, going beyond what appear to be the limits of endurance. They may do so at the cost of their own well-being and with severe deprivation and suffering to their own families. Some such women appear to be subject to compelling and powerful forces; they fail to make any attempt to free themselves and their families from parent-caring burdens that are oppressive even when options to relieve them are available and are offered. What returns do they get from their efforts that outweigh the burdens? (Options are not always available, of course, in the form of affordable or subsidized services or nursing facilities.)

Thus, a fundamental question concerns the value judgments made by professionals and society. When is continued caregiving viewed as "good" and "normal"? At what point are these women judged to need help in *reducing* their caregiving activities? Are women to be applauded because, as one of them put it (repeating this after recounting each of many crisis episodes in her long caregiving career), "I persevered"? Are the women to be criticized when placement of a parent in a nursing home occurs as soon as a parent can no longer live alone or if such placement is made after 3 or 6 or 19 years? When is caregiving "healthy," and when is it not? When is enough enough, and what limits should be set? Readers will make their own evaluations about which women should be urged to redouble their caregiving efforts, which ones are managing well, which need help to ameliorate their situations, and the kinds of interventions that may be indicated for the latter.

Chapter 6

"It's a Woman's Role"
The Struggle for Control, and
The Fallacy of Role Reversal

Beyond the belief that care of the elderly is a family responsibility, there are major "inner" or subjective themes that recur over and over again in the stories daughters and daughters-in-law tell about their caregiving experiences. Those shared themes cut across the wide diversity in the women's characteristics and situations. Not all caregivers have all of the same subjective experiences, of course, and there are many other themes that may be major or minor for a particular woman.

The first, most powerful, and over-arching theme, one that appears and reappears for virtually all daughters and daughters-in-law, is their fundamental acceptance that parent care is a woman's role. Related to this acceptance is their feeling that they are responsible for more than performing the instrumental, personal-care, and nursing tasks that are needed. The women also feel responsible for the emotional well-being of the older people. Indeed, they often feel responsible for the happiness of everyone in their families.

Another pervasive theme relates to the inner experiences of caregiving daughters, but not of daughters-in-law. (That theme is described in this chapter, however, because so many women play both roles in relation to older people; being both daughters and daughters-in-law they not infrequently help their parents-in-law as well as parents.) Specifically, this striking theme is that so many daughters explain their assumption of the parent-care role (in particular, when they are caring for their mothers) by saying "She took care of me, so now it's my turn to take care of her." A closely related and prominent issue concerns the changes in relationships that occur when a parent becomes dependent on a daughter—the difficulties of the shifts in dependency and independence, and the struggle of mother and daughter for power and control.

PARENT CARE AS A FEMALE ROLE

In exploring the reasons why women, rather than men, almost invariably and unquestioningly are the ones to assume the parent-care role, it is not within the purpose of this book to become involved in the unresolved issue of "nature versus nurture." As Weithorn (1975) noted in her discussion of women's roles in cross-cultural perspective, "Present-day literature is filled with arguments pro and con the question of whether existing relationships are determined by sex-linked biological inheritance or by enculturation" (p. 276). What is basic to our concerns here is that in virtually every culture, the nurturing role belongs to women, no matter how it has come about. That statement, of course, uses a broad brush to paint the overall picture. Differences between the genders are not absolute and mutually exclusive, but a matter of degree. Though men as well as women can be nurturing, however, there is no doubt but that women overwhelmingly are the ones to be the caregivers for anyone in the family who needs help.

Cohler and Grunebaum (1981) point out that the sexes are socialized quite differently in early life. Girls are encouraged to identify with and to be dependent on their mothers. As the ones who are taught to be the nurturers, nurses, homemakers, and "kinkeepers" in the family, they constantly receive signals that they should be like their mothers. Boys, on the other hand, are encouraged to be instrumental and active like their fathers; they learn early that work is their main role—to be the provider or "breadwinner."

A daughter's identification with her mother is further strengthened when she becomes a mother herself. As one daughter put it,

> I never regret caring for her [mother]. She's the only mother I have. When you have children you can empathize with your mother.

In that vein, Gilligan (1982) holds that the key difference between men and women stems from the disparate experience children of each gender have of the care they get from their mothers. Girls, whose basic identity is formed from experiencing themselves as like their mothers, therefore develop the inclination to sense other people's needs and feelings as their own. Women, says Gilligan (1982), "judge themselves in terms of their ability to care" (p. 17).

When little girls become women, they are particularly susceptible to demands for assistance from family and friends because they have been educated since childhood into the caregiving role (Cohler, 1983). The widespread, powerful social value that *families* are responsible for the care of the old really means that *daughters* are the ones held responsible.

Such role assignment begins early in life—even as soon as the baby draws her first breath, as this daughter indicates:

> When I was born, my mother thought I was a boy. When the nurse told her she had a girl, she said "How can that be?" But everyone tried to console her. They said "She'll be a comfort to you in your old age."

A daughter-in-law explains the process of educating little girls in the caregiving role:

> I guess it falls on women because women have children. As an architect, I always considered myself a professional. Taking care of an old person was the furthest thing from my mind. But when you're growing up you see your mother doing stuff so you fall into that. Little boys learn from their dads. So that's how it happens.

A divorced daughter, who said she had "divorced" herself from her parents' way of life and had lived a "Bohemian" life-style of which they disapproved, says:

> I say my mother take care of people who needed help. She took care of her own father whom she adored, her father-in-law whom she disliked, and also her mother-in-law. I have divorced myself from many ways of life, but this [parent care] is the right thing to do. You never really change. There are many things that are internalized, even though your thinking has changed.

Caregiving as a female role is so deeply ingrained that most often it does not even occur to daughters that their brothers could have become the main caregivers. They simply assume that when a son provides parent care it is his wife, the daughter-in-law, who carries out the responsibilities. When, for example, a caregiving daughter was asked whether her brother participates in helping their mother, she replied "A daughter-in-law is not the same as a daughter." In another family, an elderly woman, following a stroke, moved into her daughter's home. The daughter had four siblings, two sisters, and two brothers. Describing how it happened that she became the main care-giver, the daughter said "One of my sisters lives in Alaska, and the other is divorced and has to work." When the interviewer asked "What about your brothers?" The daughter replied in surprise, "My brothers? Why would I give my mother to a daughter-in-law when she has daughters?"

Caregiving daughters describe their acceptance of the gender assignment of various aspects of parent care:

> I do all the things to take care of my Mom. But my brother is the decision-maker even though he lives far away. He's always on the phone telling me what to do. He *should* be the one to make decisions. After all, he's a policeman. He's even saved lives.

* * *

Caregiving has been my whole life. As women, we're suited for that because we have that nurturing instinct. Even secretarial work is like that.

* * *

My brother worked, and I didn't. It was expected in those days and probably still is—the woman being the caregiver, it being a daughter's responsibility.

Even women who in many ways are enacting the new views of women's roles in their life-styles often behave in accordance with the traditional view.

My two brothers and I are all busy lawyers. But when my mother got sick—she lives in another state—my brothers just assumed that I would be the one to fly out to her. And you know something? I did it.

A daughter who is a bank executive stated:

My son is going through a divorce, and he and his child live with my husband and me now. When my grandchild got sick, who stayed home? You guessed it. Me! And who does my mother-in-law's grocery shopping and takes her to the doctor? Don't even guess. We all know the answer.

Daughters-in-law, for their part, also accept the proposition that caregiving is their role when a parent-in-law does not have a daughter. Asked how it happened that they became caregivers for their mothers-in-law, women replied:

My husband has two brothers, but he was always the one in the family who took the most responsibility.

* * *

My husband is an only child, so there was no one else.

MAKING PARENTS HAPPY

The feelings of responsibility of many daughters and daughters-in-law go beyond doing the instrumental and personal-care tasks required by the disabled older people in the family. More than men, women have been socialized to feel responsible for the *emotional well being* of others. This being so, it is not surprising that women feel a greater responsibility than men not only for helping parents (Gray & Smith, 1960; Townsend, 1968), but for making them happy. In one study, for example, daughters were more involved emotionally with their parents, while sons appeared better able to distance themselves, experienced less guilt, and more readily accepted that they did not have the power to make the parent much happier. Unlike daughters, the sons seldom felt responsible for their parents' emotional well-being (Robinson & Thurnher, 1979).

Acceptance of such gender assignment of responsibility for another's emotional support and "happiness" is further demonstrated by the finding that widowed elderly people generally name daughters rather than sons as their confidantes (Brody et al., 1982b; Horowitz, 1985a, b; Shanas, 1979b).

A divorced woman who is working and raising her two teenage daughters herself does all the shopping and errands for her house-bound widowed mother, who lives 10 miles away. This daughter said:

> On Saturdays I am like a robot—driving and driving to take the girls and my mother where they have to go and doing the things my mother needs. I make flow charts. I have to decide what comes first, and I don't always succeed. *By "succeed," I mean making everyone happy.*

After telling about an extraordinarily difficult caregiving situation and her mother's continuing preference for her brother, a caregiving daughter commented, "I'm glad to be able to do it! It makes her happy."

Explaining why she took her mother into her own home, a daughter says,

> It's important to have her where she's happy. . . . I don't think she'd be as happy in a nursing home [as in caregiver's home]. . . . She's happier this way, and I'm happier having her here. I would feel guilty if I put her in a nursing home.

Not infrequently, the boundaries between expressive support and instrumental help are blurred in the perceptions of caregivers. That is, they do not differentiate sharply between *caring about* and *caring for* the parent. "Care," then, is interpreted as doing whatever is necessary *for* the parent; if the caregiver does not do it all, she doesn't care enough *about* the parent.

Thus, social values about filial behavior are reinforced by women's expectations of themselves that they perform well in caregiving. Women are under considerable pressure in being held responsible for the care and the well-being of all those in the family who need it. They feel, in effect, "I have to do it all, do it well, and see to it that they are happy." When this does not happen, they experience a sense of failure.

In describing her feeling of responsibility for the happiness of other family members, a daughter said:

> I feel responsible for everyone in the family. I'm the main focus. I keep it all glued together. That's the way it is. That's what I should do. I try very hard to

please my mother, but nothing is good enough and then I feel I failed. When my
son failed a course in high school, he had to go to summer school. I felt maybe I
hadn't done enough. My job is to keep everyone in the family happy. Only I am
miserable.

Making people happy is an unrealistic and unachievable goal, of course.
Given the human condition, given the fact that some older people's life-long
personalities preclude their being made happy, and given the unhappiness
and depression of older people that may accompany their age-related losses
(including loss of functional capacity), the expectation of caregivers that they
can make the parent "happy" is often doomed to failure. The failure leads to
guilt; that is, guilt about parent care often relates to the failure to make the
older person happy as much as to the feeling that one has not provided as
much actual instrumental help as one should.

The caregiver's guilt is intensified if she tries in any way, no matter how
small, to meet her own needs and in so doing perceives that she has failed to
make the older person happy.

Having taken her mother into her household, which also contains her
own children, a widowed daughter had no privacy or free time. Occasionally, on her day off from work she wanted to go out for a couple of hours by
herself or to curl up in bed with a book. The elderly mother was so
disappointed, that the daughter felt she had to give up her outing or put the
book away. "She [the mother] has no one but me, and she has looked forward
to time with me. It makes me feel so guilty."

Thus, women become women in the middle in the sense that they try to
meet the needs (including the emotional needs) of all members of their
families and to perform well as caregivers for whomever in the family is in
need of care.

The mental health literature is replete with documentation of women's
greater vulnerability to emotional stress in general. The fact that daughters
experience more strains than sons specifically in response to parent care
meshes with Gilligan's (1982) proposition that women's nurturing nature
leads them to be more susceptible to experiencing deep stress in the lives of
people they love as though it were their own. Strong support for that theory
comes from the consistency with which daughters experience more stress
than sons when in comparable positions vis-à-vis parent care. Not only
primary caregiving daughters, but sisters of those caregivers (both proximate
and geographically distant) experience more stress than brothers (see Chapter 8). Moreover, daughters experience more stress than sons because of
parent care even after a parent has been institutionalized (see Chapter 14).

Daughters' expectations of themselves may be further heightened when
the elderly parent they are helping is the mother. Elderly mothers, by
comparison with elderly fathers, tend to have higher expectations of filial

support (Seelbach, 1977). Moreover, elderly mothers, as well as society in general and daughters themselves, expect daughters, but not sons, to be like themselves—the nurturers and caregivers in the family. That expectation may contribute to the notion that "role reversal" occurs or should occur when an elderly mother becomes dependent on an adult daughter.

IS THERE "ROLE REVERSAL"?

Cohler and Grunebaum (1981), in writing about mother/daughter relationships in general, state that "The relationship between adult women and their own mothers is perhaps the most complex and emotionally charged of all the relationships within the family." In their view, various psychological mechanisms encourage a lack of separateness between mother and daughter, and the highly charged relationship that develops is characterized by elderly mothers' high expectations of their daughters.

The "emotional charge"—whether positive or negative (it is sometimes both)—is intensified when the stage of life is reached at which a mother is elderly and needs help from her daughter. Again, mother and daughter need to interact with each other in a caregiving relationship. This time, however, it is the daughter rather than the mother who is the caregiver, and the two women have had no rehearsal for their performances in their changed roles. Some expect that "role reversal" will take place. The expectations of both mother and daughter that there should be such "reversal" intensifies the strains both women experience, since there cannot be true reversal of the roles they played earlier in life when the daughter was an infant and child.

The phrase "role reversal" is a popular but incorrect psychodynamic cliché. As an explanation of the processes that occur when a parent becomes dependent on an adult child, it is a simplistic and superficial concept at best. Some elements of caring for another member of the family are similar no matter the relationship of caregiver to care-recipient—whether the dependent individual concerned be a child, a spouse, a parent, or a sibling. Certainly, some of the tasks the adult child may perform to help the parent are the same kinds of tasks that the parent had performed for the child when the latter was a baby—feeding, bathing, dressing, or changing the diaper, for example. But there the resemblance ends. Though the roles of both parent and adult child undergo *change,* such change cannot be equated with *reversal.*

A caregiver experiences very different inner meanings when her young child depends on her and when it is an elderly parent who is dependent. People caring for those who are at the opposite stages of life—that is, for a baby and for an old person—have very different reactions to things that are normal and will be dealt with in the normal course of development in the child, but are not normal in the elderly adult. A young mother's feelings about incontinence in her baby, for example, are not in any way similar to an adult child's feelings about incontinence in her elderly parent.

In the main, young parents have chosen to bring a totally dependent being into the world; they expect and accept the baby's need for total care. In caring for that infant, the future holds promise of a gradual reduction in the child's dependency. The goal is to help the child become more and more independent. Each step along the way—the first step, the first word, going on the potty, starting school—is greeted joyfully as a success. Though there may be problems along the way, in the main the direction of the child's growth is toward self-sufficiency, with both parent and child striving for the positive changes that occur.

The contrast is sharp when an older person needs help. That situation is not expected or chosen by either the adult child or the elderly parent. Caring for the older person presages increasing dependency, rather than increasing independence. Sadness rather than happiness accompanies each change when the trajectory of the parent's dependence is downward. Both the elderly parent and the adult child strive to avoid those changes. Daughter caregivers are aware of the differences:

> I never think of it as a comparison of an older person becoming childish. It's not like having a child in the sense the older person is not getting more exciting or interesting and adventurous everyday but going into the other direction. So it is a downer.

* * *

> It burns me when anyone says this [caregiving to her elderly mother] is like raising a child. Children are malleable, curious, open to learning. They are selectively dependent, and it decreases. Old people do not become like children. Not in any positive ways. I watch my niece and nephew. They display all the positive things about children because they *are* children. Old people bring their own sadnesses with them.

Some daughters do characterize their changed relationships with parents as "role reversal," invariably in connection with illness-induced helplessness and dependency of the parent and most often when the parent is cognitively impaired. Such women are often puzzled, however. They note the differences between caring for a child and an elderly parent, recognizing on some level that "reversal" is deterioration in the relationship rather than the way things should be.

> My mother is completely helpless. I have no children, so mother is my baby. Our roles are reversed. But it's different. A baby gets better all the time, and an older person gets worse. It's sad.

* * *

Mother's brain was affected, and she became so dependent that it was a bottomless pit. It wasn't her fault, but our relationship deteriorated. She became the child and I became the mother in terms of role reversal.

Perhaps the most important reason that there can be no true role reversal in the psychological sense lies in the very nature of the parent/child relationship. No matter how much care an older person needs, he or she does not become, and cannot become, the child of the adult child in the feelings of either child or parent. Half a century or even more of a parent/child relationship cannot be discarded. Although their roles are enacted differently in late life, parents cannot become children to their children and children cannot become parents to their parents. And love for a parent is a different love from the love one experiences for one's child.

"SECOND CHILDHOOD"

Closely related to the concept of role reversal is the notion that the older person is in a "second childhood." Such a characterization comes from observations of the declining functional capacities and increasing dependency of disabled older people, particularly those with Alzheimer's disease and related disorders. Although describing the superficial resemblance of behavior and functioning at the two widely separated stages of life—childhood and advanced old age—such a phrase does not take note of the very different physiological and psychological processes accounting for that behavior and functioning. Reminiscence about early life experiences, failing memory, confusion, and disorientation do not mean that the old person has returned emotionally or psychologically to childhood. Eighty or more years of living cannot be erased. The fact that the individual may require services similar to those given to children (such as feeding, dressing, and other personal care) does not make that person a child physiologically.

Nor are other behaviors or personality traits in old age developmental, i.e., are a "normal" accompaniment to the aging process. They are not regressive in the sense that they represent a return to childhood, though there may be overtones of child-like behavior. Rather, they may be continuations or exaggerations of life-long tendencies that are less masked, become more visible, and are more clearly delineated because the older person is struggling against feelings of loss of control and competence (see Goldfarb, 1965). Or, as in the case of patients with Alzheimer's disease, behaviors may be manifestations of actual damage to the brain.

She fought getting into bed. I tried to encourage her to go to the bathroom like the book says, but she wouldn't listen. Toward the end, she refused to sit on the toilet. It was a fight every night to get her to go to bed. At night I would give her the capsule. But then I realized she wasn't taking them. She was hiding them in the bed.

DEPENDENCY/INDEPENDENCE: A DIALECTIC TENSION

The shift in the balance of dependence/independence is a constant theme that colors thinking about the relationships between disabled elderly parents and their adult children. Much confusion about intergenerational relations is engendered. The goal of parenthood is often misunderstood to mean helping the child from the total dependence of infancy, through childhood and adolescence, to the achievement of total independence and total separation. But overdependence in any phase of family life is different from normal, healthy *inter*dependence. Psychologically, there never is total separation or total independence. Yet a strong cultural value emphasizes people's independence as the desirable goal.

The psychological issue of the older person's dependency on adult children has its origin in the dependency of the helpless infant on the young parent. The inevitable shift in the longstanding but delicate balance of dependence/independence of the elderly parent and adult child is a central issue and reactivates unresolved conflicts about dependency. There is no one moment common to all families at which a shift in the balance of dependence/independence begins. For some, it occurs gradually and can be resolved in an orderly manner. For others, it may be precipitated suddenly in the crucible of an acute crisis. That stage may be omitted entirely when premature deaths occur.

The psychological issues that confront the elderly person when dependency begins and progresses are directly relevant to the interaction between parent and child. The old person's dependency/independence needs have been central to much clinical theory and writing about late life (for example, see Goldfarb, 1965; Weinberg, 1976; Butler & Lewis, 1973). Butler and Lewis (1973) feel that the issue of autonomy (self-sufficiency) is as important as that of identity (self-sameness) for older people. Though the sense of self is a continuing issue, they say, the problem of autonomy may become more important as health problems arise. That is, a critical question then may be "Can I survive independently without being a burden?" That question speaks to the fear of loss of control over one's own life, of surrendering to the direction of others, and of no longer having the essential sense of mastery.

The individual's previous life-pattern of dependence/independence qualifies adaptation to dependent conditions and situations (Butler & Lewis, 1973). Both the older person who has extreme difficulty being dependent and the one who is overly dependent (these may have been life-long characteristics) may hamper the efforts of the adult child to behave appropriately in the caregiving role. If successful adaptation is to be made, not only must the adult child have the capacity to permit the parent to be dependent, but the parent must have the capacity to be appropriately dependent so as to permit the adult child to be dependable.

STRUGGLE FOR CONTROL AND THE PSYCHOLOGICAL BALANCE OF POWER

The need to rebalance dependency/independency often sets in motion a struggle between mother and daughter for control of the caregiving situation. A struggle for power is inherent to a lesser or greater degree in all helping relationships.

No one would argue that total control over older people's lives should be transferred to others when they become disabled. Since some sense of control is central to the integrity of the human personality, it follows that it is desirable for the older person to be treated as a dignified adult whose control over her life is supported to the fullest possible extent. It is the loss of that sense of control that so often leads to depression. Thinking of and treating the older person as a child can erode that control prematurely. Maggie Kuhn, the activist who founded the Grey Panthers organizations, often exhorts her audiences "Do not turn us into wrinkled babies!"

In general, therefore, professionals emphasize the importance of permitting the dependent elderly to retain as much control over their own lives as possible—on "empowering" the elderly (for example, see Barusch, 1987). Certainly, that is a desirable goal. One must also, however, view caregiving situations from the perspective of the caregivers. Often, *the psychological balance of power is held by the elderly parent*. Multiple factors contribute to maintaining that balance of power. Culture and religion may reinforce the parent's power. "Honor thy father and thy mother," and even obedience and respect may be invoked. Moreover, in every family's history, it has been the parent who held the power, and vestiges of that relationship remain to a greater or lesser degree. As one caregiving daughter put it, "I'm still intimidated by my mother."

Whatever the dynamics, and whether or not the caregiver is a willing participant, *there is insufficient attention on the part of professionals to empowering some caregivers by helping them to extricate themselves from control that sometimes amounts to tyranny*.

Shifts in the power relationship when a parent becomes dependent on a child present many difficulties. Early in the family's history, power and control over the helpless infant and the young child were lodged totally in the parent, and there was no question about the parent's "right"—even responsibility—to control the child. As the child grew and his or her independence increased, the parent's power decreased, with the child's adolescence witnessing the classic struggle for independence. Vestiges of this struggle remain throughout adulthood to a greater or lesser degree. Thus, an additional frustration for the elderly parent may be remnants of the unresolved but inevitable loss of control over the child. Similarly, the daughter may have vestiges of her own ambivalent struggle toward independence.

Parenting implies control that is relinquished gradually. It is a generally accepted proposition that it is good and necessary for the young parent to exercise appropriate control over the child. An adult daughter's major prior rehearsal for caregiving is having cared for her own children. Then it was also her parental prerogative to be the decision-maker. When an elderly parent is disabled, some adult children think of themselves as the parent's parent with the same right to power and control. (Another reason why professionals should stop encouraging the notion of "role reversal.")

The issue of control can be a source of some confusion to both parent and adult child. Does the child have the right to exercise control over the parent for whom she is caring? Some elderly people readily relinquish control to the child, whereas others fight fiercely to retain control not only over their own lives, but the lives of the adult children. For their part, some adult children continue to accept the right of the parent to control, whereas others strive for their own total control.

I'm used to my own way. I was never fond of my mother and couldn't wait to leave home when I was old enough. Now, 45 years later she has moved in with me, and I fight with her all the time for control of my own home, my own life.

* * *

It's so different now. I look at my mother in a certain way. It's hard to cope with when she's childish. I'm the disciplinarian now, but she's still my mother.

* * *

My role as caretaker for my mother is I feel like a boss. You know, you supervise.

* * *

She has always felt that she knows best. That control thing—she is the mother and I am the child. She was used to being the mother. Now it's turned around the other way. She can't accept it. She just wouldn't stop telling me what to do. A lot of mothers are that way. They won't let go.

* * *

My father treats me like a child. He waits up for me at night and asks "Where the hell were you?" If he doesn't like what I do, he says "Why the hell did you do that?" If I hear one more "Why the hell," "How the hell," "Where the hell," "What the hell," I'll go out of my mind.

The situation is further compounded because the elderly mother, though now disabled and dependent on the adult child, psychologically is still parent to the child she has parented and controlled. Being expected to become child to one's child adds insult to the injury of becoming disabled and losing autonomy.

Thus, mother and daughter may each expect to be in control, with the elderly mother wanting her care to be provided in ways that are in accordance with her own preferences. She may resist and resent the daughter's attempt to take over. The daughter may feel that, since she is the one doing the various tasks and the caregiving is arduous, she has the right to do it her way and in a manner that fits in with her life-style and other responsibilities.

No matter what I do, it isn't enough or it isn't right. When I wash her feet, I sort of automatically begin with her [the mother's] left foot. She gets angry and criticizes me. She wants me to do her right foot first.

* * *

She [Mother] calls when I'm in an important meeting and asks me to drop off a pound of coffee on my way home. When I get to her house, she is angry because I bought the coffee in a small store that's on my way instead of going 3 miles further to the supermarket. She says I could have saved 28 cents.

* * *

I thought it would be role reversal, but she fights everything I do.

On some level, however, the daughter may have the uneasy feeling that she should provide care in the way the parent wants it. She, therefore, feels guilty if she becomes angry, even when the mother is demanding, controlling, or critical—the more so because the old person, being disabled, is seen as helpless, pitiable, and therefore deserving of patience and kindness. Older people are sensitive to such feelings, and some behave so as to increase the guilt and sympathy of the caregiver.

My mother gives me "signals of disapproval," and I cry like I did when I was a child.

* * *

I couldn't bring myself to say no. She was a very old lady, and the older she got, the more pathetic she was. She needed me more. . . . I couldn't possibly say no to her now.

* * *

She [the Mother] has her ways of making me feel bad.

This theme was captured by a cartoon in *Punch* (p. 16) showing an elderly woman with a cane talking to a middle-aged couple who are dressed to go out. She says, "Now, you young people go out and have a good time. Don't think about me back here, all alone, at the mercy of intruders pushing dope, robbing, raping. I'll be all right."

A common theme in caregivers' reports, and a measure of the parent's power, is that daughters often do not utilize outside help to relieve even the severe pressures they experience because:

My mother won't permit any outside help.

* * *

My mother won't let anyone help her except me.

* * *

I can't go out for dinner or even to a wedding because my mother is afraid while I'm gone.

* * *

We don't take vacations because my mother is unhappy when I'm not here.

Although such caregivers express frustration, anger, and feelings of being trapped, some participate fully in avoiding outside help. If they do not provide *all* the care needed in the instrumental sense, they feel guilty because it implies that they do not care enough. At the same time, providing all the care may also serve the caregivers' own needs.

No one can take care of my mother the way I can.

* * *

Mother refuses a baby sitter and is very unpleasant about it. She was a miserable patient in the hospital. I was there from 8 a.m. till bedtime. She complains when I'm not here. I'm her security blanket.

* * *

I'll be able to think I did something for her. I won't feel guilt.

In extreme cases, the older person attempts (sometimes successfully) to control almost every aspect of the caregiver's own life.

Some caregivers keep trying to please the parent, but approval is withheld: "Whatever my mother wants, I do it. Nothing I do is good enough. I try very hard but I don't please her."

Other members of the family may ally themselves with the mother:

> Should I take charge, and fight my Mom and my siblings? I'm the one who's doing everything. But I'd be fighting everyone. My brother says "Don't work. Stay home with Mom." My Mom makes me feel guilty. She says "The house is dirty. Wash the windows."

The struggle for control may intensify when the older person has Alzheimer's disease. Now, the caregiver must protect the parent, even insist on doing things to ensure that parent's very survival. The parent, for her part, is struggling against the devastation and panic of losing control—the erosion of her or his autonomy.

At times, the older person's condition reaches the point at which he or she does not have the capacity to exercise control. The long struggle is over. Some daughters state clearly how much easier—even more satisfying—their caregiving then becomes:

> If mother were still herself I couldn't live with her. [Mother has severe Alzheimer's disease.] We didn't get along. It's because she's helpless that I can do it. She's much more childlike now. She was a tough lady. Now she's sweet and gentle. The resentment and anger I used to have toward her have dissipated. As she became more helpless, they dissipated.

* * *

> The more Dad deteriorates, the easier it gets.

* * *

> It's easier now that Mother is on a feeding pump. It makes taking care of her a breeze. I have my routines.

Overdependence of a parent can be as irksome to caregivers as a parent's assertion of dominance:

> She's so dependent, she even asks me what she should wear. My father turned her into a dependent vegetable.

* * *

> If I could have one thing different it would be for her to have a couple of friends. Not to be so dependent on me for everything. It makes me feel trapped.

There are, of course, many situations in which the caregiving situation works well, and parent and daughter are considerate of each other, discuss issues openly, and sustain a good relationship. To the extent that the parent is appropriately dependent and appreciative of the caregiver's efforts, and the latter is sensitive to the parent's need to retain some control and to be involved in decisions, things often go smoothly. Receiving feedback in the form of her parent's appreciation is of major importance to the daughter. One daughter, for example, said that her elderly mother stays in her room as much as possible to give her daughter's family privacy. The older women is very grateful for the care the family provides and is very supportive of her daughter. The daughter says,

> I take care of Mother because I can give her better care (than a nursing home) and I love her. She knows that if she needs 24-hour care and we can't provide it, she may have to go into a nursing home. It's no big secret. We discuss it all with her.

To recapitulate, a powerful inner experience of caregiving daughters is their deep feeling that they, as women, are responsible for providing care and making dependent parents happy. In the process of attempting to fulfill that goal, they and disabled parents may engage in the struggle for control that is related to the inevitable shift in dependence/independence. The daughters cannot and do not achieve perfection in the caregiving that they see as their obligation. That "failure" contributes to the guilt and other emotional strains experienced by many daughters.

The daughters may have an uneasy sense that the parent wants something more and something different from them than they are able to give. When the mother criticizes aspects of her daughter's caregiving or when either of them refuses to let anyone else help, those behaviors may represent a more fundamental expectation. At some level of awareness both the mothers and the daughters harbor the expectation that the devotion and care given by the mother to the daughter when the latter was an infant and child—that total, primordial commitment which is the original paradigm for caregiving to those who are dependent and is the basis for women's identity as caregivers—should be reciprocated and the indebtedness repaid in kind when the mother, having grown old, becomes dependent.

It is that expectation—that roles be reversed—that often makes a strong contribution to the caregiver's strain, for the adult daughter cannot and does not provide the same total care to her elderly mother that the mother gave to her in infancy and childhood. This may be the inner, psychological parallel of the social myth that children do not take care of their parents as was the case in the good old days. That is, when people talk of the "good old days" those days may not be an earlier period in our social history (after all, the myth existed then too), but a metaphor for an earlier period in each individual's and family's history to which there can be no return.

There is an inevitable disparity between standards and expectations on the one hand and the unavoidable realities on the other hand. The disparity leads to guilt and other symptoms of stress. The myth persists because the guilt persists, reflecting a universal and deeply rooted human theme. That may be why we hear over and over again from adult daughters, often in these very words, "*She took care of me and now it's my turn to take care of her*" and "*I know I'm doing everything I can for my mother, but somehow I still feel guilty.*"

The fantasy is that "somehow" one could do more and do better in making the parent happy. That may be one reason that so many adult children are overwhelmed with guilt when a parent enters a nursing home. It is experienced as the total surrender of the parent to the care of others— the ultimate failure to meet the parent's dependency needs as that parent met the child's needs in the good old days. These feelings are exacerbated by the parent's spoken or unspoken reproach (see Chapter 14). The language some caregivers use talking of potential nursing home placement is striking. They say "I will not throw her away," "I don't want to give her away," "I don't want to warehouse her," and even "I don't want to get rid of her."

Guilt may be a reason that people assert that they and their own families behave responsibly in caring for their old, but that most people do not do so, as was the case in the "good old days." They need to defend against the guilt, and to deny their own negative and unacceptable emotions by feeling that others do not behave as well. Those unacceptable emotions such as resentment, anger, the wish not to be burdened, and even the wish for the parent's death add another dimension to the guilt and may account for the fact that guilt does not seem to lessen as the caregiver increases the intensity of help. By exacerbating the guilt, the myth contributes to the strains of the parent caring daughter, thus completing the feedback loop. Not only does the myth persist because the guilt persists, but the guilt persists because the myth persists.

That point is emphasized because it is so central to the daughter's inner experiences. The strains of many adult daughters are intensified by their constant, but fruitless efforts to close the gap between what they *can and actually do* in caring for their parents, and what they and their mothers think the daughters *should do*. Surely, their efforts derive in part from oft-cited motivations such as family, religious, and cultural values, a sense of duty, strong bonds with the parent, and affection. (These values are often strongly reinforced by the urging of the clergy and members of one's ethnic group.) But it is the inner striving that compels some women to go beyond what appear to be the limits of endurance in caring for their parents and trying to make them happy, doing so for many years at the cost of severe suffering for themselves and their families.

SPECIAL ISSUES AROUND CARING FOR ELDERLY FATHERS

Fathers as well as mothers expect daughters rather than sons to become caregivers. However, virtually nothing is known about how the daughters' inner experiences differ when they become caregivers for their fathers rather than for their mothers or whether the emotional strains experienced are similar in caring for parents of different sexes.

As seen above, both the elderly mothers and their daughters often expect daughters to repay in kind the nurturance and care the mothers earlier provided to daughters. "She took care of me, so now it's my turn to take care of her." Daughters' stories suggest, however, that *elderly fathers and their daughters expect the daughters to replace their deceased wives/ mothers in providing care*, rather than for their roles to be reversed. That is, daughters maintain their identification with the mother in caring for either parent. But they think of caring for mothers as the way "she took care of me" and think of caring for fathers as the way "mother [as wife] took care of him."

As a result, daughters often define "care" of the father as doing housekeeping, laundry, and cooking, not because the father is disabled, but because he never did those things when his wife was alive. Care of mothers is defined in that way only when the mother no longer has the capacity to do such tasks.

The day my mother died was the day Dad moved into our house. He could have done for himself, but he never did. He was spoiled and used to having everything done for him. So I stepped in, picking up where she left off. I get his breakfast, do his laundry, whatever he wants. He asks, and I do it.

* * *

I went to work 20 hours a week for my own sanity. Father was resentful. He had to make his own lunch. He's the only one in the house who gets a choice of menu. He's picky with his food. That's what my mother used to do. If I don't, he won't eat. He goes with his nose up in the air. My mother created a monster. She used to say to me "If anything happens to me, take your father in." I used to say "I won't pamper him." But here I am doing it.

* * *

Three times a year I take a train and go to give his house a thorough cleaning and get his clothes in order. I call him in November to tell him to get his coat out—not the raincoat, the wool coat. I don't want him to get pneumonia.

* * *

I more or less forced the help on him. He didn't need it. But there were certain things my mother [deceased] did for him.

* * *

When my father became ill, she [the deceased mother] cared for him incredibly well. The best thing I can do for my mother now is to take good care of Daddy.

The last quoted daughter also says that she provides care for her father because,

Who else is there? And he gave to me so much and so caringly, and so completely. There's no way there's too much I could be doing. It's not an exchange. He just deserves it.

Thus, that daughter indicated her wish to reciprocate the father's love and caring ("caring" in the emotional, not instrumental sense of the word) and draws a subtle distinction in saying it's not an "exchange," but that her father "deserves" the care.

Whether the parent is a mother or a father, the fact that the parent has earned the help is often mentioned. That is, in addition to providing care as an obligation or as reciprocity for receiving care as a child, caregivers who have been loved generously and treated kindly by parents talk of the goodness of the parent. "She was a good mother." The parent *deserves* and has *earned* affection and help that goes beyond obligation and the simple call of duty.

The inner processes described above occur in the context of the daughters' and daughters-in-law's particular stage of life. The stage of life as it intersects with parent care is another major theme among the multifaceted "internals" of caregiving. The next chapter discusses the question, "Is parent care a developmental stage of life?"

Chapter 7

Parent-Care Stages of Life

A major theme in the stories of daughters and daughters-in-law who help the disabled elderly is their awareness of the stage of their lives when such caregiving takes place. In broad terms, these are the stages of relatively young adulthood, the middle years, and the years during which the caregiving women themselves are approaching or are actually engaged in the aging phase of life.

The differences in the life stages at which parent care occurs suggest the question: "Is parent care a normal developmental stage of life?" Although providing help to disabled parents is *normative* in the sense that most people have that experience at some time in their lives, the notion that parent care is a *normal developmental stage* of life is incorrect. The distinction relates directly to the strains many filial caregivers experience.

There have been various theoretical formulations about what happens during the life course of individuals and families. The normal, expected life stages have been conceptualized from many different vantage points. Among the most familiar conceptualizations are those with psychodynamic orientations such as Freud's developmental stages, English and Pearson's "normal life crises" (1937), Erikson's eight stages of ego development (1950), and Peck's elaboration of those stages (1968). The best known sociological conceptualization of life stages characterizes the last phase of the family life cycle as the "empty nest" stage.

The gerontological literature has given considerable attention to role transitions that occur after the prematurity stages of life: the menopause or climacteric, the empty nest, retirement, widowhood, the processes of aging, and grandparenthood (see George, 1986). Family therapy theory, which only recently has begun to turn its attention to the later phases of the family life cycle, identifies stages such as launching, postparental, retirement, widowhood, grandparenthood, aging, and illness and dependency (for example, see Turnball et al., 1984 and Walsh, 1980).

None of those theoretical formulations, however, addresses the issue of parent care and its place in individual and family development and the life course.

In the 1960s, when it was observed that a greatly increased number of people were being confronted with the need to help a parent, Blenkner (1965) attempted to place the stage of parent care in people's life course in a developmental framework. In reaching for some criteria of what constitutes "mature" filial behavior, she tried to illuminate what the inner, subjective experiences of adult children might be at such a time. Proposing the idea that parent care is a developmental stage, she characterized it as "filial maturity," defined as the capacity of the adult child to be depended on by the aging parent and to be dependable. If successful, Blenkner hypothesized, filial maturity marks the healthy transition from maturity to old age.

According to Blenkner (1965), in general, the "filial crisis" occurs during one's 40s and 50s when the "individual's parents can no longer be looked to as a rock of support in times of emotional trouble or economic stress but may themselves need their offspring's comfort and support" (p. 57). When filial maturity occurs, she said, the parent is seen in a new light as an individual; this is a way in which the adult children prepare for their own old age as when, in childhood, they prepared for adulthood.

Where there are psychological difficulties in resolving the filial crisis, Blenkner (1965) stated, "One of the major roles of the therapeutic professions can be that of helping the middle-aged client or patient accomplish this task to the best of his ability, for it will inevitably determine how successfully he meets the challenge of growing old" (58). (The way in which adult children resolve their own "filial crisis" may also determine the ways in which their own children will meet *their* own filial crises in the future.)

The concept of parent care as "developmental" is not just a theoretical issue, but has very practical implications. If meeting all of a parent's dependencies is the desirable goal, for example, then therapeutic approaches should (as Blenkner stated) aim to help the adult child to accomplish the task of becoming filially mature. If that reasoning is taken a step further, it releases society from any obligation to help the disabled elderly since the implication is that the adult children should do it all.

Certainly, the model of Blenkner (1965) illuminates some aspects of how it feels to become the support for a parent on whom one previously depended. However, *parent care is not a developmental stage of life* in the same sense that other life stages are developmental. Although parent care is a major transition, it is not a transition in the traditional sense that an individual or a family is moved from one stage to another. Accordingly, the transition is not symbolized by what Neugarten (1968a) has called "punctuation marks along the life cycle" (p. 18) as in the case of weddings, christenings, Bar Mitzvahs, and other ceremonies. There are no such punctuation marks to signal the start of parent care.

But *the fundamental reason that parent care is not a developmental stage is that developmental stages are specific to age-linked periods of time, whereas parent care is not.*

Compare parent care with other stages of life in that respect. The developmental stages or "normal life crises" of earlier life usually occur in a somewhat orderly sequence and progression as people move through more or less well-defined age categories. Those categories (such as infancy, childhood, or adolescence) are linked by age to specific cognitive (intellectual), emotional, and physiological developments and capacities. In sharp contrast, the demands of parent care are often incompatible with the psychological, emotional, and physiological capacities of the adult child concerned. For example, the trajectory of the demands on aging children usually goes upward over time (that is, in the direction of providing the increasing amount of help being required by the parent), a direction that may run counter to the declining capacities of an aging child to meet those demands.

Parent care is not a single "stage" that can be fitted neatly into an orderly sequence of stages in the life course. Among the elderly, age and stage are not the same (Peck, 1968). Young children are "programmed" developmentally for a gradual reduction of dependency, whereas the dependencies of old age appear with great variability and irregularity, over much wider time spans, and in different sequential patterns. Disability can occur at age 65 or at age 85, for example. In addition, the timing of the marriages and parenthood of both parent and child influence the ages and stages of adult children when their parents need help. If the parent was 35 years old when her child was born, that child may be 30 or 40 years of age when parent care becomes necessary. But if the parent was 18 or 20 years old when the child was born, that child may be 55 or 60 or even 70 years of age when parent care becomes necessary.

Parent care, then, can overlay many different ages and stages in different people and different families, occurring as it does in young adulthood, in middle age, or even in old age. Although the largest proportion of parent-caring daughters, for example, are in their 40s and 50s, as many as one-third are either under 40 or over 60. The caregiver may be a grandmother who is experiencing the processes of aging, or she may have preschool children at home. People who are experiencing the same kinds of other life events may vary widely in age. One filial caregiver may be widowed at age 45, for example, and another at age 65.

Even when they are in the same age group, the situations of parent-caring children are extraordinarily variable. One woman in middle age may be engaged in adapting to the onset of chronic ailments and disability; another may be enjoying excellent health and playing tennis regularly. Health, marital and economic status, living arrangements, geographic distance from the parent, personality, adaptive capacities, and the quality of parent-child relationships vary. The caregiver may or may not be employed. She may be working upward on her career, or her retirement (or that of her spouse) may be imminent or already have taken place. Meeting a parent's dependency needs may be concurrent with the "letting go" of one's young adult children. Or, the theoretically empty nest may contain young adult children who have not left it or have returned to it, a phenomenon that has been increasing.

Because of the different life stages at which parent care occurs, its demands often do not synchronize with the adult child's capacities. In general, the roles played during the life cycle and the social definitions of appropriate behavior in those roles are in synchrony with emotional and physiological developments and capacities. Thus, the child-bearing years are those in which young adults not only may wish for children and have reproductive capacity, but have energy levels commensurate with the care needs of young children. At present, when there is emphasis on the need to develop new roles for older people, sensible suggestions for those roles implicitly recognize the physical changes attendant upon aging. No one suggests, for example, that the retiree embark upon a new role as a pro-fessional athlete, truck driver, or parent of young children.

Still a further complication is that parent care often is a time-extended process, with some women helping a parent for more than 20 years; it may span several of her age periods or stages. Moreover, for many women, care of a parent at a particular time is only one phase of their "caregiving careers" that may extend well into late middle age and early old age. Many women help several older people in the family simultaneously or sequentially (see Chapter 2).

"OFF TIME" AND "ON TIME"

Because parent care is not a "developmental stage," the age and stage at which parent care becomes part of the daughter's life may be perceived as being what Neugarten and Hagestad (1976) call "off-time." They write:

> . . . social timetables serve to create a normal, predictable life course. Role transitions, while they call for new adaptations, are not ordinarily traumatic if they occur on time because they have been anticipated and rehearsed. Major stresses are caused by events that upset the expected sequences and rhythms of life. . . . To be off-time usually creates problems of adjustment for the individual, either because it upsets his sense of self-worth, or because it causes disruption of social relationships. In either case, the consequences of a role change . . . depends on whether or not the same change is prevalent among one's associates" (p. 51).

Because of the variability in the ages and stages at which women are confronted with the need to provide parent care and because that experience is not "developmental," it is often regarded by caregivers as off-time. That perception may add to the stress they experience.

Daughters and daughters-in-law in their early thirties often mention spontaneously that they are at the "wrong" age and stage for parent care:

> I am doing the same things the people across the street are doing for their parents, and they are in their 50s. Even my boyfriend's mother is taking care of his grandmother. And here I am, my life is on hold.

* * *

> Our group of friends are still not there yet [at the parent-care stage]. My friends don't have to face this. Mostly it's people whose children are grown who have to do it.

When the caregivers are at other ages and stages of life, other considerations may be at work. If, for example, they are married and have young or adolescent children at home and/or have a strong career commitment (or both), their supply of psychic energy or emotional investment may be overextended. Thus, psychological overload is added to the objective role overload of sheer time and energy. The psychic overload is intensified by internal conflicts over which responsibilities should take priority and whether they have a right to take something for themselves rather than the leftovers after other people's needs have been met.

The pull of having to meet the needs of the older and younger generations is heightened by tension between the daughter's role as child (the historical precedent in the relationship) and her role as caregiver (the historical precedent for which was her role in parenting her own children). Gary Trudeau captured this dilemma in his cartoon strip *Doonesbury*. An adult daughter about 40 years of age is talking to her mother on the phone, giving her instructions on how to travel, but the mother is refusing to take advice. The daughter hangs up the phone and says "God! She can be exasperating sometimes." Her husband says to her "Joanie, have you noticed you've reached an age where you speak to your parents and your children with almost exactly the same tone of voice?" Joanie, stunned for a moment, then replies "I don't even want to *think* what that means." The husband replies "It means don't die. Everyone's counting on you."

When they are further into their middle years, caregiving daughters and daughters-in-law may have the sense that their lives are different from what they had hoped or planned. Particularly striking is the frequency with which women in the "empty-nest" stage say their anticipations of what their lives would be at that time have been disappointed. They say again and again that they had not expected to be taking care of their parents and have had to modify their expectations of freedom and ability to pursue enjoyable activities. The future may seem bleak rather than something to look forward to.

Our nest was empty, and now it's full. My husband and I had decided to work part time. Neither of us is well—he's had heart attacks, and I have ulcers. We decided to spend more time together and to travel. We've always wanted to see California. We've raised our children, and now they're grown and live in different places. But now there is no one else to care for my mother who has gotten forgetful and confused. She can't be left alone. We thought we had seen the light at the end of the tunnel after working hard all our lives.

* * *

I thought I would be working full time. It was my insurance. I hadn't thought of other options.

* * *

I have to reevaluate my goals now. I have to reevaluate what I want to accomplish. It's a turning point.

* * *

I didn't expect I'd be caring for my mother. She said she wouldn't ever live with her children.

* * *

I looked forward to this time. I expected to be free and to be able to come and go as I pleased.

Equally striking is the frequency with which the women say they had expected to travel. (Does travel symbolize freedom from responsibility?)

Our children are grown and developing. If parents are well, it's a beautiful stage. I wanted to travel. We would live our own lives. The things I'm doing are different from what I expected.

* * *

I wanted to be going on cruises and weekend vacations. I'm bored, and I'm in a rut. I feel lost, sad, everything.

* * *

The main thing I expected to be able to do was travel, be free of regimentation and financial responsibilities.

When the role of caregiver to an extremely disabled, very old person must be assumed in late middle age or early old age, the demands of that role may not be synchronous with the psychological, emotional, and physiological capacities of the caregivers. The physical care of an extremely impaired old person requires strength and stamina. For the adult child whose own beginning processes of aging require major adaptations, the parent's dependency may make too great a demand on the supply of sheer physical energy.

> She [the 91-year-old mother] is so confused that if I take her any place she wanders off, and I have to run, run to catch her. She wakes up two or three times a night, and I never get any rest. I'm exhausted. I'm 71 years old. My back aches from struggling to get her dressed in the morning. I'm too old for this. I simply don't have the strength I used to have.

*   *   *

> I can't leave the house for too long. Physically, I can't do as much as I'd like. I expected a bit more freedom. I expected my health to be better. I didn't expect I'd be caring for Mom. I'm going downhill physically.

*   *   *

> I'm lonesome and hungry to be with my children at this stage of my life. I feel old. I *am* old. Most of my life is over. I thought I would have a lot of free time—perhaps to be travelling, taking some courses, doing some volunteer work, spend time with the family. The things I'm doing now are different from what I expected. I can't do much. I'm responsible for my mother's care even if I don't do it myself.

Their situations inevitably stimulate caregiving women to think about their own old age and the children who might bear the responsibility. "I don't want to live into my 90s. How can I expect my children to take care of me? When I am 99, I don't want my 75-year-old child taking care of me."

The dissonance between the demands of parent care and the older adult child's physical capacities has its parallel in the psychological factors at work. In Cohler's (1983) thoughtful examination of interdependence in the family of adulthood, he points to theories of personality development in late life that show the aging individual's increasing "interiority" or self-absorption (e.g., Neugarten, 1973). He argues that family relationships that are satisfying and appropriate within young and middle adulthood may not be so in later life. Citing the evidence of increased interiority after midlife, he suggests that older people may wish to reduce the time and effort they spend helping other family members. Cohler (1983) reviews various studies showing that continued family responsibility among older persons may be associated with lower morale and increased psychological distress, *particularly among older women*. Essentially, he states that if older adulthood involves increasing interiority—more self absorption—then acknowledging the needs of others can become a source of stress.

In thinking about Cohler's formulation as it might apply in the context of caregiving to the disabled elderly, it may be that an aging daughter's strains are accounted for in part by the tension between her inner developmental processes (increased interiority) and the counterdemand for increased caregiving. That being so, parent-caring children in late middle age and early old age are confronted with increased demands on themselves at the very time of life when, because of normal personality developments that are part of the processes of aging, they want to reduce the dependency of others on themselves.

Parenthetically, an unanswered question is the extent to which the disabled elderly are sensitive to the limitations of their children. Are the parents aware of the declining energies and capacities of children who are in late middle age or early aging? People generally think of their children as young and vigorous, and it is natural to deny (in the psychological sense) the aging of the next generation.

The evidence shows that *the role of caregiver is not a "natural" developmental stage of life for an adult child,* no matter the child's age or stage. It is not an expected "on-time" event. In effect, *younger caregivers say, "I'm too young for this," middle aged caregivers say, "I thought I would be free at this stage of my life," and older daughters say, "I'm too old; I'm old myself."*

A most important consequence of the fact that caregivers do not share a single developmental stage of life is the absence of behavioral norms for this normative life crisis. Since behavior in different people and families cannot be measured by the same yardstick, there is no simple answer to the question that is asked so often: "What should adult children do to help their elderly parents?"

Chapter 8

Caregiving Daughters and Their Siblings

The themes of parent care described in Chapters 6 and 7 are only a few of the many that exist and interact. Among other issues are those that pertain to the daughter's family of origin—the relationships of all of the adult siblings with each other and their parent as they focus on the caregiving situation. Many questions about those relationships are unanswered or have been answered incompletely: How does it happen that a particular daughter in the family becomes the principal caregiver? What reverberations does the caregiving situation have on the other adult children? What are the perspectives of those siblings? What are the problems and the positive aspects of the siblings' interactions with each other?

Sibling relationships, of course, are significant throughout the life cycle. Their nature and salience in early development is well documented, as are the roles of gender and birth order in, for example, determining personality, intellectual development, and parental attitudes (Lamb & Sutton-Smith, 1982; Sutton-Smith & Rosenberg, 1970). The literature stresses the uniqueness of the sibling relationship (the shared genetic heritage, cultural milieu, and early experiences) and its long duration (for a review, see Cicirelli, 1982).

Relationships among siblings, even among those who have lived relatively separate lives, tend to be renewed when their own children mature and leave home (Manney, 1975) and may become even more important when the siblings grow old. Not only do four out of five older people have at least one surviving sibling with whom they have frequent contact (Shanas, 1979a), but their relationships with each other are salient to maintaining morale (Wood & Robertson, 1978). Elderly siblings provide tangible help to each other as well as emotional support (Cantor, 1980; Gold, 1987), notably when the disabled person has no spouse or children to do so, though siblings do less than such relatives. To the extent that fewer adult children are available to provide intergenerational support than have earlier cohorts of older people, it may be that older people will rely more on intragenerational support (Gold, undated).

Sibling interaction in midlife as it pertains to parent care is virtually uncharted territory, however, despite the fact that even those who have lived relatively separate lives must interact in unrehearsed ways. The illness of a parent may constitute a "critical event" in the sibling relationship, with the possibility of a positive or negative outcome (Ross & Milgram, 1982).

Though intersibling issues are recurring themes in caregivers' stories, they have received relatively little attention from research. In general, investigators have had a *vertical* perspective on family caregiving. That is, they examine parent/child relationships during the phase of the family life cycle when the parent is elderly and needs help. There has been less consideration of the *horizontal* relationships—that is, among adult siblings who have a disabled parent.

Another factor contributing to a lack of sufficient attention to siblings is that practitioners and clinicians see caregiving situations primarily from the perspectives of the older people concerned and their principal caregivers. When an older person is in contact with a service agency or health professional, it is usually that primary caregiver who accompanies her and whose account of the situation is heard. As a result, most information about the behavior of the various siblings and the family dynamics that operate is not supplemented to a significant extent by reports from the siblings themselves.

The main parent-care pattern is for one daughter to become the primary caregiver and to provide the bulk of help (see Chapter 2). The other adult children in the family, who often help to some extent, are referred to as "secondary" caregivers. Typically, the main caregiver sustains her efforts, sometimes for many years, despite any negative effects she and her own family may experience. Even when it becomes necessary to place the parent in a nursing home, the same woman usually remains the steadfast responsible other who maintains the closest connection with and does the most for the parent.

The lack of a rich body of information about the secondary caregivers leaves a vacuum easily filled by opinions and biases. The siblings may be viewed as having abdicated their responsibilities and allowing their responsible sister to bear the burdens alone, while they go "scot free." In a related vein, emphasis has been placed on intersibling conflicts about the parent-care situation and the deterioration in their relationships with each other. The many instances in which sisters and brothers collaborate with each other in decision-making, cooperate in caregiving, and give each other emotional support as well as instrumental help go relatively unnoticed.

Though situational factors may play a role in determining who in the family becomes and remains the principal caregiver, there are many subtle forces at work as well. In beginning to unravel this extremely complicated matter, it will be approached from several perspectives:

- The principal caregivers' views about how they happened to occupy that role
- Reports from caregivers and their local siblings in the same families as to the amount of parent care each provides
- The effects caregivers and their local and geographically distant siblings experience as a result of the parent care situation
- The accounts of caregivers and their local and geographically distant siblings of the problems they have with each other and the positive side of their interactions

While reading this chapter, it is important to keep in mind that family relationships, whether positive or negative (most often there is a mixture), do not arise anew at the parent-care stage of life, but are part of the natural continuum of the family's history (see Chapter 5). Old loyalties and alliances among siblings as well as old rivalries exist, and the problems and strengths stand out in bold relief when the older person becomes the focal point of their interactions. Among adult siblings, as with all types of family relationships, vestiges of unresolved relationship problems from earlier phases of family life are reactivated and recapitulated during subsequent family crises. The older person's dependency is just such a crisis; it disturbs the family homeostatsis and requires a rebalancing of the roles and relationships of all family members.

In exploring questions about how a particular daughter happens to become and to remain the principal caregiver, it is emphasized that there is nothing intrinsically "wrong" when a daughter occupies that role. In many situations it works out well. Siblings help as much as indicated or as much as they can, and relationships are amicable. Obviously, when the disabled parent can no longer live alone, she cannot live with all her children and a selection must be made. Serious intersibling problems are by no means inevitable. In most families, sibling relationships fall between the extremes of severe conflict and being "ideal." Moreover, it would be naive to view any human relationship as totally "good" or totally "bad," since both positives and negatives invariably exist simultaneously, though the balance is different in different families and among different sets of siblings in the same families.

When serious latent or existing relationship problems exist, however, the parent may become the storm-center of a chaotic family situation. The stimulation of intersibling tensions that may have been relatively quiescent have been described in reference to situations in which the parent requires assistance or is at risk of institutionalization (Brody & Spark, 1966; Simos,

1973; Spark & Brody, 1970). Practitioners frequently hear complaints from caregivers about their siblings, much anecdotal material from support groups of adult children highlights sibling conflicts, and there are some research reports of widespread deterioration in sibling relationships as an effect of parent care (e.g., Kinnear & Graycar, 1982).

Some patterns will be described that emerged in the course of qualitative interviews with caregiving daughters. Then information will be presented that was elicited directly from the siblings in what were essentially quantitative studies.

BECOMING THE PRINCIPAL CAREGIVER

The value that older people *should* receive care is accepted here as a given, as is the proposition that it is the responsibility of the family to provide that care within the limits of its capability and to arrange for nonfamily care if that capability is exceeded. Belief in those values, together with love, affection, and genuine caring are potent and constructive forces. Some of the women who provide the bulk of care do not experience undue strain, and some obtain and utilize help from other family members and from nonfamily sources as well. What determines the selection process by which one daughter or daughter-in-law becomes the main person to provide care?

Gender, Geography, and Being an Only Child

Three powerful determinants of the selection process are relatively straightforward: gender, geography, and being an only child.

The virtually universal acceptance of the proposition that care of elderly people is a woman's role was discussed in detail in Chapter 6. (Note that the power of gender in determining who becomes a caregiver extends to other relatives as well. When disabled older people do not have a spouse or an adult child, female relatives—sisters and nieces, for example—predominate over their male counterparts (Horowitz & Dobrof, 1982).)

Geographic proximity is often a major determinant of becoming the main caregiver. It is obvious that when an adult child lives at a distance from the parent, she is simply not available to provide day-to-day assistance, no matter how close the emotional bond and no matter how much she wants to help. Though geographically proximate daughters recognize the practical reasons for their caregiving role, there may be an undercurrent of resentment nonetheless.

I don't mind being the principal caregiver. That's the way it is. I'm up the street from her and that's all there is to it. The main reason I'm the principal caregiver is because I live closest. They all live comfortably away. They can be away and be comfortable because they know I'm here. I think if I wasn't here, they would probably do a little more.

It can be argued, of course, that a parent can be moved to be near a child or that an adult child can move to bring the parent within caregiving range. This happens at times, particularly if it brings the parent closer to a daughter.

· After my mother's heart attack, it seemed logical for my mother and step-father to move near me since my brother and his wife were both working full-time and I wasn't working.

To adult children who have no siblings, it is self-evident that they should become the caregiver. They invariably say "Who else is there?" or "There wasn't any option." Some only children report that they were aware very early in their lives that parent care would be their responsibility and accordingly prepared themselves for that role.

Way back then [as a child] . . . I figured I'd have to be responsible for one or another of my parents. I guess I had that in back of my mind all these years . . . it wasn't as if I was making a huge sacrifice [not getting married] because I like to work. I figured . . . if the day came and the need arose [for parent care] I could probably handle it. . . . That's how it went."

* * *

It was up to me. I have no siblings. I prepared for this all my life. An ounce of prevention is worth a pound of cure. I'm a preparer. . . . A stitch in time saves nine.

Some caregivers become only children later in their lives because their sibling(s) have died, a situation that is increasing in frequency as more people live to advanced old age and outlive one or more of their children.

I knew I had to take care of them [parents] and that there would be no one else to help. . . . I regret my sister wasn't alive to share the changes.

* * *

My mother-in-law moved into our house after her stroke because my husband's only brother died.

Beyond gender, geography, and being an only child, no strong patterns of selection have been identified, and there are many subtle forces that operate. Though birth order (being the youngest or oldest child) is often mentioned as influential, overall it has not emerged as important in the few studies that have been done. Nevertheless, some caregivers do attribute their role to their position in the birth order.

> I'm the oldest, and I always took most of the responsibility.

> * * *

> I'm the youngest, so I was still home when Mom started needing care.

In a small percentage of situations, the elderly parent and adult daughter have always lived together (even after the latter marries), and the caregiving situation is a natural extension of that life-long relationship.

Some caregivers, when asked, "How did it happen?," offer reasons such as feeling responsible; being better able to provide care; having more appropriate housing, money, or time than a sibling; the elderly mother's preference; or emotional closeness. Since such responses tell us little about the processes at work, further exploration is required.

An intriguing theme is that, whatever the various reasons or combinations of reasons offered, a daughter often votes for herself in the informal election that is held to select the principal caregiver. (The election is rarely contested.) Listening to the accounts of other siblings about how it happened is part of the unfinished agenda about parent care.

It Just Happened That Way

"It just happened," "It just worked out that way," or "That's the way it is" are explanations offered by some caregivers.

> When mother needed a place to stay, I was the only one to offer. It wasn't a conscious decision for me to do it; it just worked out that way. Things happened, and I picked up. When she came to the house, it was for a visit. No one expected it to be permanent. It just worked out that way. Everything just ran together. It all fell into place, and here I've been.

> * * *

> We knew we would have to take care of her. Mom trusted us to make decisions about her care; that was how it was. I felt I was home, so I might as well do it. It was a natural thing.

> * * *

> It just happened that I made the offer for my mother to come and live with us, and I became the principal caregiver. I don't know if my sister would have made the offer or not. It didn't really enter into my decision.

In many instances, caregivers begin by providing very little help, but the amount of assistance grows incrementally over time as the parent becomes more and more disabled and dependent. Because such situations develop gradually, there is no clear point at which the setting of limits is indicated, and the boundaries of care are expanded almost imperceptibly. When parent care expands so that it encroaches on and displaces all other areas of the caregiver's life, other dynamic patterns are at work as well.

Fewer Competing Responsibilities

A selection process may go on in some families so that the role of caregiver falls to the child with fewest competing responsibilities (Ikles, 1983; Stoller, 1983). Thus, daughters who are not married (widowed, never-married, separated, or divorced) may be over-represented as parent carers (see Chapter 2). This was illustrated in a survey of three generations of women in which all three generations were likely to expect more of not-married daughters than of married daughters or sons—to adjust their work schedules for parent care and to share a household with an elderly parent, for example (Brody et al., 1984). That expectation was expressed in the women's actual behavior, with married daughters providing less help to their parents than not-married daughters (Lang & Brody, 1983).

It is not unusual for daughters to offer their siblings' competing responsibilities as the rationale for their own selection as caregiver.

> Being a widow made it easier. I just feel sorry for [caregiving] women who have children or even boyfriends.

> * * *

> I felt I was the person to take on her [mother's] care because I was a single person. That was definitely a factor.

> * * *

> I don't have any other family obligations *per se*. I'm not married, I don't have children. And my sister has emotional problems.

> * * *

> If I had a family of my own I would have had to give it a lot more thought. . . . But I felt I was the person to take on her care because I'm divorced."

Although fewer competing responsibilities may indeed be a factor, another influence may also be at work with women who are not married, especially if they are childless as well. The parent fills the human need we all have for a close relationship with another. (see Chapter 10.)

Burden Bearer

No matter how many siblings there are in a family, it is not unusual for one of them to assume all major family responsibilities, of which parent care is only one. Such individuals have been characterized as the family "burden bearers" (Brody & Spark, 1966). This woman's plaint is typical:

> I am always the one who has taken responsibility for my mother. I am the one who shops and takes her to the doctor. I am the one she depends on to take care of her. I am the one she calls late at night if she feels ill.

These women may present themselves as long-suffering, patient, martyred, self-sacrificing, and even oppressed. Sometimes the burden bearer protects and excuses her siblings. "My brother is not well. He cannot be expected to help," or "My sister has emotional problems." Sometimes resentment and bitter envy is expressed. "My sister [and/or brother] does nothing, but is always telling me what to do." Although the behavior of such women may be viewed as admirable, one wonders what gratification they may be obtaining from the very burdens that ostensibly weigh so heavily. Exploring these dynamics is also part of the unfinished agenda.

Favored Child and The "Rejected" Child

The child who was favored by the parent or the one who always "got along best" with her may be elected to the role of principal caregiver.

> Of all of us [children], I always understood my mother the best.

> * * *

> Maybe mother chose to live with me because growing up she and I got along the best of the four children.

> * * *

> I didn't mind being the principal caregiver. All our lives my mother was my friend. My one sister and her never got along. My one sister was never a giver, and that was all right. My other sister was willing but couldn't manage mother.

At other times, however, it is the child who felt rejected or the least loved who provides the care in the hope that the parent will come to love her the best. Such daughters yearn to become the favorite child and are constantly trying to win the acceptance or love they had been denied earlier in their lives. They continue their efforts to do so even when they are "children" in their eighth decade of life, exhausting themselves in a fruitless and neverending effort to please the parent they are helping.

I'm the one who does everything for my mother, but my brother is still her favorite child.

* * *

My mother does nothing but complain and criticize me. When my brother visits, she's a different person.

A variation on this theme is that of daughters who did have their parents' approval early in life, but lost it because of their behavior (an unacceptable marriage or life-style, for example). Such a woman may see caregiving as a means of regaining the parent's love or vindicating herself, "I'm a good person [or daughter] after all."

I remember a lovely relation with my father when we were small. . . . Some of that warmth has come back in taking care of him. It's sort of nice to experience his total acceptance of me after so many years.

Mother/Daughter Enmeshment

Some caregiving daughters say they have been extraordinarily close to their mothers since early childhood. Time has not weakened the powerful bond, and the caregiver seems unable to separate from her parent. In extreme cases, the mother/daughter tie remains central, even superseding the daughter's relationship with her husband and children. These women feel that no one else is satisfactory as caregiver to the mother, or no one else is able to provide care as well.

I wouldn't be happy if mother didn't live near me. I need her near me. I need to be there and know what my mother is doing and know what kind of care she is getting. So it is good she is here and I can check on her all the time and be there for her. I don't think my mother would have been happy living near my sister. My sister doesn't know what is right for mother.

* * *

My sister-in-law offered to come over for a few days so we could visit our kids, but I told her that my mother will not let her do what I have to do for her.

* * *

My husband did not object when I brought my parents to our home, but he withdrew into himself. Now Dad is dead, and Mother is in a nursing home. My husband would like me to turn to him now, but there is still the connection with my mother. I am not free yet.

* * *

Now that I'm 50 years old, I've decided that I would like to marry. But the man would have to understand in advance that my mother will always come first.

* * *

Mother said when I was a girl "You don't want to get married." I did get married, but I never really left her.

Being Worthwhile

Caregiving gives some women a role in life, a sense of competence and of being a responsible individual. Their behavior elicits approval and admiration from those around them, and their sense of adequacy and self-esteem is enhanced: "I'm doing a noble thing," and "The doctor tells me 'Nobody gets the care your mother gets'."

"Professional" Caregivers

Women who might be characterized as "professional" caregivers seem to seek opportunities to enact that role, often providing help to other elderly people in addition to their parents or parents-in-law.

I also helped my aunt [in addition to both parents]. She had other people to help, but I was the only one around. . . . It just evolved. It started out a little bit and ended up a lot. My father and mother did it, and when my father died it fell on me.

* * *

I helped my aunt before she moved in here. We would go over every week and take her shopping, and my husband would fix anything that had to be fixed in her apartment. My husband and I decided together to have her live with us. My mother was living with us at that time. The reason we brought my aunt over was because she had tiny strokes. It was when my aunt had a stroke that I quit work. I also have an uncle on my father's side that I help.

Some of these women began to take care of their parent(s) very early in childhood. Caregiving becames a way of life, and parent care continues that longstanding pattern. The early socialization of these "professional" caregivers sometimes occurs when the parent had a physical or mental disability that was present when the child was very young.

My parents were born totally deaf, and I began to take care of them when I was a child. I took care of my younger brothers as they came along. You have to be a certain kind of person to deal with deaf people. My brothers are loving and caring but . . . my mother wouldn't be happy except with me. She cares about me, nobody else, just me. Maybe my brothers, but not so much because they aren't with her. Anybody else could do the same things that I do for my mother, but it wouldn't be the same and it wouldn't satisfy her. I took care of my aunt, too, and I have another aunt who is beginning to need my help. I want my house to be the halfway house where all the family gather.

* * *

Beginning when I was a child, my mother didn't leave the house for 22 years. She was afraid to go out. We used to do all the errands and bring the stories of our days to her.

* * *

My mother was so sick when I was little that I lived with my grandmother for 6 years. My father was sick too. For a long time, I though that's the way things are: You grow up, you get married and have children, and then you get sick.

Deathbed Instructions

The instructions of a dying parent are sometimes offered as a reason for the caregiver's assumption of that role:

Daddy said I should be the one to care for Mommy. My sister took mother for a while, but it wasn't right. Daddy said mother should be with me. I'm the only one who could take Mom. Daddy wanted most of the care to fall on me. I didn't have a choice. Just before he died he asked me to take care of Mommy. He said I was to be in charge.

Being Responsible and Nurturing

Being responsible, capable, or especially nurturing are traits some caregivers attribute to themselves as accounting for their role.

My sisters think I can handle it better. I'm the backbone of the family. I guess I always acted old for my age.

* * *

When she was dying, my mother-in-law told my father-in-law "Go to your son's house. That's the place to be." She knew we had a happy household.

Low Expectations

Some women accept the caregiving role because others in the family expect it of them and continue on for years without protest. These women often appear to be unusually passive and to express very low expectations for meeting their own needs. They may attribute severe emotional symptoms or stress-related physical problems to caregiving, but make no effort to extricate themselves or even to obtain family or nonfamily services that would give them temporary relief. Some live extremely restricted lives. When asked what they would like to ameliorate their situations, they reply "I would like to be able to take a walk by myself once in a while," or "It would be wonderful to have a whole day all to myself."

Transferring the Role to Another

Occasionally, an overburdened caregiver will try to transfer care of the parent to a sibling, usually without success.

At first, my mother was shuffled around among us sisters, but they wouldn't keep her.

* * *

When I was breaking down, my sister took my mother. But after a couple of weeks, my brother-in-law put her in a taxi back to us.

* * *

I asked my sister in Chicago . . . if she could take her. She said she could take her for 2 months. . . . After 3 weeks, my sister couldn't wait to get her on the plane to get her back to us.

Equitable Sharing

Sometimes siblings—almost invariably a pair of sisters—collaborate so closely that they have difficulty identifying one or the other as the principal caregiver.

I don't know which of us is the principal caregiver. My sister lives in Washington, and my mother lives about a mile away from me. Sure, I do the day-to-day things like shopping and taking mother out to dinner and running over if there's an emergency. But my sister comes in regularly, and we save up things for her to do like going to the doctor and the podiatrist and shopping for clothes. She comes in right away if we need her. She takes Mom to Washington for visits. I always know she's there. I count on her and she counts on me."

* * *

My sister and I are each better at different things. She's more assertive, so she deals with the doctors and the Medicare people and so on. I'm better at dealing with our mother. So we each do our thing, and it works out.

The kind of sharing described in those excerpts is better characterized as amicable and equitable rather than equal. The particular tasks are not divided, but each sibling sees the other as willing to do what she can—a *fair*, rather than an *equal*, share.

SECONDARY CAREGIVERS: THE SIBLINGS' PERSPECTIVE

In turning to the perspectives of the caregivers' siblings, it is reiterated that the data presented derive primarily from quantitative studies; it remains to gain in-depth understanding of those siblings' inner processes.

Having become the principal caregiver, the daughter provides the bulk of care, with her siblings providing a much lesser amount of help. Reports from those daughters, however, indicate that emotional support from siblings and from other relatives is very important in buffering their strains (George, 1986; Horowitz, 1982; Sussman, 1979; Zarit et al., 1980).

In one study, the siblings themselves (those who lived locally, defined as within 50 miles of the parent) confirmed the imbalance between their own helping contributions and those of their caregiving sisters (Brody et al., 1989). The caregivers reported they provided an average of more than 24 hours of help weekly (including virtually all the ADL help needed), whereas their local sisters and brothers reported providing 8 and less than 4 hours weekly, respectively.

The lesser amount of help siblings provide should be seen in relation to the mother's living arrangement. Certainly, a daughter whose household includes the mother absorbs many tasks like the mother's shopping and cooking when she does those things for her own family. Nor can personal care such as feeding and toileting be postponed until someone else can visit. In addition, there may be a tendency to view the older person as having become part of the caregiver's immediate family. That being so, other family members assume that the elderly parent's needs are being met. Whatever factors are at work, the net result is that the caregiver's contribution is greater when the parent shares her home; her siblings do less than when the parent lives alone (Brody et al., 1988). Although other members of the caregiver's own household may help a bit more, their help does not offset the reduction in the help from others in the extended family network.

There is another qualification about the roles of the caregivers' siblings. Because estimates of help in surveys are based on day-to-day ongoing assistance with ADL and IADL, certain important forms of help usually go uncounted. Sisters and brothers often rally to provide major services at specially demanding times or during emergencies—acute medical illnesses of the older person, the caregiver, or her immediate family, for example, or when the older person moves from one household to another. The sense that siblings can be relied on at such times gives the caregiver a feeling of security and support.

Comparing the Effects on Caregivers and Siblings

An extensive literature shows that approximately one-half to three-fourths of daughters who are primary caregivers report effects such as various emotional strains, negative effects on their physical health, and life-style interferences (with privacy socialization, vacations) and feelings of anger and resentment (see Chapter 3). When the effects of care experienced by siblings were elicited directly from them in a PGC study of caregiving daughters and their siblings (Brody et al., 1989), it was apparent that siblings do not go unscathed, however. Half of them reported experiencing some problems similar to those of the principal caregivers (see Brody et al., 1989, for complete report.).

It is particularly significant that findings about gender differences in parent care proved to be consistent. The daughters who were the main caregivers experienced the most negative effects of parent care, the local brothers experienced the fewest negative effects, and the local sisters fell in between. To emphasize, though the strains of the siblings were fewer and less severe than those of the caregivers, the latter's sisters reported more overall strain and more severe strain than the brothers; more of the physical, mental, and marital strains; more emotional symptoms such as feeling drained, nervous, frustrated; and more interferences with their family responsibilities.

The brothers' reports that they experienced fewer emotional symptoms than both groups of their sisters may reflect the fact that the men provided the least help. Or, it is possible that as men, they are more likely to repress or deny their emotional reactions than women. It is most likely, however, that sisters experience more strain than brothers because they are more involved emotionally and see the responsibility for the care and happiness of their parents as their role as females (see Chapter 6).

An effect of care about which the caregivers and their local siblings did not differ significantly is of special interest. Most of the caregivers and their siblings agree with the statement, "Somehow I feel guilty about not doing more for my mother." The siblings outdid the caregivers in the frequency with which they experienced such guilt, however. Being the one who does most for the parent appears to alleviate (if only slightly) guilt about "not doing more." Some of the adult children felt guilty about other aspects of care as well. Both groups of daughters exceeded their brothers in feeling guilty when they became angry with their mothers. The sisters outdid the caregivers in feeling guilty about not doing more for their mother and in wishing that they were not so busy so that they could assist their mother more.

Nevertheless, one complaint unique to the main caregiving daughters is particularly poignant. Two-fifths of them said that even though they were doing the most for the parent, another sibling was the favorite child.

Sibling Interactions

Other information from the same study spoke directly to the problematic and the beneficial aspects of the siblings' interactions with each other about the caregiving situation—interactions that were categorized as intersibling "hassles" and "uplifts." As expected, the sibling relationships ranged from those that were close and mutually helpful to those that were extremely problematic, with most falling in between.

Once again, daughters reported more strain than sons. Overall, approximately 30% of the caregivers, 40% of their sisters, and only 6% of the brothers reported a great deal or a fair amount of strain from interactions with their siblings about parent care.

There were many differences between caregivers and their siblings. It was the former who reported the most problems about ways in which their siblings were failing to meeting parent-care responsibilities by doing such things as visiting the mother, volunteering to help without waiting to be asked, helping more, or doing a fair share of parent care. Such complaints were characterized as siblings' "nonfeasance." Other kinds of complaints were called siblings' "malfeasance"—that is, more active negative behaviors such as criticizing the caregiver or trying to make her feel guilty.

The caregivers describe their negative interactions with their siblings:

My sister took mother for a period of time but felt very resentful about it. We were not communicating very well.

* * *

I'm not satisfied with the amount of help they give Mother. They often take turns having her for weekends but have to be reminded that she sat home for some weekends in a row. With eight of us, it shouldn't be that way.

* * *

My brother and sister used to help, but when Mother moved in with us they considered the problems solved.

Again, there was a striking finding about the sisters. They exceeded both the caregivers and the brothers in saying that a sibling had tried to make them feel guilty for not helping more, had tried to have the mother appreciate what s/he does more than what she does, had complained of doing more than she does, or had said how burdened they felt.

Positive interactions existed side by side with problems in the very same situations, however. The other side of the picture is that the caregivers and both groups of her local siblings reported many rewarding aspects ("uplifts") of their parent-care interactions. The vast majority of all three groups felt that a sibling was dependable about helping their mother and understood their caregiving efforts. *Again, the sisters and brothers differed.* The sisters experienced more rewards from their sibling interactions and felt more benefited by them than the caregivers. In particular, the sisters were the ones who felt good when permitted to share decisions about the mother.

Many of the rewards reported by the main caregivers were the obverse of the problems they had expressed; specifically, they felt benefitted when socioemotional support was forthcoming from their siblings and hassled when it was not. The siblings, too, were benefitted by the same behaviors that caregivers found rewarding and, in addition, appreciated the approval of their siblings and the willingness to share decisions with them.

The caregivers describe rewarding situations:

> Mother had a heart attack, and my father went to a nursing home. My brother went back and forth several times. At a family conference, we arranged for them to move to an apartment in Philadelphia. My brother is very supportive and appreciative. He and his wife come east [from Denver] three or four times a year so we can go away each time for a week, and he calls every week.

* * *

> My sister and I both work. We really tried to share the responsibilities of my mother, and we still share them. We are better at doing different things. I'm better at talking to the staff at the nursing home and getting my mother's needs met because I'm more assertive. My sister was much better at filling out all the forms at the nursing home. We really try to share. There is no resentment that one does more than the other. If there was a difficulty, if one wasn't satisfied or something, we would just talk about it."

Overall, the PGC study of siblings made it apparent that parent care has repercussions not only on principal caregivers, but on their siblings and on the relationships among them. The caregivers and siblings who were most troubled by their interactions were those whose mothers were more difficult to care for because of cognitive impairment and irritability, and whose relationships with their mother and families were not satisfactory. Conversely, those with more positive relationships had mothers needing less help, and better relationships with the mother and the family. This suggests that as the mothers' care needs increase, the pressure felt by her children is expressed as increasing tension among them. The caregivers, on whom the burden is greatest, become more aware of the inequity and more sensitive to any failure of their siblings to provide emotional and instrumental support. Close and warm relationships with the mother and among her children, however, appear to mitigate the strains among them.

Perhaps the most intriguing finding of the study was that once again, in comparison after comparison, daughters proved to be more vulnerable than sons to emotional strain relating to parent care.

It is understandable that the main caregivers should feel more strain, but their local sisters are a particularly interesting group. To recapitulate, local sisters fell in between the other two groups—caregiving daughters and local brothers—in reporting overall strain and negative emotional and physical consequences of caregiving. They exceeded even the principal caregivers in reporting strain from the intersibling interactions. These sisters were especially sensitive to any implications that they were not meeting their parent-care responsibilities and were appreciative when included in decisions about the mother's care. They were the ones who felt the most guilty about not doing more for their mothers and who most often wished they were not so busy so that they could do more. They joined the caregivers in feeling guilty more often than the brothers when they became angry with the mothers, and they joined the brothers in feeling guilty more often because they were doing less parent care than the principal caregivers.

The overall sense conveyed is the discomfort of the local sisters (but not the brothers) about being in the role of secondary, rather than primary caregiver.

The information in this chapter about the siblings' perspectives was derived from survey data. We, therefore, do not have the benefit of case material derived from open-ended, in-depth interviews with those "secondary caregivers." However, in the PGC study the siblings were asked to write briefly about the nature of the problems that may exist among siblings when a parent needs care. Their replies spoke to equitable sharing of responsibility, problems of communication, disagreements over the mother's needs and care, and unresolved sibling rivalries:

> Her care is unlikely to be equally shared, which leads to guilt and resentment. Children may have different ideas about what is most important in her care and how she should be treated; those who are not primarily caretakers have little voice in what happens to her.

* * *

> Problems with siblings and rivalry come up with conflicts over who does more for mother. This creates tension and often hostility and resentment; jealousies emerge.

* * *

The problem is finding ways to work out an equitable sharing of the help so that old family patterns are not simply reinforced; also, coping with the ways in which different values or different senses of mother's real needs can create tension and distance rather than cooperation and closeness.

* * *

The main problems are the unequal degrees to which siblings help (or are perceived to help), the differing extents to which siblings are able to help, and indifference on the part of some siblings.

Geographically Distant Children

Geographically distant children have somewhat different problems than those who live close to the parent. The direction of social and demographic change undoubtedly will render them increasingly significant in the lives of elderly parents. The continuing trend towards small families, as well as the increase in the number of families having only one child, means that successive generations may have fewer or no siblings with whom to share parent care. In addition, more of the children of future cohorts of the elderly may live at a geographic distance (Treas & Bengtson, 1982). Children of higher socioeconomic and educational status tend to live farther away from older generations (Cicirelli, 1981; Sundstrom, 1986). Although in most cases it is children who move away from parents, the elderly themselves are migrating in increasing numbers. During the past decade, there has been a 54% increase in the number of American of retirement age who migrated from state to state (Longino et al., 1984).

Geographic distance between elderly parents and children is not the main pattern by far. It is important, however, to understand the problems and perspectives of such children who are constrained in their ability to provide regular and sustained instrumental support to an aged parent though a sibling is proximate to the parent and is the main caregiver.

In the PGC study described, geographically distant children were compared with their sisters who lived close to the parent and were the main caregivers. Once again, *women (the caregivers' sisters) proved to be more vulnerable to parent care strains than men (the caregivers' brothers)* (Schoonover et al., 1988). The caregivers' sisters were more likely than their brothers to express feelings of guilt about the mother's situation—in particular, about not doing enough for the mother and the fact that a sibling (the main caregiver) was doing more. In comparison to their brothers, the sisters also felt more guilty about living far away and about getting angry or losing patience with the mother at times. They were more likely to express the desire to spend more time with the mother and to want to live closer so that they could provide more help.

The sisters, more frequently than the brothers, reported negative emotional effects from the caregiving situation—the now familiar litany of feeling helpless, nervous, frustrated, depressed, drained, overwhelmed, tired, and pulled in different directions by the mother's need for help. They also reported higher levels of strain deriving from the mother's situation and from living far away from her, and from the intersibling problems that occurred. The sisters were more likely than brothers to say that a sibling had complained of doing more for the mother than they had, had not understood how much help the mother needed, had tried to make them feel guilty about not doing more, had not done his or her fair share, had criticized what they did to help the mother, had complained of doing more, had not visited the mother enough, did not understand how much help the mother needs, and thought he or she knew better what was best for the mother.

Like the local siblings, majorities of both geographically distant brothers and sisters also reported benefits from the social and emotional support provided by their siblings—from their dependability in helping when needed, moral support, reliability in visiting and calling the elderly mother, and understanding of the effort he or she made to help the mother.

Certain themes appeared for sisters and brothers alike in their replies to an open-ended question about the main problems or concerns facing geographically distant children of disabled elderly parents. Their responses included their inability to respond to the mother's needs in a timely fashion or on a regular basis because of family obligations and/or financial restraints; feeling cut off and left out of decision-making and uninformed as to the mother's day-to-day conditions; feelings of guilt for not being able to do more or to relieve the sibling providing the help; and the competing demands of their own families and careers. They wrote:

> I feel sad and guilty both for my mother and my sister's always being 'on call'; I worry about being unable to get there on time when needed, and I worry a lot about responsibilities of my own here and the stress of not being able to accept a commitment that might be interrupted, or unfulfilled, should I be needed at my mother's side.

* * *

> It takes a major effort to visit her, particularly as my children get older. These visits are usually instead of a family vacation. When she is here, we give up our room, as space is limited, and arrange our lives around her. All of this puts a strain on my family, and I feel guilty that I can't please them or help mother enough.

> The major problem is not being able to provide help, and not being sure what is really wrong or what is taking place. I never really am able to feel secure about my mother.

* * *

Major problems are finding ways to provide something like a fair share of the help while living at a distance; feeling that I have little right to assert my views of her needs because others are providing most of the care. There is little sense of a sustained relationship that make a large difference toward her comfort instead of a periodic one that makes little difference on the whole.

* * *

. . . not being able to visit or invite her on a regular basis; helping to make financial decisions when she is not able to do this; the feeling of being almost helpless when certain situations arise.

On another write-in question, the distant siblings were asked if there were any other ways in which the mother's needs affected them and their families. Both sisters and brothers described arrangements whereby they attempted to participate in and relieve their sister's caregiving burden, as well as the ways in which these arrangements affected their and their families lives. In addition, some described the effects of their parent's condition on their own children. For example:

I have developed a pattern of making visits to relieve my sister and brother-in-law several times a year. That is, I take over for a few days and let them get away. This has been very beneficial to me as well as to them.

* * *

We do feel responsible for emotional support and for frequent visits; these visits are wrenching and a strain for the whole family. My children have a pessimistic view of aging and the terrible changes it works on people they love. We often feel caught between the needs of helpless parents and siblings who take the major burden. We feel guilty about taking vacation time for ourselves. Our jobs are often stressful, and we need time for ourselves. It's horrible to see people you love lose too much of their personality and dignity.

The responses of those geographically distant children reinforce other research (Marshall & Rosenthal, 1985; Mercier, Paulson, & Morris, 1987; Shanas, 1973) documenting the persistence and durability of emotional bonds linking parents and their adult children despite the barrier of geographic distance. Though those bonds transcend distance, the degree of social interaction and nature of help such children provide is necessarily different from that of proximate siblings.

Advice for Others

Still another write-in question in the PGC study asked the siblings if they have any advice to offer others who are in, or anticipate being in, their situations. The dominant themes focused on planning, communication and cooperation, and flexibility among siblings:

> Set it up front what is to be shared and include the older person; then all will know what was said. Remember, what you wanted to do in 1976 you may not want to do in 1984. Also, have all meet with the doctor so all hear the same story.

* * *

> Be prepared! Understand well in advance what might happen. Attend any and all information meetings, seminars, whatever, concerning older parents and their effects on children.

* * *

> Talk to each other. Try to state needs and limits clearly and without placing blame.

* * *

> Obtain agreement in advance between siblings as to the sharing of responsibilities.

* * *

> Be patient, sympathetic, and permissive towards the other members of the family in terms of their reactions and emotional needs.

Undoubtedly, distant children whose parents do not have a proximate adult child experience more pressing and distressing problems. Anecdotal reports describe their frustration about making arrangements for care at a distance, confusion about service availability and eligibility in a different state, inability to monitor care, financial strain of frequent trips, feelings of helplessness, guilt, and worry. Research, service organizations, and the media have begun to address the unique problems of such children (for example, see Litwak and Silverstein, 1987; Collins, 1983), and a network of professional case managers has sprung up to help by providing referral, monitoring, and counseling services.

A COMMENT

In light of the concerns of this book, it is reemphasized that *daughters experience more negative effects than sons in relation to parent care.* Not only do daughters do more and experience more strain than sons when they are in comparable positions as principal caregivers, but also when they are siblings of the caregiver, whether they live close by or at a geographic distance. Gender differences occur consistently, then, in comparisons of strains experienced by sons and daughters of the disabled elderly.

Though this chapter offered a glimpse of some of the themes present among adult children when a parent needs care, those issues are by no means fully understood. Professional and public attitudes often blame the caregivers' siblings for not helping her more, but there is not a great deal of information about why additional help is not forthcoming. Caution must be exercised before critical judgments are made about the behavior of the caregivers' siblings, however. We do know that in some instances the primary caregiver selects herself for that role and sometimes refuses help, feeling that only she can do the caregiving properly or submitting to the parent's refusal to let anyone else help her. Moreover, though this chapter includes some information elicited directly from the siblings, their views on how it happened that they did not become the primary caregiver still remain to be explored.

Undoubtedly, there are some situations in which the sharing of care among siblings could be more equitable. But siblings who are "secondary caregivers" are not uninvolved. Sisters in particular experience bothersome strains, though in the main they are fewer, less severe, and often stem from different sources than those of the principal providers of care. At the least, more complete knowledge is needed about the psychological dynamics and relationships that are at work in families when an elderly parent becomes disabled.

Chapter 9

Married Daughters (and Their Husbands and Children)

In addition to experiencing many of the themes described in the previous chapters, there are issues for married caregivers that are unique to their marital status. Not only do they have husbands who inevitably affect and are affected by the caregiving situation, but most married women also have children whose ages and stages vary. (Issues concerning children and caregiving are also present in the lives of some caregivers who are widowed, divorced, or separated, of course.)

This chapter identifies the major themes articulated by women that relate specifically to the intersection of parent care with their status as married women. Available information about their husbands (the sons-in-law) and the couples' children will be summarized as well—their perceptions of the caregiving situations, the effects they experience, and the roles they play. Brief case excerpts will illustrate the themes married daughters share. Then, eight longer case studies will show the context in which the themes and issues are embedded, and the changes over time in caregiving situations.

CAREGIVERS AND THEIR HUSBANDS

A major theme for many married daughters is the emotional support they receive from their husbands. That form of help appears to be more important to them than any instrumental assistance the men may provide. The women emphasize that having a husband provides them with someone to talk to about their parent-care problems—someone who understands and who can share in decision-making. They are quick to point out, however, that such benefits depend on having a supportive husband with whom one has a good relationship. Many women describe their husbands in just that way, confirming the observation that some sons-in-law are "unsung heroes" (Brody, 1985b). A contrapuntal theme that is apparent even when husbands are supportive is that the latter and the children in the family often represent competing demands for the daughter's time and attention. Those "pulls" add considerably to her strains.

When competition and interpersonal problems erupt between the husband or children and the elderly parent, the daughter experiences even more stress. Her struggle to mediate the conflicts and to set her priorities is intensified. Whose needs come first? Although, in general, daughters try to honor the loyalty and priority responsibility they see as owing to their husbands and children, it is often a delicate balancing process. A helpless, ill, disabled parent who is unable to survive on her own must take precedence at times, for example, when children are old enough to take care of their own basic needs.

The women themselves are aware of the simultaneous presence of those positive and negative aspects of being married during the parent-care years. One of them, when asked who in her view has the hardest time among women whose marital statuses differ, replied tersely, "Married women." Who has the easiest time? She laughed and again replied, "Married women."

These daughters describe the benefits of having a supportive husband:

> For 3 years, my husband stopped in everyday to check on my parents. He did even more than I did. Finally, he said, "Why don't you move into our home?" Our relationship has not been affected [by caregiving] because it was established long before. We had our ups and downs, but we have weathered it.

* * *

> My husband is the balancing point. When things get on my nerves about the help I give to my mother, I go to him and he calms me. If anything happens to him I would have no support, and I would go crazy.

* * *

> My husband would help her. At night, he would care for her completely. It was rough on him, and it's not even his mother. I am very grateful for this.

There are also situations with considerable marital tension:

> Mother was up all night, we weren't sleeping, it was terrible. My husband was working then. I was between the two of them. When I reduced my work hours, my husband was all for whatever would help.

* * *

My husband moaned, groaned, and complained. He said we should put her in a nursing home. My husband complained about the constant bickering between my mother and me.

Those themes and others also emerge in research in which the sons-in-law themselves were interviewed (for a complete report, see Kleban et al., 1989), confirming the vast body of literature regarding the repercussions throughout the family system of the experiences of individual family members.

Though most sons-in-law in the study played a minor role in the day-to-day provision of instrumental services to their elderly mothers-in-law (Brody & Schoonover, 1986), most of them said they were under strain because of the caregiving situation, some for many years. They too were troubled by the life-style restrictions so often noted by their wives. Substantial minorities of the men reported interferences with time for themselves and with their wives, and with their social lives, privacy, and family vacation plans. Almost one-fourth of them had experienced work interruptions because of the need to help their mothers-in-law, and a small proportion had actually missed work on occasion. Many of the negative effects of parent care on the sons-in-law were associated with the same objective factors that caused their wives' strains—sharing their households with the mothers-in-law, for example, a living arrangement associated with the older people's poor cognitive functioning and severe disability.

The husbands were quite aware of their wives' problems. Approximately two-fifths of them viewed their wives as being "caught in the middle" between them and their mothers-in-law. Moreover, they viewed the parent-care situations to be more burdensome to their wives than the women did themselves, particularly when the elderly parent lived in the couple's household.

In comparing the perspectives of the daughters' and their husbands, the study found both similarities and differences. The spouses agreed about the kinds of disruptions that can be observed with some objectivity—to vacation plans, to the family budget, and to household chores, for example. The wives, however, were much more likely than their husbands to report that caregiving caused problems in the marital relationship, interfered with the time the spouses spent with each other and with the couple's children, and with relationships with those children. The husbands were more likely to cite interference with relationships with relatives in the extended family. Despite the fact that almost half of the men said they argued with their wives at times about the caregiving situation, very few thought it had driven them apart and most said it had made no difference in their relationship.

The fact that the sons-in-law reported less marital tension than did their wives is consistent with literature to the effect that men are more likely than women to repress or deny their emotional reactions (e.g., Walum, 1977). It may also be that family lives are more central to women, and that therefore they are more sensitive to relationship problems. The sensitivity of the wives in the study, however, may have been heightened because the dependent elderly women were *their* mothers and the daughters, therefore, felt responsible when problems occurred.

Though the quality of the marital relationships and the interpersonal interaction patterns varied greatly, it deserves emphasis that the vast majority of couples felt that the caregiving situations had not affected their basic relationships with each other.

GRANDCHILDREN

There has been virtually no research about caregivers' relationships with their own children, the effects on those grandchildren, or the roles grandchildren may play when an older person receives family help. Yet, most filial caregivers have children of their own, all of whom are witness to the situation and who inevitably are affected themselves to some extent. Some of those grandchildren live or have lived under the same roof as the disabled grandparent, whereas others have not, either because the grandparent maintained her own household or the children had already left the nest when the older person moved in (see Chapter 3 for data on the prevalence of three-generation households).

Most studies involving three-generational family relationships have focused on issues such as the transmission of values (e.g., Bengtson, 1975) or the roles, styles, and meaning of grandparenthood (see Bengtson and Robertson, 1985, for a collection of papers about grandparenthood). In the majority of those studies, the grandparents were primarily the younger cohorts of older people, including those who had not yet reached the age of 65. The grandparent's health and functional capacities are rarely addressed, though one study did include the grandparent's health as a variable in the contacts of grandchildren and grandparents (Cherlin & Furstenberg, 1985) and another as it related to the happiness or distress of grandchildren (Troll & Stapley, 1985).

Although grandchildren are often viewed as a "competing responsibility" for their parent-caring mothers, in-depth interviews with such women showed that there is a positive side as well. When they are old enough to do so, grandchildren often become part of what might be described as an invisible back-up system for their mother—"invisible" because the help they give is rarely counted in surveys. Some grandchildren are important sources of emotional support for their mothers. They may provide some instrumental help on a day-to-day basis, but move closer to center stage when emergencies (such as acute illnesses) arise or special events (such as moving the older person to a new living arrangement) call for added help.

There are no reports of studies that have elicited directly from grand-children what their roles and perspectives are in helping disabled grandpar-ents or the effects they experience for good or ill. However, a study of caregiving women that compared the effects of parent care on women in three different household types offers some insight into the consequences to women of having responsibilities to their own children as well as to an elderly parent. The household types were those shared by the disabled older person, her daughter and son-in-law (no children present because in the main they had "left the nest"); those shared by the older person, her daughter, son-in-law and their child(ren) (who ranged in age from preschool-ers to young adults in their 20s); and those in which the elderly mother maintained her own separate household (see Brody et al., 1988).

Households with three generations of people in them not only may have problems of space and privacy, but widen the arena for potential interper-sonal conflicts and for women's role strain in meeting the needs of husband, child(ren), and parent. Thus, the daughters whose "nests" contained both their own children and the disabled elderly parent had the poorest mental health. More of them reported symptoms of depression, restlessness, and feelings of isolation and missing out on something because of caregiving. In addition, they were more likely to view their elderly mothers as critical of the sons-in-law and grandchildren.

The daughters whose mothers lived in separate households fared the best in the effects of care they reported, a finding that supports those of previous studies comparing shared and separate households. As might be expected, the elderly mothers who lived alone were the most capable functionally and cognitively. Of the three groups of daughters, fewer in this type of living arrangement experienced caregiving strain, limitations on space, privacy, and social activities, or interference with time and rela-tionships with their husbands, children and friends. In fact, there was not one variable on which caregivers providing interhousehold help equalled or exceeded the strains of the two groups who shared their homes with the disabled older people.

When the disabled elderly mothers and their daughters shared two-generation households, both generations of women were older than their counterparts in the other two groups. Theoretically at the "empty nest" phase of life, these daughters and their husbands exemplify the concept of the "empty nest refilled" (Brody, 1978). More of the older women in this type of living arrangement evidenced symptoms of Alzheimer's disease and impairments of hearing and vision, and they received more hours of help each week. More of the daughters reported strain from caregiving; they felt less in control of their lives, experienced more interference with time for themselves and with the family budget, and reported more problems with their husbands that related to the caregiving situation.

In open-ended interviews, the daughters described their perceptions of some of the effects that grandchildren may experience as well as their roles in caregiving and in contributing to or alleviating the strains of their mothers. The ages and stages of the grandchildren varied greatly, and their roles varied accordingly.

Grandchildren who were in their late teens or young adulthood served as a back-up reserve of assistance. The help they provided was not negligible. Sometimes it was provided directly to the grandparents and sometimes indirectly through assistance to their mothers, ranging from giving advice and emotional support to their mothers to extensive instrumental help. Some cleaned and cooked for the grandparent at times of special need or helped them to move from one home to another. Some did "sitting" to allow their mothers respite to take a vacation or to go to work, or to fill in when she was sick.

The other side of the picture is that grandchildren who were teenagers or young adults often found their social lives disrupted. They could not play music or have parties for their friends, or the grandmothers' behavior was irritating or embarrassing when friends came to call. Some were upset by bickering between their mothers and grandmothers, and some resented the burdens their mothers were carrying and the reduction in the time she spent with them.

Daughters sometimes felt they were setting a model of how their children should care for them in their own old age: "I want to set an example." "I hope my children will treat me the same way I treat my mother." Others tried to protect their children from involvement. One of them even sent the granddaughter away to school so that she would not become the "grandparent-care person," and another said "I hope this isn't a turn-off for them."

Daughters in three-generation households are quite literally in the middle in feeling that they must be the ones who mediate conflicts among various family members—not only between elderly parent and husband but also between elderly parent and grandchildren.

I was always in the middle, trying to keep grandmother off the kids and the kids off of grandmother.

* * *

My children [an adolescent son and daughter] are good children, and they help my father a lot. My son gets my father's bed ready at night. My daughter gets the bathroom ready for his shower. They make sure he has his medicine.

But he doesn't want them to bring their friends home. But I can't tell my children not to do that. My son is very sloppy. But a 16-year-old boy is supposed to be sloppy. My father doesn't like it. He's a good kid—he doesn't do drugs, he doesn't drink. But my father was angry when he got his ears pierced. My husband says I'm *his* wife, but my father thinks I'm *his* daughter and he should take priority. When they fight, I jump in the middle of it. I jump in with my kids, too. I'm the mediator. I'm worn out physically and mentally from trying to keep it all together. I have an ulcer, and it kicks off.

Daughters have varying degrees of difficulties in sorting out the needs of children and parent.

My mother always sided with *her* mother even if she embarrassed me in front of friends I brought home. I won't do that to my children.

* * *

My son [age 11] would come home from school and try to tell me what happened during the day. My mother would interrupt him and finish his sentences. At first I told him he had to be polite and then I realized . . . I stopped her. My son had to be allowed to talk. That was hard. Telling my mother what to do.

* * *

I knew before my mother moved in that there would be difficult adjustments for all of us. Everyone had always catered to my mother. She was not used to having kids around and objected when my girls [two teenagers] brought their friends home. I said to my daughters "We have to tough it out on this one. Bring your friends. This is your home. We have to hang tight, and Grandma will come around." Well, there were some tears and some door-slamming [by the grand-mother], but she adapted.

Although grandchildren may be involved in care of the elderly when their parents become caregivers, an undetermined number of them find themselves in the role of primary caregiver to grandparents when deaths or illnesses of their parents leave a gap in the generational caregiving chain. Some become responsible for two generations of disabled older people— their parent(s) and grandparent(s). If the values and attitudes of today's young women are indications of their future behavior, grandchildren will be reliable helpers to older people when need be (for example, see Brody et al., 1983 and Brody et al., 1984).

The following case studies of married caregiving daughters illustrate the delicate task they face in balancing the needs of their elderly parents, their husbands, and their children. The daughters' own needs often come last, if at all, in the way they set their priorities.

"We're Missing Out on the Empty Nest Syndrome"

A supportive family

Mr. and Mrs. Green have three grown children who have left their nest and have children of their own. Mrs. Green's parents lived in Chicago until 11 years ago. When the mother had a heart attack and the disabled father went to a nursing home, Mrs. Green's brother went back and forth from his home in Detroit several times. At a family conference, it was arranged that the elderly couple would move to an apartment in Philadelphia. Mr. and Mrs. Green both went out to Chicago to get them. A brother-in-law and a friend accompanied them to do the packing and to help manage the move. A granddaughter did all the unpacking and arranged the Harris' furniture to get things ready for them in their new home while they were driven to Philadelphia by the Greens.

The caregiver's husband: an unsung hero

Enough money

During the next 3 years, Mr. Green stopped in every day to check on his in-laws. "He did even more than I did," said Mrs. Green. She and her daughter did all the housekeeping, and there was a visiting nurse once weekly. Then both parents began a series of hospitalizations, including several surgeries. When the mother was in the hospital, the elderly father stayed with the Greens. When the father was hospitalized, one of the Green's daughters stayed with her grandmother. Finally, Mr. Green said to his in-laws "Why don't you move in?" They had deliberately planned their home to accommodate the older people. "We knew it would happen sooner or later." A niece and nephew helped with the move. There was no financial strain because the parents had enough money to support themselves and the Greens were well off.

Many services purchased

The elderly couple continued to be in and out of the hospital. When the father was incontinent and comatose, Mrs. Green cared for him. She arranged physical therapy, homemaker service, a visiting nursing, and got all the equipment needed. He improved "amazingly" and was cared for in that way until his death 5 years ago. Now, the elderly mother is often seriously ill. She stays in her room a lot to give the Greens privacy. She is very grateful for the case the family provides and is very supportive of Mrs. Green. The daughter says: "I take care of Mother because I can give her better care [than in a nursing home], and I love her. She knows that if she needs 24-hour care and we can't provide it, she may have to go into a nursing home. It's no big secret. We discuss it all with her."

The daughter quits her job

Mrs. Green had given up her job when she had children. "Back then you did what your husband wanted you to do." She went back to work part-time later. "I enjoyed it, it was supplementary income, and the children were proud that I did something besides just being a mother. I was still there for them and could be home."

After her parents moved to Philadelphia, Mrs. Green did not
return to work. "I felt I was investing my time in them."

Grandchildren help

Mrs. Green says, "My children have really helped. When I was
sick, my eldest daughter took care of things. My youngest daughter would stay with my parents so that we could go out to a movie.
Our middle daughter sometimes stays with Mother. My brother is

A helpful brother

very supportive and appreciative. He visits three or four times a
year so we can go away for a week and he calls every week. His
daughters visit and call. Even my husband's family is supportive.
My husband is a saint, and I try not to slight him. We are very
close. Our relationship has not been affected because it was established long before. We have had our ups and downs, but we
have weathered it."

Empty Nest re-filled

Mrs. Green occasionally feels fatigue, frustration, or being
pulled in different directions. She feels it's very important to know
what you can and can't do where your parents are concerned. "A
lot of it has to do with personality. It's an individual matter. If
everyone was complaining it would have been different. I am very
lucky." She adds wistfully "The only thing is, we are missing out
on the Empty Nest syndrome."

In many ways, the story of the Green family is a best-case scenario.
There were good interpersonal relationships and cooperative behavior
among many members of the nuclear and extended families. Mrs. Green's
brother, brother-in-law, nieces and nephews, grandchildren—even family
friends helped. Mr. Green is one of the sons-in-law who can be described as
"unsung heroes." The elderly mother's personality and understanding of the
family's need for privacy and her appreciation of the care she was receiving
facilitated caregiving.

The excellent financial situation of both the elderly parents and their
children permitted the purchase and mobilization of a battery of supportive
services. Equally important, those services were used constructively. The
elderly mother did not refuse help from anyone but her daughter, and for
her part, Mrs. Green did not say "No one can take care of my mother but
me." Ample family finances also permitted the creation of an appropriate
environment for the elderly people, one that permitted privacy while maintaining closeness so that care could be monitored.

At the same time, however, Mrs. Green had reluctantly given up
the job she enjoyed and has some emotional symptoms. Like the vast majority of women, she accepts parent care as a woman's role and allows that
role to supersede her wish to work. She is uncomplaining, but she and her
husband have given up much of the freedom they had looked toward as
part of their stage of life. "We are missing out on the empty-nest syndrome."

"Promise Me You'll Always Take Care of Your Mother"

Mrs. Carter is the youngest of six siblings. Her household includes her second husband, two teenage children from her first marriage, a 5-year-old and a 7-year-old from the second, and Mrs. Carter's mother.

A promise to a dying father

For Mrs. Carter, it started with her "doing food shopping, laundry, and going to doctors" for both of her parents. Her father was "definitely senile" so could not drive a car. Once in a while, one of her sisters would help, but not very often. When her father was on his death bed, he extracted a promise from Mrs. Carter that she would always take care of "Mommy." "I would have died for Daddy," Mrs. Carter says. The mother had always been a very difficult woman. Mrs. Carter's siblings strongly advised her against moving the mother into her home, but she did so anyway.

Financial problems

Goes to work

When Mr. and Mrs. Carter married, they agreed that she would not work. Mrs. Carter says she had a dream, "I guess everyone has a dream." Hers was to be a "regular" mother. She felt she had neglected her older children because she had to work. But the elderly mother's care strained the family's finances because she must have a diabetic diet and her insulin is expensive. Mr. Carter began to work overtime to pay for these things. Finally, he told his wife reluctantly, "You'll have to go to work. We're drowning. We could lose the house."

Teenagers under pressure

Mrs. Carter worked on the afternoon-evening shift as a waitress so that the younger children could be cared for by the older children after school. The teenagers cared for their grandmother as well, but they complained of all the responsibility. They had no time of their own. "It isn't fair," they said.

The future: mother-in-law care

Mrs. Carter said: "My first husband took no responsibility. I would beg him and say we had to do something with Mom. He would just go and have another drink." Mr. Carter "did not ask me to remove my mother from our home," says Mrs. Carter resignedly, "Someday I'll have *his* mother here. I know it."
When the elderly woman moved into the Carter home, she made the daughter "nuts." At times she was "shuffled around" among the sisters, but they wouldn't keep her.

Total disruption of family life

Someone had to be in the same room with the elderly woman almost all of the time. "I had to leave the door open when taking a bath," says Mrs. Carter. The mother presented extraordinary difficulties that were getting worse. The whole family had to eat diabetic food because she ferreted out and gobbled up anything with sugar in it. She embarrassed her daughter in the supermarket by grabbing sweet things off the shelves, stuffing them into her mouth and telling the other shoppers that Mrs. Carter was starving her. If the children or the Carters brought friends to the house, she was nasty to them, so they stopped having visitors. She ruined the Carter's sex life by turning night into day. If they shut their bedroom door, she banged on it. Twice, she went out of the house at night and laid down in the roadway. "We are lucky she wasn't run over," says Mrs. Carter.

Granddaughter needs mental health care

The teenage children could not bring friends home because the behavior of their grandmother was disruptive and embarrassing. A granddaughter begged for a high school graduation party. She had never had a party before. Mrs. Carter agreed and planned to send her mother to another daughter's house for the evening. But the mother, in order to thwart the plan, "pulled one of her little tricks." She only pretended to take her insulin for several days before the party and went into shock. There was no party. The granddaughter is now receiving psychiatric care.

Can't be managed in dom care

At one time, the state social worker found a domiciliary care home, but the mother gave them a terrible time. "She would run away just like she did here, but they weren't used to calling the state police to look for her. They said they couldn't deal with it." The sisters tried to have her with them, but she caused so much trouble they would bring her back to Mrs. Carter. Once, when Mrs. Carter was on the verge of a breakdown, a sister took the mother. After a couple of weeks, the brother-in-law put the elderly woman in a taxi and sent her back to the Carters. Mr. Carter started not coming home. "He deserted us mentally. He tuned out."

Sibs can't manage her

No Medicaid nursing home bed

Depression

Finally, Mrs. Carter needed psychiatric care. Her older sister said firmly, "This is the end of the road. Mom must go to a nursing home." But it was many long months before a Medicaid bed could be found. The older woman is now in a nursing home, and her daughter says, "It's better without her. It's being able to go in the bathroom and take a shower. It's not having the TV on full blast all day and all night." But she adds despondently, "I think Daddy is looking down and is angry with me. But it ruined my life. I can understand why two of my sisters don't see Mom at all."

The chaotic Carter situation was characterized by disorder and conflict between the extraordinarily difficult elderly mother and everyone else in the family. The caregiver was driven to a "nervous breakdown," both of her marriages suffered, and her adolescent children were experiencing severe emotional problems.

All of this was aggravated by the family's poor economic status. Mr. Carter had to work overtime, and Mrs. Carter had to get a job to pay for things her mother needed but that are not covered by Medicare. Appropriate services and facilities were not available even when Mrs. Carter finally was ready to use them. The domiciliary home sent the mother back to the Carters, and a Medicaid nursing home was not available for many months.

In contrast to the many women who give up their jobs reluctantly when it conflicts with parent care, Mrs. Carter wanted to stay home with her second family. Finances made it necessary for her to work, however, in order to pay for things her mother needed. Although Mrs. Carter's sisters tried to intervene, they were unable to influence her. Mr. Carter does not complain, and his wife hints that he may be anticipating that she will care for his mother in the future. "Someday, I'll have *his* mother here. I know it."

Ultimately, when nursing home placement was unavoidable, Mrs. Carter's depression deepened. She had failed to fulfill her adored father's stern injunction to take care of her mother.

"Our Whole Lives Revolved Around Her"

A caregiving career

Mrs. Anthony is now 64 years old, and her husband is 68. Their grown children are dispersed in other cities. In a long caregiving career, the daughter took care of her mother for more than 6 years before the older woman entered a nursing home. Before that, she had helped to take care of her father.

Early symptoms of dementia

"I guess we didn't notice a lot of things while my Dad was alive. Soon after he died, the first symptom we noticed was that she didn't know the time. I was working full-time, and I'd ask her to meet me at a certain time and she wouldn't be there. I'd come home and find her, and she would say she waited for me all afternoon. She had no idea what time it was. She would try to go to the bank on Sunday morning, or she would pay the same bills three times. We would stop by her house every day. She would come and stay the night with us, and in the morning she would be gone."

Dementia progresses

"Then one of my mother's neighbors called and said she was going out of the house at 2:00 a.m. I knew she was going around to the grocery to check what time it was. When we went to visit our children in Columbus or Washington, we would take her with us. When she came back, she couldn't remember where she had been."

Reduces work-time

"I was beside myself because I didn't know what to do with her. I didn't know which way to turn. I saw an ad in the paper about a meeting to help people dealing with the elderly. I couldn't attend the meeting because I was working full-time. But when I called, they suggested that we go to a clinic that diagnosed people like my mother. So I decided we would go there. It was a very stressful time—working full-time and dealing with her, going back and forth. Between my job, my mother, and my husband, I was going baloney. I told my husband I couldn't handle everything, so I went part-time in my job."

"I always enjoyed my work. It was an interesting job, a nice job,

Career becomes "just a job"

and very well paid. I think if it hadn't been for my mother, I would have stayed full time. But that was the last straw. The work was very important. I enjoyed it. I just couldn't take it all—work, mother, and husband. I thought I would explode. Before I reduced my hours, I thought of my work as a career. I was good at it. Now that I work part-time, it is just a job."

Diagnosis made

"We went to the clinic. They were very lovely. My husband and I went to the final evaluation. It was Alzheimer's disease. They said she wouldn't get better. They don't call it senility anymore. They ruled out all physical problems."

In the middle

"She stayed with us more and more after that. Then we took her to our house. She was up all night, we weren't sleeping, it was terrible. My husband was working then. I was between the two of them. He would ask her if she was going to go to bed sometime today. I would try to calm him down. She wouldn't do what you told her. I was in between there, and then it got bad."

Picked up by police

"Prior to this was our first episode with the police. We came home from work, and she wasn't there. When we got home, all the lights were out and the doors were wide open, but she wasn't home. We went to her house, but it was dark. I said to my husband that I bet the police have her. She probably got confused and started walking. They sort of regress to previous years. Maybe she went back to when she walked to my other house and helped me when my children were babies. I called the police. They had found her, but she couldn't remember where she lived. So we went and got her."

Frightened and exhausted

Sister sends her back

"That did it. I called my sister in Chicago who wasn't working and asked her to take her until we could catch our breath. I was frightened and exhausted. We weren't sleeping, and I had the tension between my husband and my mother. She couldn't be by herself. That's what they told me at the clinic. We couldn't leave her all day because it was dangerous. We didn't know what to do. My sister said she could take her for 2 months. We put her on the plane. After 3 weeks, my sister couldn't wait to get her on the plane to get her back to us."

Day care

"The doctor suggested a day-care center at a nursing home. So that is what we decided to do. Otherwise, we would have to come home to an empty house and the fright. So we applied for day care, but we had to wait a few weeks before she could start. I was still working part-time. We got someone to babysit on the days I worked. But my mother was very bad, and the woman quit. We still had one more week before my mother could start day care. So my brother-in-law and his wife took her for the days I worked. They just did this for 1 week."

"Then she started day care. She gave them a run-around. They told me she needed some medication. The doctor prescribed

Difficult to manage

some medicine, Haldar. All the medicine did was make her doze. When she was awake, she was still the same. I told the doctor that one of us needed a prescription. So the doctor tried one medication for the day and one for the night. That worked. She fought getting in bed. It quieted her and made it so that at least we could exist. It helped when she was at the day care—before she had been very bad and uncooperative. That continued for a while."

"My mother had two more trips to Chicago. One time she visited my other sister, and another time I went with her. At least it was a different set of walls."

Incontinent and resistive

"We tried and gave it our best. I was very afraid they were going to put her out of the day care. They were really good. Then she started to be incontinent. I tried to encourage her to go to the bathroom like the books say, but she wouldn't listen. I spent my days worrying about the fact she wasn't going to the bathroom. I tried to get her to go to the bathroom, but she refused and invariably would wet the carpet. Towards the end, she refused to sit on the toilet. That was a continuing stress. I was always worried. At the end, I was just satisfied if she would stay in her room. It was a fight every night to get her to go to bed. Sometimes she wouldn't, and I would blow up. That went on for a while. I counted it good if I could get her to her room."

"She was still supposedly taking the medicine. At night, I would give her her capsule. But then I realized she wasn't taking them. She was hiding them in the bed. The woman at the day care suggested I put the medication in a cookie. I tried it, and it seemed to work."

Management problems

"One time we went on a short trip, and I fought with her all day to get her to go to the bathroom. I was going bananas. In a restaurant, I finally got her into a stall, but she wet herself. She was soaked. I had a change of clothes with me, but then she fought me when I tried to help her change. She also refused to bathe. But they wouldn't keep her at day care unless she was clean. We got a home health aide. One time she cooperated, but never again. She couldn't understand. That was the big problem—lack of communication. So the home health aide didn't work out. Everytime I tried to give her a bath my stomach would turn over. At the end, my husband had to pick her up and carry her to the tub. This was horrible."

"Our lives revolved around her"

"I was off the wall. I was never myself. I was never me. I was always concerned with her. Our whole lives revolved around her. If she had a decent day, we had one too. At the end, we couldn't take her out. At the shopping center, she wouldn't stay with us. She would take off. It was bad. I was getting to the point where I didn't know what to do. I was concerned that they were going to say "no more day care," but they didn't complain.

"I didn't care what happened the rest of the week if we could get her in shape for the day care. That was what we revolved around. At the end, it was a real fight to get her clothes off for bed, and my husband had to hold her."

Sisters can't help

"My sisters must work for a living. My mother visited several times with my sister in Chicago. The other sister is in Baltimore. The sister in Baltimore would occasionally babysit so we could go away. She always said, 'I'll give money, but count me out.' I had suggested we take turns—each of us caring for mother for 4 months. My sister in Baltimore said "absolutely no." My sister in Chicago at one point saw I was having a hard time and said I could send Mother out and she would manage somehow. But I knew she couldn't manage. She is really sick. If I sent my mother out there, I would have had to go out and bring her home again. It would have been impossible. That's why that sister never got involved. When my sister in Baltimore cared for her, mother always got away. The same thing happened in Chicago. Mother got to know the police in both places because they always picked her up."

"The whole thing prevented my husband and me from taking vacations or seeing our friends. But it has made me appreciate my husband even more. My children really couldn't help because they were married and lived far away, but they were always very good to my mother. They are good children and grandchildren."

"My mother was my friend"

"I didn't mind being the principal caregiver. All our lives, my mother was my friend. She was a nice woman and didn't have much of a life with my father. My other sisters and her never got along. I never faulted them. One of my sisters was never a giver, and that was all right. My other sister was willing but couldn't manage mother. No one was making me do it. [The brother is not mentioned as a potential caregiver.] I could have put her in a home before. I didn't feel resentful, and here we are. We were always friends beside being mother and daughter. We were able to communicate. That was the worst, when we couldn't communicate anymore. That was the greatest strain."

"My sisters and others said, 'Why don't you put her away?' They said this long before. I said, 'The day she doesn't know me is the day I will put her away.' But our lives became impossible, and I couldn't take care of her. My mother said she hated me."

The time had come

"I felt the time had come. She was unhappy here, and she hated me, because I was the one dealing with her. At the end, she wouldn't let me do anything for her. So we started looking around. We were wondering how to go about it and what to do. We were in touch with a social worker. I realized I couldn't handle it. She was fighting with me, and I couldn't let it go. I could deal with it, but not when she wouldn't let me. That was horrible."

"Before that I had sent away for some booklets on nursing homes. One booklet gave a listing of nursing homes that were run with the patient in mind and did not make a profit. In the private ones, if you can pay for 2 years, they take you in, depending on how many people they have on Medicaid. When you run out of funds, they may keep you and put you on Medicaid. I got a lot of feedback from the girls at work who had to place relatives in nursing homes."

"So we sent for some literature on some of these homes, and the three of us visited some of these places. One consideration was financial—how much money mother had to put down. I tried to look at the places through her eyes."

"I had investigated a nonprofit religious home for my father before he died. I thought it would be a good spot for her. To be a resident, you needed $38,000. We had already filled out forms for another place, but something in me made me want to call the nonprofit home. My husband and I went there, and I said to my husband, "This is it!" My mother has an income of $8,000 a year until she dies, plus $35,000 in cash. They figured she had enough to full pay for 3 years. But they wanted to meet my mother. Thank G— my mother was good. She was Miss Congeniality. My husband and I were saying, "Thank you, Whoever!" that she was so well behaved. They said she would get the first available space. We were delighted."

"But the time wore on, and we were having our hassles with bathing and the whole thing. She was still going to day care. By this time, my husband was retired, so he babysat her. Before when we were both working and she went to day care, he would get off of work early so he could pick her up. He was wonderful. At the end so his bosses wouldn't complain, he took it as vacation time."

"After 3 months, we got a call and the next day we took her into the nursing home. I didn't know what to do. I wanted to explain it to her. I couldn't tell her because she couldn't understand. My husband and I were there. I asked the Director of Nurses what we should do. I didn't know how long to wait before visiting her. She told me to do whatever I wanted. I stayed away for 3 days. She was fine."

"But I worried about the care. For anyone to get care, you need one on one, and where are you going to get it? You get it when it's yours, like I gave it to her. I thought she won't get her daily piece of fruit. I wondered what would happen because she can't communicate about anything. That's really hard."

"One afternoon, the Director of Nursing told me she was fist fighting with all the attendants. She wouldn't cooperate about anything. They had her on a lot of drugs. She wound up on

Drugs to quiet   Thorazine, so she is really spaced out. If I hadn't lived through it,
her   I would be very dissatisfied with that. I know how it is. They have
                        to fight with her to make her do. They are very nice, and she was
                        never alone. I am very satisfied."

                        "In the beginning, I went every day. We would walk inside or
"She doesn't   sit outside. I told my husband I would love to bring her home, but
know us"   I was afraid it would upset her when I took her back. I didn't know
                        what to do. But I figured I'd chance it. We did it, and she was
                        happy. I took her back, and she didn't say anything, but her face
                        was glum. Since then, I bring her home once a week. It's been
                        fine. She is not as lively because of the medicine. This last Sun-
                        day, she didn't know me. I was glad in a way because it lets me off
                        the hook a bit. If she's got complaints it's not me they're directed
                        to as the daughter. One time she confused me with my sister. She
                        must come in and out. This last time, there was no recognition of
                        me or my husband. It will be interesting to see if she knows me
                        next time, but she wasn't antagonistic and she seemed glad to get
                        back to the home. She may be going into another stage."

                        "My mother right now has enough money to support herself for
                        3 years in the Home. When she only has $1,500 left, the rest will
                        be covered by Medicaid. The nursing home will take her checks
                        and use them toward the cost of care, and the rest will be paid by
                        Medicaid. This is all arranged now so Mother will not be put out of
                        the home."

The Anthony family is a striking example of a prolonged Odyssey of
caregiving to an elderly mother who was deteriorating because of Alzheimer's disease, a situation that went beyond the family's limits of endurance.
During their long ordeal, the Anthonys sought and used whatever help
was available. Mrs. Anthony was willing and able to secure services: a diag-
nostic work-up, day care, an in-home worker, a support group, social work
counselling, and educational information about management of the parent. But ultimately, the services did not work because of the mother's incontinence and disordered behavior. As often happens, it was not only
the older woman's intractable behavior and the exhaustion of her caregivers that prompted nursing home placement, but, finally, her inability
to communicate or even to recognize her daughter. Fortunately, there
was enough money so that the elderly woman was accepted by such a
home, and both she and her daughter were able to adapt to their new
situations.

Mrs. Anthony's story is classic in its description of the development and
progression of Alzheimer's disease. It also illustrates many findings from
research studies of caregiving. Mrs. Anthony suffered severe stress effects.
Parent care competed with her job; she had to reduce her work hours and

give up her career. Her husband also was deeply affected and under strain. Though he was "wonderful," at times Mrs. Anthony was "caught in the middle" between him and her mother as well as between her job and her mother. Her mother's premorbid personality and their good relationship were among the reasons why she become the caregiver and endured the situation so long. Despite the horrors caregiving entailed, her long-standing, good relationship with her husband was not damaged.

When caring for her mother was no longer possible, Mrs. Anthony did not "dump" the older woman, but was careful to find a nursing home that she felt would give good care. After placement, she did not abandon her mother but still worried about her, visited faithfully, took her home on visits frequently, and gradually adapted to the situation.

"If Only Someone Would Be More Forceful with Me"

Eleven years of care

Sixty-seven-year-old Mrs. Rossman says in an exhausted voice, "How much longer can I do it?" She has been taking care of her 93-year-old mother for 11 years. Although the elderly woman is cognitively intact, she is depressed. Her vision is very poor, and she is almost totally disabled as a result of arthritis and having had several hip fractures. Wheelchair bound, she can manuever the chair in the house to some extent.

Multiple falls and depression

The Rossmans took the mother into their home a decade ago after her first bad fall. "I was the only daughter," Mrs. Rossman says. Her brother lives in another state, and his house isn't suitable because it has stairs. Each time the elderly woman fell, she became more depressed and more emotionally dependent on her daughter.

Quits her job

When her mother first moved in, Mrs. Rossman was still working full time as a teacher. But when she came home, she never sat down because of the cooking, laundry, and other chores. Then she stopped working full time and did substitute teaching 2 or 3 days a week. Finally, 6 years ago she stopped altogether when more fractures meant more care for her mother. During the mother's hospitalizations, Mrs. Rossman spent hours at the hospital every day. In addition, Dr. Rossman was pressing his wife to retire. He felt it wasn't worthwhile financially for her to work, and he was already retired. Mrs. Rossman admits she was having trouble coping. "But I loved the work," she says.

Can't leave Mother alone

Now, the Rossman's lives are so circumscribed that they can hardly go anywhere. Mrs. Rossman does not even attend family functions such as weddings. She sends her husband without her because the elderly mother would not feel comfortable with a paid caregiver. "My children and grandchildren feel bad that I can't come to visit, but it hasn't estranged us," she says. "After all, it's their grandmother, and they love her."

Mother refuses paid help

"I can't use paid help," says Mrs. Rossman, "because my mother resents it. My mother feels she cannot afford to pay for a baby sitter. She thinks in financial terms of way back. Anything over $10 is a lot of money, and she never had a lot of money. I told her before when I worked and had someone come in . . . I told her 'I have the help not for you, but for me; because I don't want to worry about you, and I don't want my husband to feel he has got to stay home.' But she didn't want it. Now whenever we go some place, she says, 'You can go. Don't worry about me.' But she knows we will only stay 2 or 3 hours."

Problems with services

From time to time, some nonfamily help was obtained. "But they only do the minimum, and each time you have to start all over again to tell them what to do. I just get sick of having people around. The physical therapist did a lot. She was excellent. But I was still confined to the house. Medicare didn't give me a penny for outside help. My mother has so little money. Medicare said as long as she lived with family, she couldn't get anything. I told them I saved them thousands of dollars. We're in the middle—too rich to be given help and too poor to buy it."

Options not feasible

Mrs. Rossman never seems to get out from under and attributes this to a variety of factors. "I want you to know why my case is different," she told the interviewer. "If Mom did not live with us, it would be easier to send her to a nursing home. Or, if we lived in a smaller city, nursing homes would not be so impersonal." The Rossmans want to move close to their son, but can't find a place even though they yearn to spend more time with their grandchildren.

A husband's advice about nursing home placement

Dr. Rossman resents the restrictions on his life and the fact that his wife can't go places with him. He always respected his mother-in-law and is nice to her. Nevertheless, he often complains to friends and relations that his life is limited because of the elderly woman. He can't go away on vacations or go out with other couples. But when they went to look at a nursing home, he was "wishy, washy" about it. Mrs. Rossman didn't have anything against it, but her husband said "Well, she isn't that bad right know. She wouldn't like it in such a place. I don't know if your mother would be happy there, seeing all those sick people." He thinks too many people place parents in nursing homes nowadays. So they didn't follow it up. "If *only* he had said 'Enough!'," Mrs. Rossman laments. "If only he had said 'Your mother must go to a nursing home'."

Friends' and cousins' advice

Mrs. Rossman's friends told her she had to place her mother in a nursing home. "She might not like it, but she will adjust to it like all the other parents," they said. Mrs. Rossman's cousins told her she would be killing her mother if she sent her to a home. "You know how that makes you feel," says Mrs. Rossman.

Mrs. Rossman's brother worries about his sister and the strain she is under. She describes him as a "big man" in Washington and a community leader. He is very busy, very harrassed, but he's good about helping with money. Their family relationships are described as close, with considerable visiting back and forth. The sister-in-law even offers to come to Philadelphia when on vacation from her job to stay with the mother, but Mrs. Rossman says to her: "Mom would never let you do for her. She wouldn't be happy with anyone but me."

Brother's advice

The brother thinks his mother should go to a nursing home because he sees what it is doing to the Rossmans. He talked to his mother, and she said "Okay." But when he left, the mother would not mention it. The brother even found a place near his home, but she didn't mention that either. "She wavers in these conflicting feelings," the daughter says.

Professionals' advice

When the Rossmans were in the process of moving to a new home, the mother was about to be discharged from the hospital to convalescent care in a nursing home. It would have been enormously helpful not to have to take care of her temporarily during the chaotic move, but Mrs. Rossman took her home instead. "If only someone had been more forceful with me." She blames the doctor and social worker who said, "If you put her in a nursing home, you'd feel too guilty." She says they should have been forceful in urging nursing home placement. As it was, she didn't have a chance to catch her breath. "If I'd had the luxury of it, I would have had a nervous breakdown."

"My turn"

Mrs. Rossman says she goes on with this caregiving situation because, "My mother took care of me. Now I guess it's my turn. I have been brought up with the ethic that you should really take care of your parents. I have a sense of obligation." Besides, her mother is so pathetic. Her mother used to say years ago, "I hope God takes me before I have to go into a home." Mrs. Rossman says the older woman knows logically that she should be in a nursing home, but cannot face it emotionally.

Mother can't face it

Emotional problems

As a result of all this, Mrs. Rossman says she is depressed, sleepless, and nervous, and has headaches. She describes herself as a worrier, and sometimes her hands tremble. She is acutely aware that caregiving frequently interferes with privacy, social activities, vacation plans, and responsibilities to other family members. She claims progressive views about women's roles, but at the same time she does not think sons should take time off from work as a daughter should do to help an elderly parent, nor should sons do household chores. She says she became the caregiver because she's the only daughter and her brother "would have to consider his wife's feelings." She sometimes feels guilty about losing patience with her mother.

"Its changed my life"

Mrs. Rossman says, "It certainly changed my life. I wouldn't stay home even if I wasn't working. I'd take a course or do volunteer work. I'd do something with my mind. My husband and I would travel and spend a lot of time with our children, visit friends, go to see my brother. We would be out more and entertain more. It has changed my life. She is my priority instead of my husband and children. I have to watch about giving her a lot of attention. I make an effort to be more solicitous of my husband. I feel a strain from this."

Competing demands

Son-in-law helps

"My husband has helped a lot with my mother. He has been a moral support in many ways. He has never said we have to get rid of my mother, but I think he feels he has sacrificed."

Not only the immediate family, but members of the extended family, professionals, and friends offer Mrs. Rossman advice. Cousins and professionals are clearly against nursing home placement ("You'll kill her" and "You'll feel too guilty"), whereas friends are for it ("She'd get used to it"). Dr. Rossman sends his wife mixed messages; he complains about the situation, but advises against placement. Mrs. Rossman's brother urges placement, but cannot implement the plan. The elderly mother herself recognizes the detrimental effects of caregiving on her elderly daughter and son-in-law, verbally expresses her willingness to go to a home, but subtly sabotages such a step. Mrs. Rossman cannot bring herself to get some relief. Her values tell her that it's a woman's role to take care of parents (even if it means giving up her job) and that adult children owe it to their parents to care for them. Immobilized, depressed, and unable to go against her mother's resistance to placement, she says "If only someone had been more forceful with me" and "If only he [her husband] would say 'Enough!'." Her plea for help has gone unanswered for 11 years.

"What Would It Be Like To Be Alone in the House with Only My Husband?"

Never alone

Mr. and Mrs. White have not lived alone since the day they were married 35 years ago. First, Mr. White's mother lived with them; then the children were born. An unmarried adult son still lives at home. He lost his job and stays home most of the time. Mrs. White's mother moved in 8 years ago after she broke her leg. Mrs. White feels "torn"—juggling her time between her mother, her retired husband, and her son. The elderly mother usually "wins out," says Mrs. White.

A caregiving career

Mrs. White traces her caregiving career: "Ten years ago my father took sick—he had cancer. Everything fell on my husband and I and the family. After he passed on, we disposed of the house, and my mother moved into an apartment so she could be closer to me. I had an elderly aunt who lived in the same building. It was a little easier for me at that point for whatever I did for the one, I could do for the other. Then my aunt died, and my mother fell. She was in the hospital for a long time, and then she went into rehabilitation. I could see from that that there was no way she could go back into her apartment. Her leg was in a brace, and she was on a walker. My husband said 'Do you think your mother should come and live with us?' We decided we would bring her here for a while. We worked from day to day. We didn't make any firm decision. We felt it was her decision. If she wanted to come here and live, she should make the decision, and if she made it it was fine with us. Then my other son got married and emptied the room out. It was more or less a mutual agreement between the three of us that she would come to live with us."

Helps an aunt

Mother moves in

Emotionally de-pendent

"My husband and I have been discussing going away for a couple of days. My daughter asked my mother to stay with her, but my mother hesitated. She went, but I don't think she really wanted to. She is very dependent on me. She has gotten more so since my father died. It is an emotional dependency. She also has this type of dependency on her doctor. She doesn't want to be too far away in case she needs him. I don't think it is good, but I don't know how to get out of it. She transferred this—she was depending on my father, and when he died she transferred all dependency on to me. It's the way it is."

"My mother said to me that if my husband and I feel she's too much care, we can put her in a nursing home if we want to go away. I said, 'Yes, I know. Isn't it better to stay with someone you know and love rather than some place that is impersonal?' "

Brothers' roles

A nursing home?

"My brothers haven't given her much care. After my mother came out of the hospital and rehabilitation, my husband and I wanted to go away. So we left her with one of my brothers for 2 weeks. The other brother is very impersonal. All she needs is an invitation, but he won't ask. I think I have grown away from my brothers. They don't do much in the way of caring and definitely have no involvement in decisions, though I try. If there is a major decision to be made, I try to include them. I have already told them that if having my mother here affects mine and my husband's health or our marriage, which it could, then she will have to go into a home. If it reaches that point, I won't call and ask them to be in on that decision. It is not theirs to make. Neither one of them offered to take her in. They assumed I would do it."

"When my mother was in the hospital, my older brother came up to see her. She said to him, 'I don't know what I'm going to do if I can't go back to my apartment.' He never answered. I know they would never take her in. My sister-in-law told me that my brother would never take her in—she would have to go into a home. I said it was nice they could be so firm in their plans, so they don't have to make that decision. You should never say "never." I said what if something happened to Dan and I? She said they'd put mother in a home. I said what if she doesn't have any money? Are you going to pay? She didn't answer. I hope my kids are different."

Aunt's care

It fell on me

"I helped my aunt because I was the only one around. It just evolved—it started out a little bit and ended up a lot. I helped her with decisions financial and otherwise. For 5 years, I helped both of them with grocery shopping, housekeeping, doctors, and transportation. She and my mother were half sisters, and she was always part of our family activities. My father and mother did it before, and when my father died it fell on me."

"I haven't really thought about using paid help especially since my husband retired. Now it is the two of us caring. I did think of getting duplicates of some things like walkers for up and downstairs. But since my husband retired and my son is out of work, there are three of us now."

Work

"I have thought about working again, but I don't really have the desire. I turned down a couple of jobs before my mother came. I felt I didn't want to go all the way into town to work. But I didn't think of my work as just a job. I felt it was very interesting. I worked for a sociologist as a research assistant.

"It's my turn"

"If I didn't take care of my mother, I feel I would not be fulfilling my daughterly duties. My mother cared for me, and it is my turn to care for her. I was the only one around. I did as much as I could for my father, and I'll do as much as I can for her.

Wouldn't it be amazing to be alone?

"Since I've been married, my husband and I have never been by ourselves. We've always had somebody. His mother lived with us. I can't change my life any because I've never had it to change. I said to my husband the other day, 'Wouldn't it be amazing some morning to wake up and have just you and I in the house.' "

Separate lives

"My friends ask me how can I stand having a kid still at home. But he has never left, so I never had to adjust to him leaving. He has his life, and we have our life. I don't try to influence him. It is the same with my mother. I try to keep her separate. She is not in our decisions. We have our own life, and we live it."

An understanding husband

"My husband is very understanding. I don't think my mother could have come here to live if he hadn't been. If it hadn't of been for him being so understanding, I wouldn't have been able to say

'Come and live with us.' Since he is retired, it's made it nicer because he is here to help. He does help. He would do a lot more if she would let him."

Mrs. White feels her husband is very supportive of her in her care for her mother because when they were first married the husband was the sole support of his mother who lived with them for 12 years. "That's why he's like he is."

The Whites' situation illustrates the caregiving careers many women have in that they help several older people in their families. They have helped Mrs. White's mother-in-law, her father, an aunt, and her mother. She is typical, of course, in being the caregiver because she is the only daughter. She feels "it's my turn" to take care of her mother as the mother took care of her as a child.

Mr. White is not unusual in helping with the care of his mother-in-law now that he is retired. Other older daughters, too, mention their husbands' availability and willingness to help when the latter no longer have the demands of a job. Another reason for Mr. White's help is to reciprocate for the help his wife had given to his own mother. This pattern of parent-care reciprocity between husbands and wives will reappear in the stories of daughters-in-law (Chapter 11).

"I'm Living My Mother's Life"

Gave up her career

"I was going to be a career woman," says Mrs. Rossi, who is now 51 and feels that time is running out. A social worker, she had planned to go back to school to take a doctorate so that she could teach at a graduate school. But her mother was her priority so she took a lower level job with less pressure. It meant less money, and she and her husband will need the money in the future. "No one is going to take care of us," she says. "We have no children, and my husband is not a bank president." Mr. Rossi is a psychologist who works in a state hospital. "I didn't know whether I should be home or at work. I was torn. People [her family and her husband's family] said I should be home. Work is therapy for me. But I had to choose between a human being—my mother—and money. The hardest thing is the loss of freedom, not the physical things. There's no break. Going to work is like getting out."

No one is going to take care of us

Work as respite

Parent care is your job

When she was 12 years old, Mrs. Rossi's father died. When he was dying, he told her, "Now you have to take care of your mother and brother [who then was 6], that's your job." "My mother and I saw to it that he had education to start him off," says Mrs. Rossi. "It's clear to me that caring for mother is my job. It was instilled in me. It's my duty. It becomes your own idea."

The elderly mother, now 79, has always been sick. Mrs. Rossi cannot imagine having healthy parents. Her mother was so sick when Mrs. Rossi was a child that she lived with her grandparents for 6 years after her father's death. Mrs. Rossi wept as she recalled the loving grandmother who cared for her. "I've never known a time when I wasn't taking care of someone. As a child, I thought that's the way it should be." When Mrs. Rossi married, her mother came to live with her at once. They have never lived apart.

Caregiving since childhood

The elderly mother is now in a wheelchair because she has rheumatoid arthritis. She needs help with everything except eating. Mrs. Rossi bathes, dresses, and transfers her. The home has been fully equipped for care. There is even a chair-glide for the steps.

Almost total care

Mrs. Rossi says, "I'm thinking about this a lot lately. I think it'll be one of us next. I guess I'm getting older. I think 'Why me? Why didn't I put mother in a nursing home like other people?' I wouldn't do it, but why not? Why didn't my mother die? Then I think 'My God I don't want that. The house would be empty.' I wonder, 'why?' I have these terrible feelings. My husband says it's normal. I say 'Why didn't God take her and give me a little break?' And he says 'It's normal. You're tired.' I feel guilty about my thoughts."

Unacceptable feelings

"But she devoted her life to me and my brother; she thought only of us when she was widowed. So how can I throw her away now? I would only put her in a nursing home if it were not humanly possible to have her here. I don't know what I'd do if she got worse. If I went part time, I wouldn't get any benefits. I'm worried about money. We'll need it when we're old. Sometimes I think families take advantage of one person. Like me. My mother always has some problem. Now she has a decubitis ulcer. It's frustrating. No matter what I do, it's not getting better. I've tried everything the doctor says. It's like going around in circles. And ulcers on her toes. I have to bandage them when I come home from work. I feel consumed by it. It's terrible. Do I have to wait for my mother to die before I begin to live? I'm living my mother's life, not my own."

I'm living my mother's life

Mrs. Rossi calls her husband her "saving grace." "He takes care of Mom as though she were his own mother. *His* family would be angry if they thought we might put her in a nursing home." She takes care of her mother, she says, because in her ethnic group the daughter is always left with the mother. Also, her mother took care of the children when her Dad died. She never even looked to marry again. I guess it was her duty. I ask myself, 'Is it my duty to take care of her?' "

The pressure of culture

The son-in-law takes his mother-in-law to the bathroom in the middle of night and gets her up in the morning. He's a comfort to his wife and helps her in relation to the rest of the family. They used to say to Mrs. Rossi, "It's your job. You have to take care of your mother." He sets them straight. He told my brother, 'You have to be there when a decision has to be made.' My brother is wonderful, but he sees it as my job. I get angry at him sometimes. Why doesn't he take her off my hands once in a while? He's so involved with his wife and daughter and his job that he's unavailable. It has brought my husband and me closer. Maybe it's not good. The emotional bond is so tight. We don't do anything without each other. We're very close, in some ways like a newly married couple. I look at him and think 'why isn't he complaining more?' ".

Why doesn't husband complain?

Mrs. Rossi is getting tired. She and her husband haven't had a vacation in 5 years. They need to get away. She was so energetic, but now she's tired and recently had a bad case of shingles. When she was sick, everyone worried about who would take care of the mother. The daughter is depressed, resentful, and angry. "I'm at the helm all the time. I have to manage." She would like to have 1 day all to herself or go out to dinner or go to a movie or go away for a weekend.

Fatigue and depression

I'm at the helm

"My mother took care of me, but she had me. I didn't have her in that way, but I do want to take care of her." Her mother is "a good person," and they're good friends. "If she were a difficult person, I don't think we'd put up with it." Mrs. Rossi asks "When do I get what I want? My whole life is around my mother." But it could be worse, she says; "Mother could be senile." She advises other people in her situation to look for help and asks "What's going to be done?"

Is it my duty?

Unlike the couples in the first three cases, the Rossis are childless. They, therefore, have a worry that is shared by other childless caregivers. Who will take care of them when they are old?

Mrs. Rossi, pressed by her own personal history as a life-long caregiver and a powerful cultural injunction, which reinforce each other, has given up the career she had hoped for. Her father, her siblings, her husband's family, and her husband all see caregiving as her role. Even in her childhood, she was socialized to giving precedence to males; it was up to her to take care of her brother and see to it that he was educated. She still works, but has curtailed her vocational goals. She has unacceptable thoughts about her mother, but feels guilty about them because the mother is a "good person." But she has no life of her own and wonders why her husband doesn't complain. Why doesn't he?

"My Friends Don't Have to Face This Yet"

Gives up career

Mrs. Roberts is a vivacious, attractive, cheerful, successful professional with a graduate degree. Her marriage is obviously happy

"Off-time"

and satisfying. The couple do not have children. Mrs. Roberts
gave up her job the previous year during her father's terminal
illness. After his death, her 75-year-old mother moved into her
home. "My group of friends don't have to face this yet. They're not
there yet," says Mrs. Roberts, "I'm only 34."

*"It's completely
changed my life"*

"It's completely changed my life. I stopped working because of
my Dad's illness. Mother couldn't do it. I had to help her through
it. I knew she'd have to come to live with us when he died. They
couldn't afford nursing care. My husband and I picked up the tab.
But they couldn't adjust to nurses, so I quit my job. Then I had to
get her through selling the house. Going to their house after work
and sometimes spending the night was too much, so I quit. Now I
take mother to the doctor, write all the checks, do all the paper
work, cook, do all housework, see to it that she eats. She un-

*Provides much
emotional sup-
port*

derstands English, but doesn't speak it, so she has great trouble
making friends. [Her mother was born in South America.] I have
to be her therapist and morale booster. Her short-term memory
has been poor for about the past 6 months, and she's very depressed. She resists going to a mental health program and says she
wants to join her husband. She had a very hard time adjusting to
moving in here, though she has her own bedroom and bath. She
had to move in. She could not live on her own, and, besides, her
neighborhood was bad, and she wasn't safe."

Mrs. Roberts describes the curtailment of her life-style as going
from "total freedom" to being tied down. If she and her husband
want to go out, there are always arrangements to be made. She
wishes her mother were more independent. The older woman
didn't marry until her late 30s, then quit her job as a manicurist
and stayed home. "Women weren't expected to claim any
responsibility for their lives when she was young," says the independent daughter.

*There's someone
here all the time*

"It's a big change for me and my husband. All of a sudden
there's someone here all the time. That's the biggest adjustment.
She tries so hard not to get in the way that she gets in the way.
Mother is so dependent, and that's hard, and the time alone that I
don't have any more, and the constant emotional support I have to
give her. It's taken almost a year for me to get to being myself
again. I still sometimes feel trapped."

Not role reversal

"I get really upset with people who say 'They become like
children.' Not in any positive ways. I watch my niece and nephew.
They display all the positive things about children because they
are children. Old people bring grief, and they're tired of living. It
burns me when anyone says this is like raising a child. Children
are malleable, curious, open to learning. Children are selectively
dependent, and it decreases."

Mrs. Roberts' deep affection for her mother is readily apparent.

A *loving mother*

She tells the interviewer, "If you met her, you'd be drawn to her instantly. She is a warm, caring person. She radiates warmth. She has a language barrier, but she's very smart and very sweet. We've always been very close, and I feel responsible and protective towards her. She never meddles." Mrs. Roberts didn't get along as well with her domineering father, who was much older than her mother. He was arrogant, whereas she was submissive. The father never said "thank you," but the mother is very appreciative. "She knows what we've given up and gone through. Dad just expected it."

What do you do?

It was very hard for Mrs. Roberts to give up work. "That's the biggest thing. I had been getting a paycheck for many years. And I was getting recognition from society as a professional person. Now people look at me and say 'What? What do you do?'." She says she probably will do some consulting work but will not resume full-time employment.

A supportive husband

Mr. Roberts is very supportive of his wife. He is helping her to get over the disappointment about not going back to work and tells her that what she is doing is important. He gets along well with his mother-in-law. The latter tries so hard to stay out of the way that he gets a bit irritated, but the mother's temperament is such that there are no problems.

No options

Mrs. Roberts' one sister has young children and also works. In contrast to the caregiver, the sister cannot afford to quit her job. They have had some words about the fact that the sister does little to help their mother. Mrs. Roberts would appreciate some emotional support and thinks that perhaps the sister should take the mother shopping on a weekend day. As the older sister, Mrs. Roberts has always had more responsibility, so she feels there is no other way and she has no choice. The mother doesn't belong in a nursing home and cannot live alone, and this arrangement is best for her. "I owe my mother to take care of her because she's my mother, *not* because she took care of me. It's a family responsibility."

Not because she took care of me

I come last

Among the effects of care is the inability of the Roberts to take a vacation. Mrs. Roberts gives her husband and his schedule top priority before her mother, but "I come last," she says. She and her husband have decided to have a baby. If it happens, it will be more important to her than helping her mother.

Women's roles

Mrs. Roberts comments on caregiving to parents. She says, "Women are still responsible for nurturing relationships, for making the home comfortable, for getting the birthday cards out. There are a lot of expectations on women these days." She feels parent care is easier if you're married. Then you are not in it alone and don't have to work for financial reasons. It has opened her eyes to being old and she has resolved not to be dependent. She

On being old

feels it's unrealistic to expect old people to change, however, because they probably can't. She is sympathetic. "Don't hold it against the old people. They don't want this situation. As you get older, you lose so much independence, and they've lost this too. It's not their choice."

Get help! Do it!

She advises other caregivers, "Always go for outside help if you can. I see this in my mother-in-law. She takes care of my husband's grandfather who is in his 90s. She refuses to get outside help. She claims he wouldn't like it. I say '*Do it!*' Take as much burden off you as you can if you can afford it." When my mother needs physical care, I'll get someone. I'm not going to be a martyr. I'm a lot more aware now of all these issues, first of all because of the experience with my father. So many things were not covered by Medicare or any third-party pay. Things that would help *before* they need to move in, to help keep them independent and out of nursing homes.

A women's issue

Mrs. Roberts says: "This problem is going to be a major issue for women. A lot of people think this is the main issue. Day care will pop up, but other things are needed. Women, whether daughters or daughters-in-law, will always have the biggest burden of care. The situation will be a major problem. It can sabotage the successes women have had in the past. Unless the funding rules get changed, they will quit their jobs. They need flexible and understanding employers. Not a lot of people have started to address this problem."

One wonders whether in the future many women like Mrs. Roberts will quit their jobs for parent care as she did. Although research findings show that a significant proportion of caregiving women do give up their work lives, they are most often the ones in late middle age who have been working many years and who are of low socioeconomic status. Because they are older, they are less likely to hold the "new" views of women's roles (see Chapter 13). Because Mrs. Roberts is young (in "off-time" for parent care), is highly educated, and holds views associated with the Women's Movement, she may not be typical in having given up her job. She also has a strong positive bond with her mother, excellent financial resources, and a devoted husband, and is hoping to have a baby.

Although Mrs. Roberts has given up much already to care for her mother, she is clear about her limits. She will get outside help when it is needed. "I do not plan to be a martyr." She advises women to "Get help! Do it!" She is aware of parent care and the lack of services as a major social issue and suggests what industry should do. Mrs. Roberts also comments thoughtfully on women's socialization to the nurturing role and says that things must be done or the situation will be a major problem.

The elderly mother is part of the current minority of old people who do not speak English. Combined with her dependent personality, the handicap in communication increases her isolation and places an additional burden on her daughter. The number of such people may increase in the future as people in the new wave of Asian and Hispanic immigrants grow old.

"My Mother Still Intimidates Me"

An only child

"My mother still intimidates me," says Mrs. Wood, who is an only child. "She was very strict with me as a child. She always had to know exactly where I was all the time, and she still does it. She keeps asking about what I'm doing and whether I plan to go out. If I'm on the porch, she looks out the window to see what I'm doing.

She's always with me

I have no privacy. If I close the door to have a telephone conversation, she walks right in. She'll even walk in when I'm in the

No privacy

bathroom. That's the most strain—no privacy. Sometimes I take a walk even if it's raining, just to be alone. I'd like to do some things without her. I do crafts upstairs, but I can't do it when I want to. She keeps asking what I'm doing."

Mrs. Wood is 58 years old, and her mother is 84. Mr. Wood,

Cannot take a regular job

age 67, is a retired corporation executive. The couple has been married for 40 years. Mrs. Wood works 1 week a month as a switchboard operator. She says that the work she does "anyone could do," and she just does it to get out of the house a little. She would like to have a regular job that uses her skills, but she can't be away that much.

Mrs. Wood had been going back and forth from her own home

Mother move in

to her mother's to help and found it very stressful. The mother was not functioning properly, but moved to her daughter's home reluctantly. She was forgetful, her personal hygiene (formerly meticulous) was very poor, her house was dirty, and she was not

Signs of Alzheimer's disease?

eating. In addition, her arthritis was getting worse. At first, Mrs. Wood was relieved to have her in her own home, but now, she says, there are days when she'd gladly put her in a nursing home.

The elderly woman causes many problems. She's sarcastic with

Behavior problems

visitors. She's spoiled. She, like her daughter, was an "only" child, and her husband "did it all her way." Sometimes, if the Woods have guests and sit on the porch, the mother slams the door and locks them all out.

Mrs. Wood and her husband have five children, all married and

Competition with grandchildren

living close by. Her mother had objected to the daughter's pregnancies. "She would make me feel bad. She would go through all the reasons I shouldn't be pregnant." Now, when Mrs. Wood's grandchildren visit, the elderly woman resents the attention Mrs. Wood gives them. "I'm her only child, and she doesn't like to share me. She's jealous. But I don't let her get on the kids."

Guilt

Mother wouldn't like outside

If Mrs. Wood talks back to her mother, she goes on a "guilt trip." Once the Woods went away for a week's vacation and put the older woman in a nursing home just for the week. One of the grandchildren stopped in every day, but she was very angry. "I felt so guilty. I can't have help in during the day because I don't think she'd react well. I talked to her about it and she said 'I wouldn't like that'."

Mental health symptoms

Mrs. Wood has many mental health symptoms. "Some days I can't handle it, so I go out for a bit, and my neighbor looks in on her. I can't just go away for a weekend. I get headaches. I don't have the get-up-and-go I used to have. I worry. Is this the way I'm going to be? I don't want my children to have this. I'd want them to put me in a nursing home. I tell them to do it even if I complain. Just because I'm a good mother, I don't feel they have to take care of me when I'm old. My mother does feel that way."

"That's the way it is"

"I take care of her because there's no one else. That's the way it is. I'm resentful because she always said 'You have to do this because I'm your mother.' It would have been different with my father. He was more understanding of the way I felt."

Care of father-in-law

This is not the first time Mrs. Wood has taken care of an older person. Her father-in-law had lived in the Wood's home for several years when her children were preadolescent. But he was easy. He enjoyed the kids, and they could discuss things with him.

Off-time: the Empty Nest Refilled

Also, the Wood's were at a different stage of life. Mrs. Wood had to be home a lot anyway with the kids. Now that they are grown, she feels she should have more freedom. "I always thought I'd be traveling at this age."

"It's going to be me someday

Mrs. Wood concludes her interview by saying her situation is getting more and more prevalent. She says, "I'm the generation that's going to be involved. It's going to be me someday. We need to understand what to do."

In some ways, Mrs. Wood has made her life separate from that of her mother. The older woman tried to avoid sharing her daughter with others— objecting to Mrs. Wood's pregnancies, for example. But the daughter had five children and protects her grandchildren from her mother's criticisms. She even works part time to get away from the situation at home. The elderly parent, however, apparently sees no boundaries between her daughter and herself, intrudes intolerably on the caregiver's privacy, and acts out by locking her daughter and son-in-law out of the house when they have guests. Mrs. Wood submits to her intimidating mother by not having outside help and not going on vacations. Her strains are evidenced in mental health symptoms, and she does not want to do to her own children what her mother is doing to her.

COMMENTARY

The eight women whose stories appear in this chapter illustrate many of the themes described in earlier chapters. Their reasons for taking care of their mothers varied. Some felt "it's my turn," and some felt a deep sense of obligation (It's a family responsibility). Some daughters loved their mothers deeply; the daughters cared *for* the older women because they cared *about* them. Others had poor relationships with their mothers, but cared for them anyway. Factors were apparent that affected the situations for good or ill—the quality of their relationships with parents, siblings, and husbands and the personalities of the elderly mothers. In particular, mothers who were nonintrusive, appreciative of the care they were being given, and who had been "good" mothers at earlier stages in the family life earned the devotion of their daughters. But even when the mothers did not have those qualities, even when the struggle for control was bitter, the daughters were steadfast in fulfilling what they perceived as their filial obligations.

The daughters' guilt and ambivalent feelings related not only to the nature of their relationships with the mothers, but were reinforced by powerful cultural, social, and religious values. The intense pressure of those values reinforced the daughters' commitment that they *must* be the ones to provide care, no matter how long or how arduous, even if it meant that they were deprived of opportunities to grow and develop through education and employment. Some daughters, however, like the one who said she did not plan to become a martyr and those who were able to seek and use services, were able to strike a balance that was comfortable for them and their families.

The cases showed that the roles of services and of money are not to be underestimated. They may not alleviate many of the distressing emotional symptoms, but they can ease the paths these women are following. The Carters, for example, needed an array of supports: counselling, a thorough assessment of the elderly woman, economic support, resources and services to supplement or substitute for family help, professional case management to mobilize and monitor those services, and education in techniques of managing the resistive parent.

Many of those issues will also be apparent in the stories to follow that are told by not-married women. Unique to the married women in this chapter is the salience of the support they receive from their husbands and children and their appreciation of that support. Not all husbands were their wives' "balancing points" or "saving graces," of course. But at the least, the behavior of many as seen through the eyes of their wives justifies their characterization as unsung heroes. At the same time, however, the pulls exerted by competing needs of husbands, children, and mothers were also apparent.

Chapter 10

Not-Married Daughters (Widowed, Divorced, and Never-Married)

Considerable attention has been paid to the special problems of various groups of not-married women—that is, those who are widowed, divorced, separated, or had never married. The strains of widowhood *per se* have been well documented (Larson, 1978; Lopata, 1973; Lopata & Brehm, 1985). Divorced women also experience special problems, such as sharply lowered income and feelings of loss and failure (Bell, 1981), which are currently receiving much publicity. [There is an average reduction of 50% in the incomes of divorced women 35 years of age and older (U.S. DHHS, 1985, p. I-22)]. Moreover, morbidity and mortality rates for divorced adults tend to be higher than for persons in any other marital status (U.S. DHHS, 1985, p. I-23). Although never-marrieds have had different life-styles and do not experience the desolation of widowhood or divorce (Gubrium, 1974, 1975), they too have problems unique to their family status.

There have been virtually no studies, however, about those problems as they intersect with the parent-care years, although almost half of all daughters who help an elderly parent care are not married (see Chapter 1 for data).

A large study of not-married women who are in their parent-care years is currently underway at the Philadelphia Geriatric Center to identify the differential strains they experience (Brody, E. "Marital Status, Parent Care, and Mental Health"). Though definitive information is not yet available, in-depth open-ended interviews were held with a sample of such women. Some of the case material from those tape-recorded sessions appear in this chapter. Those case studies offer some clues and tentative information about the inner experiences of not-married women that are specific to the parent-care situation.

Overall, the stories of those women indicate that daughters who are not

160

married during their parent-care years are aware of the benefits and problems their married counterparts report—the emotional support that husbands provide on the one hand and the difficulties of trying to meet competing demands on the other hand. Women without husbands also are aware, however, that good spousal relationships are important for their married peers. The main themes for those who are not married are often the obverse of those described by married women. They may feel the absence of a supportive spouse keenly but, at the same time, point out the benefits of not having competing demands on their time and energy. As one of them said, "I couldn't bear it if I had people pulling on me saying 'You're spending more time with her than with me'." The inner experiences of not-married women have other overtones as well. They may have the sense that parent care gives them a role in life; for some, the presence of the parent gives them the feeling that they are not alone.

In this chapter, we meet parent-caring women who are widowed, divorced, or separated, or have never married. Each group has unique problems that will become apparent in their narratives. Among them are women who are uniquely alone in that they had never married and are "only" children as well.

WIDOWED DAUGHTERS

"There's No One to Talk To About Little Things"

Working at age 70

A jovial 70-year-old woman with a good sense of humor, Mrs. Levy has her father in her household but is still working as a hairdresser. She enjoys the young people who work in the beauty salon. She was widowed a few months ago after being married for 50 years to a man she obviously loved dearly. The couple experienced no conflict about parent caring. Mrs. Levy's own parents had loved each other, she says. "It was a comfortable house."

A happy household

When Mrs. Levy's father and mother moved in 25 years ago, her father-in-law had already been in her household for 2 years. Her mother-in-law had told her husband, "When I'm not here, go to your son's house. That's the place to be." The older woman had known that the Levy's had a very happy household and that Mrs. Levy would be compassionate and caring. Though the mother-in-law also had a daughter, she didn't think the son-in-law would like it if the elderly man moved in.

Two Dads and a Mom

Mrs. Levy nursed her mother before she died. For many years afterwards, both fathers lived there amicably. The father-in-law has died, and her own father, now 97 years old, is getting weaker all the time. Until just a year ago, he played cards at the Senior Center all the time. Occasionally, he got dizzy, and then his

Getting weaker and confused   granddaughter would pick him up. Now he is deaf and has trouble walking. He has begun to pick up his food with his hands and is a bit confused as to the day and the time. Sometimes he forgets to turn the stove off. He no longer can make his bed or cook and needs help with taking a shower. Mrs. Levy takes him to the barber and puts his clothes away.

Mental well-being has not suffered   Though she says she is never tired, Mrs. Levy does feel helpless when her father is not feeling well. He complains of feeling very cold, and she doesn't know what to do. As a widow, she now has all the responsibility. Her husband had been retired and had helped a lot. She feels lonely and angry sometimes, but knows its normal. Occasionally, she feels emotionally drained and depressed. Though she feels some strain, on the whole she does not feel her mental or physical health has suffered because of parent care. Right now, her concern is not to leave her father alone too long. She likes her father and "wouldn't have it any other way."

It's all up to me   Her parents lived with her because she is more tolerant and patient than her siblings. Her father gives her emotional support, but she is pretty much alone in parent caring. "It's all up to me," she says.

Compassion as a tradition   Mrs. Levy's two daughters are kind and considerate. One of them lives in Philadelphia and gives her mother respite. She stays for a few days and lets her mother go to a wedding or another event. The other daughter is in California and is as supportive as she can be. Mrs. Levy praises her daughters. They give her a lot of emotional support. She feels her parent caring has helped her girls to see how things should be and to be compassionate.

On widowhood   Mrs. Levy's widowhood is fresh. She is grieving and having to adapt to being without her husband. She has had to learn to do the things her husband used to do. She feels alone. "Married friends don't treat you the same. Your social equity has changed. You're a single person to them. My friends are nice to me, but there's a difference. You feel that you're alone when you're out with couples. There's no one to talk to about little things—what channel to watch, what restaurants to go to. And my income has dropped. My daughters are wonderful, but your husband is your best friend. You can say anything."

Dad is a reason to come home   As for caring for a parent when you're widowed, "You can't talk about it to your husband and turn to each other when you're frustrated." But there's a positive aspect to having a parent at such a time. "If you have someone to care for, you're not living alone. I have a reason to come home, a reason to be." She wishes she could afford to have someone stay with her father in the afternoon.

Get help   Mrs. Levy advises other women: "You have to care to do it. If you can't do it, that's different. If you can afford help, get it."

Mrs. Levy has a history of warm, loving family relationships—with her parents, her husband, her in-laws, and with her daughters, of whom she is proud and whose support she appreciates. In addition to that tradition, she is transmitting another tradition—caregiving. She has had a caregiving career; she cared for three disabled older people in her home while she was raising her own children. Though Mrs. Levy is feeling the effects of being a widow during her caregiving years, she remains essentially optimistic and enjoys joking with her young fellow workers at the beauty shop. She is a self-described "plain woman" who had a solid, loving marriage. She thinks parent care is easiest for a "plain married couple. They have each other." As with some other caregivers without husbands, she gets emotional support from her very old parent, and caring gives her a "reason to be."

Mrs. Levy is managing well right now. As her father deteriorates, she may face a dilemma because she cannot afford to purchase help.

"Mother Wanted Me for Herself"

Doing a noble thing

"I'm content," says Mrs. Gordon, "I'm doing a noble thing." At age 73, Mrs. Gordon is a childless widow caring for her helpless 93-year-old mother in their large suburban home. She had nursed her husband through several severe strokes before he died 13 years ago. During the subsequent 2 years, Mrs. Gordon travelled extensively and loved it. It was her "reward." Then her mother began to need care and has gotten progressively worse for the past 11 years so that now she is bedbound. Recently, Mrs. Gordon's only sibling, an unmarried brother, joined the household. He helps by lifting the mother and doing other chores. Mrs. Gordon can now go food shopping without anxiety.

Spouse care

Brother helps

Attuned to mother's needs

Though Mrs. Gordon had worked for 30 years and enjoyed her job, she finds caregiving more satisfying. It is much easier with her mother than it had been with her husband. "I always know what she wants. I have always known even if she doesn't speak. I wasn't as successful with my husband but am attuned to mother. Mother complains when I'm not here. I am her security blanket. It's not an obligation. I'm glad to do it. It's my job, and I take pride in doing it well. I get a feeling of well-being—wholeness. It's a natural female function. There isn't any other way. I never considered fighting it."

A feeling of well-being

A set routine

Mrs. Gordon has her household organized and has a set routine. The first floor of her home has been converted to a hospital-like setting. She is in complete control every moment of the day. Caregiving is even easier now that her mother has a feeding tube. "It's a breeze." When the older woman was able to walk, Mrs. Gordon was always worried about her falling.

Only daughter care is good

"There's no other way," says Mrs. Gordon. "Mother would be miserable in a nursing home. She wouldn't last 2 months. She was very uncooperative in the hospital, and I stayed there from 8 a.m. till bedtime." When Mother came home from the hospital, nurses came in, but the daughter was eager to terminate their services and get into her own routine. "I'm a do-it-yourself-er. I'm better off doing it myself." The doctor who attends her mother praises Mrs. Gordon. He says "No one gets the care your mother gets."

"She never lost me"

Mrs. Gordon and her mother have always been very close. "We were like sisters. I would have taken care of her no matter how many children there were." They've lived together all their lives except for a few years after Mrs. Gordon married. "Mother didn't want me to get married; she wanted me for herself. She used to say 'You don't want to get married.' She didn't want to lose me. She never lost me. We were always together anyway." The mother never pampered her daughter. If the latter got into a fight as a child, "Mother would say 'It's your fault. You must have done something.' It made me more self-reliant." Even when Mrs. Gordon was widowed, the mother offered no sympathy. "Help comes from inside," says the daughter.

Once was enough

No tug-of-war

Mrs. Gordon points out the advantages of her situation. "It's safe and secure," she says, and protects her from establishing a relationship with a man, which wouldn't have worked out. This way she leads a healthy life. "I'm better off for not having met anyone. Once was enough." Being widowed and childless make it easier. There is no "tug of war." She feels sorry for parent-caring women who have children or husbands.

Misses some things

Care is heroic

Asked about disadvantages of parent care, Mrs. Gordon says she misses playing the piano (she gave it up because it disturbed her mother) and taking trips. Her social life and community activities have dwindled, but "I'm not a lonely person. I'm not really social. I'm self-reliant." She says she used to feel stressed and that she was giving things up, but no longer. She has a hankering for a smaller house as the big one is a financial hardship. On balance, Mrs. Gordon is content. She says "It's a heroic thing to take care of someone."

Despite the fact that she is old herself, Mrs. Gordon's relative lack of strain and the satisfaction she takes in caregiving are striking aspects of this situation. The current picture is part of the continuation of 73 years during which the enmeshed relationship of the two women has been the central feature of their lives. Although Mrs. Gordon says it's "sad" to see an old person deteriorate, she finds caregiving easier as her mother's care comes more and more under her control. Being in control of the situation fits perfectly with Mrs. Gordon's personality, and her self-esteem comes from doing her job well. She points out the advantages of not having competing demands and has systematically stripped her life of potential diversions from caregiving—dating and hobbies, for example. "I'm better off this way." Caregiving provides her with an important role in life, one that enhances her sense of doing something worthwhile and that earns her the admiration of the doctor and others.

DIVORCED DAUGHTERS

"There Was No Love in My Family"

"I was not loved"

"There was no love in my family," says 61-year-old Mrs. Hill. "My mother was not the type who was warm and loving to me when I was a child. When my own children came along, she said 'You had them, you take care of them.' I can't remember any hugging or kissing. My father was violent. He beat my mother, and he beat me. I was not loved. I was afraid to death of him. I hated my father till the day he died. I never would have cared for him. No, never! Maybe that's why I try to do for her. She had such a rough life. If she didn't get anything, how could she give anything? I was 14 the last time he beat me, and I quit school at 16 to go to work so I could get away. But my mother went to the authorities and had me brought home. She wanted my board money. So I got married at 17 and got out of the house."

Beaten with a strap

Mother two hours away

Mrs. Hill does indeed try to "do for" her mother who is now 84. Divorced for 20 years, Mrs. Hill lives with her son and daughter-in-law, who had invited her to move in when she came back to Philadelphia from Pittsburgh. She works as a cashier in a restaurant. The elderly mother lives in senior housing located a 2-hour drive away. Until the housing manager threatened to put her out unless Mrs. Hill kept the place clean, the latter had been unaware of what was going on. The mother's apartment was like a "garbage dump"—full of stacks of newspapers, garbage, maggots, and roaches, and with spoiled food in the refrigerator.

An apartment like a garbage dump

Mother refuses paid help

Mrs. Hill now drives to see her mother every week on her day off. She cleans the apartment, bathes her mother, dresses her in clean clothes, changes the dressings on the older woman's legs, and does the banking. Her mother refuses to have any paid help, has no idea how exhausted the daughter is, and complains that she doesn't come to see her on both of her days off. Mrs. Hill has a brother. She says to her mother, "Why can't he help and spell me once in a while?" The mother replies, "He's a man and you're a daughter. You should do it. You're supposed to do that stuff." The brother laughs and tells Mrs. Hill, "Keep up the good work." She

Women's roles

Guilt says, "I have no life of my own. It's work and go to Mother's. If I don't go, the dressings on her legs don't get changed, and I feel guilty."

Mrs. Hill discussed the situation with her mother's doctor and told him how mother will not even permit Meals on Wheels or any *A doctor's* other service. She refuses to allow anyone into the apartment. The *advice* doctor told the daughter, "Do not put her in a home. They don't last long when they go into a home." She went to a support group. The other participants said, "You have to change your feelings." *Support group* They didn't give her support. They didn't understand what she goes through. "They just sit there and tell each other stories. They say you can't change the old people. You have to change. They have no suggestions."

Mrs. Hill raised her five children by herself and has no money. Her four other children live far away. She is alone most of the time, having been unable to make friends when she moved to *Takes anti-* Philadelphia because going to see her mother uses all her spare *depressants* time. She hates the long drives, feels guilty and nervous, and has been taking antidepressants. Her arthritis is painful. She won't do it when she's 65 or 70 years old, she says. She won't be able to *On being di-* drive back and forth. She thinks being divorced makes it harder. *vorced* She feels alone and has no one to do things with. But on the other hand, she feels at least she doesn't have to worry, "Am I giving enough time to people?" Married women have to deal with a husband, a job, and children.

Mrs. Hill worked all of her life. When she was raising her children as a divorced woman, she worked two jobs, and she had *Mom preferred* to do the washing and ironing on weekends. "I never got any help *son* from my mother. I don't ever remember her asking if I needed any help. Her son was more important to her. Even today, her *Makes Mom* face lights up when she talks about him. He never visits her. Now *happy* she kisses me when I leave. She does it out of need—she needs me." Summing up the caregiving situation, Mrs. Hill says "I'm glad I'm able to do it. It makes her happy."

Having received so little from her mother all her life, one wonders why Mrs. Hill is exerting such strenuous efforts to help her at this time. Perhaps she is still seeking the affection and approval that she had been denied as a child and through the years. She gets no help from her brother, her mother's physician, or a support group. Like some other daughters, Mrs. Hill accedes to her mother's refusal to allow any formal services. Also, like some other caregivers, her protests about her brother not helping are feeble. Her mother tells her, "You're a daughter. You do it." Though Mrs. Hill is overburdened, depressed, guilty, and taking antidepressants, she says she is glad she is able to do it and wants to make her mother "happy."

"He Didn't Put Me in an Orphanage, So How Can I Put Him in a Nursing Home?

"I may as well open a center for Senior Citizens"

Mrs. Jackson has two elderly men living with her, both of whom require considerable care: her father, age 96, and her uncle [her father's older brother], age 97. "I may as well open a day center for Senior Citizens," she says. Mrs. Jackson means that literally and is now in the process of establishing such a center. She has already purchased a building, hired staff, and arranged for a doctor, a dentist, and a podiatrist to visit the center. The building is named for her father.

Divorced

Now 51 years old, Mrs. Jackson has been divorced for many years. She raised her three sons by herself, experiencing many of the problems of a single-parent family along the way. The two older boys, in their 20s, are living on their own now. The third, 16 years old, goes to boarding school.

Mom care

Quits job

Mrs. Jackson cared for her mother before her death because her father couldn't manage. At that time, her children were young. She had to quit her job to do so and solved her problem by opening a day-care center for children. In that way, she was able to care for her mother, be with her children, and earn a living. It was a good decision, she says.

Moved to Dad's house

After her mother died, Mrs. Jackson went back to work. Her father lived on his own until 5 years ago. Mrs. Jackson then moved from a neighboring state into her father's home because he needed care and was refusing to leave his house. First, there was a conference in which Mrs. Jackson, her sister, and her brother participated. They would have put their father in a nursing home. Mrs. Jackson was the only one willing to move to their father's house, so she was "elected" to take care of their father. "I voted for myself," she says. The siblings felt it was easier for her because she had no husband. But Mrs. Jackson doesn't blame them, since she made the choice. The siblings don't help, though lately her brother takes their father to church and the sister once took him on a visit for 1 week.

"Dad didn't put me in an orphanage"

An adopted child

"I owe him"

Mrs. Jackson explains why she will not put her father in a nursing home: "That's where the guilt comes in. He didn't put me in an orphanage. I owe him. He's not really my biological father. He's my biological father's cousin. My parents gave me away, and he adopted me. I think of him as my father. His wife I thought of as my mother. She was so sweet. My biological father and mother had six other children. This Dad always treated me like a daughter, and his wife treated me like she had given birth to me. I have such gratitude. That's why I do this. They didn't put me in an orphanage. I do get tired, but I don't complain. Getting tired is the hardest part. But I have a responsibility. The people I call my sister and brother are his biological children. But I feel more of a bond with him. I know my biological parents and siblings. They are sarcastic about my Dad. They say 'She just loves him to death'."

"I'm grateful, grateful"

"I grew up grateful to those two people. I'm just grateful, grateful that they let me share their lives. Its repaying a debt. Doing for them what they did for me. I'm a helping person. I'm always trying to help, even though sometimes I can't help myself. My minister says, 'Just accept it'."

Uncle arrives

Her uncle lived in New York, and her father used to talk about him a lot. Then Mrs. Jackson had a phone call from a hospital in New York. Her uncle was in the hospital, and they were refusing to discharge him to go home alone. Mrs. Jackson said, "I'll come and get him," and she did. "That was a bad decision," she now feels, "but he's here, and he didn't have anyone else."

Dad confused and cooperative

Both elderly men are confused. Her father is forgetful. He forgets to eat and bathe, and his clothes are dirty. He opens the door for strangers and once was mugged by an intruder. After being awake for a couple of hours, he dozes. He calls Mrs. Jackson by her mother's name. His personality, however, is kind and sweet, as it always had been.

Uncle confused and difficult

Her uncle, on the other hand, is grouchy and complaining. He cannot see well, can barely walk, and has to be fed, bathed, dressed, and taken to the bathroom. He doesn't like anyone, not even himself. His mind is back in the 1950s and 1960s.

A toddler and a diaper baby

Mrs. Jackson quit her job a month ago to devote her time to planning the day center. She has a strict routine and times all her activities. She breaks her neck to do it all. It reminds her of how she did things when her own two older boys were small children. Again, she now has a "toddler and a diaper baby." She cooks and freezes meals so her father can put them in the microwave when she's not there, but lately he forgets to do it.

Like a TV sitcom

Mrs. Jackson's sense of humor comes to her rescue at times. She says the two old men are like a television sitcom. She comes home and finds the meals uneaten. She says, "Why didn't you eat?" Her father says to her uncle, "Didn't we eat breakfast, Tom?," and Uncle replies, "Maybe." Her father takes her uncle's medicine and gives her uncle his own medicine. The crotchety uncle calls to his deceased wife when he's upset, "Here I come, Anna!"

Stressed out

One night her father was upstairs, and she heard a thud and ran up. He had fallen asleep and tumbled from chair to floor without awakening. Her uncle thought her father was dead and began calling "Here I come, Anna." Mrs. Jackson says, "I thought 'Oh no.' I put my Dad on the bed and said 'Uncle, what's wrong?'

Uncle was jealous of the attention I was giving Dad. Then when it was over, I began to cry. I guess I was just tired and stressed out."

The teenager had to go to boarding school

Caregiving has made major changes in Mrs. Jackson's life. She told her 16-year-old son there was no room for him. Jokingly, she says, "I threw him out." On his own, the boy found a fine boarding school where he is doing extremely well. "It's really better for him," says Mrs. Jackson. The boy "had to accept it." At first he was disappointed, says his mother; then he understood. Mrs. Jackson told him, "I have to do it. It's the only thing I can do." She could have put her uncle in a nursing home, but figured if she had to take care of her father, she might as well keep her uncle too. She says, "My son said the other day that when he wants to see me he has to make an appointment. But I have to take care of my Dad. My son can do other things. When I told him I was going to have a day center, my son said, 'Oh no. Now I won't even be able to bring my friends home. It will be smelling like urine'."

Effects of care

No homemaker service

Exhaustion and sleeping pills

Mrs. Jackson says caregiving is not as hard physically as it is mentally and emotionally. "I don't sleep well. I'm listening for them with one ear. I gave up my social life. We've been on the waiting list for a homemaker for a year. After I get them dinner and to bed, I can't do anything but shower and go to bed. Uncle was turning day into night so the doctor gave him sleeping medicine. He was hallucinating and running through the house. I've been so stressed that I've been taking their medicine. That's so easy to do. I try to practice not being upset and drained. I have to exclude other things from my life. I have to say "no" when men ask me for dates. It's too much trouble. A month ago, I met someone and he's being very supportive, but I don't know how long it will last."

"You have to rearrange your life"

Support group not available

She hopes the day-care center she plans will make it better. "I'm going to hire an assistant and a cook and an aide, so I'll be able to get away at times. And I won't be away at work worrying about them. I got phone calls at work. I still have to figure out what to do at night. Maybe my assistant will have to work 1 night a week. Maybe I can get away for a few hours, even if I only read a book. You have to rearrange your life. When you take care of an older person you have to sacrifice some things. Sometimes I take a deep breath and say to myself 'Take it easy. It's not that hard.' Once I called a support group. I saw the phone number on TV. But it was far away. I called Philadelphia Corporation for the Aging [the local Area Agency on Aging agency] and they said I wasn't in the right location. Frustration gave me an idea. I'm going to start my own support group when I open the center. I'm going to have a nice place. I've arranged a doctor to come and a dentist and a podiatrist. It's going to be like I'd like for my own two old people. Not take them to the doctor and wait all day like I

Plans for the day center

have to do now. I'll have little outings for the people. The real reason I'm opening the day-care center is because I identify with the caregivers. I want them to have a place to bring their old people. There's not a place available in the area where I live for me to take my old people."

Lonely

Mrs. Jackson is lonely. "I'd rather go out with someone than put my uncle in the bath tub. Then it passes. You just have to grin and bear it. The first year, I thought I'd have a breakdown. Then I developed supports. My minister. He'd send someone from the church to spell me for a bit. I wish my sister and brother would offer to spell me a bit, but I won't ask. I have too much pride. Dad deserves to receive my care. It's different with Uncle. But I have to do it. I'd like to spend more time with my children. But I have to turn down their invitations."

Divorce and parent care

As for parent care and being divorced, Mrs. Jackson says "I was divorced before my Dad needed help. But being divorced gave me the freedom to do it. Your time isn't divided. A supportive husband would help, but it would have been harder if I had a husband. My other boyfriend said that taking care of my father and uncle was a great idea, but then we broke up because I wasn't able to spend time with him. This boyfriend cares for me and that makes it easier for me to care for them. He'll let me take a nap or bring dinner. It lessens the burden. Little things. But I don't know how he'll react when things are bad. Like when there are emergencies and when I am stressed out and cry."

A lack of services

Mrs. Jackson says there should be more help for caregivers. "Certain services aren't available. Or if they are available, there's a long waiting list. You're limited by your economic situation. The alternatives are a nursing home, or a homemaker or staying home and doing it yourself. If you choose homemaker, their wages are too high. Your own salary doesn't really take care of it. That's not very fair. Senior citizens have paid their dues, and they don't get much in return. We've been on the waiting list to get a homemaker. Medical service is OK. Medicare pays for that."

Mrs. Jackson describes her situation and the powerful need to care for her "Dad" so well that little comment is necessary. That need is so great that not only all of her own needs are superseded, but her son must leave her home. Generalizations cannot be made, of course, but for this particular woman, her adoption appears to have intensified to the ultimate degree her feeling that she must repay in kind what her "Mom" and "Dad" did for her.

"I Saw My Mother Do It"

Fifty-seven years old and divorced for 32 years, Mrs. Harris is now caring for her 80-year-old mother, who has Alzheimer's dis-

"What do poor people do?"

ease. Her father had taken care of his wife for many years. When he died, Mrs. Harris moved into the mother's home. The daughter asks, "What do poor people do? It must be terrible for those who cannot afford help. *You must have help*." She is in the midst of a successful career as an executive of a professional organization. Considerable paid help aids her in caregiving. She employs

Paid help

someone full time during the week, and a second person comes in on weekends to supervise the elderly woman. Both are "gems." Nevertheless, she has reduced her work day by one-half hour at the end of the day so she can get home earlier. Though Mrs. Harris does no housework, she does the cooking and dishes, and bathes and dresses the mother. She and the workers she employs share the shopping. The expense is worrisome, and her savings are being depleted. The mother has some money, and she hopes it lasts.

"I'm the logical person"

Mrs. Harris' sister works and has children—a full life. She says. "I was the logical person. The demands are different for my sister and me," but she doesn't mention her brother as a possible caregiver. Being divorced and childless was a major factor in becoming the main caregiver. She feels her sister does as much as she can.

Old values and new

"I saw my mother do it," says Mrs. Harris of caregiving. "It's the way I grew up. When people needed help, she did it. Mother took care of her own father and both of her parents-in-law." Mrs. Harris comments, "When I was divorced, I divorced myself from many ways of life, but this is the right thing to do." She is referring to the very different and freer life-style she had adopted and lived for many years in an artistic community. Her mother was not supportive. "I think you're crazy," she told her daughter, but later accepted it. But, Mrs. Harris says, "You never really change. Many things are internalized even though your thinking has changed."

A prisoner

She goes on. "I have an obligation. I was free as a bird and could do whatever I pleased. I can't do that now. I'm a sort of prisoner. That's the thing I mind the most." Her emotional well-being has been affected. She is often angry, always tired, depressed, and so drained that sometimes she doesn't feel much.

Easier because of Alzheimer's

The mother is helpless now and much more childlike. She thinks she's 40 years old, and her father is still alive. She was a "tough lady" in the past, but now she's very sweet, gentle, and friendly. "If she were still herself, I couldn't live with her," Mrs. Harris says. "We didn't get along." On an "elemental level," she says she gets some emotional support from her mother. Nevertheless, at times the older woman drives her crazy because she repeats the same things, asks the same questions, and cannot follow the simplest instructions. Still, the resentment and anger she once felt toward her mother has dissipated.

Being divorced   The fact that she's divorced makes parent care easier, Mrs.
makes it easier   Harris thinks. She adds that if she were younger, it would have
had a major effect on the course of her life. Now she has no
responsibilities to anyone else, and at her age life is not "unrol-
ling" before her.

Mrs. Harris continues to work and does not mention the possibility that
she might do otherwise. Nevertheless, she described the conflict in values
that many women experience nowadays. She had lived for many years in
accordance with "new" values about women's freedom and chose a life-style
that was not traditional. When parent care became necessary, she found that
she held a powerful traditional value—that care of a disabled parent is a
daughter's responsibility. She refers to the role model her mother had been
in that respect.

Mrs. Harris also illustrates what some other caregivers relate. When
her mother became relatively helpless, she also became "sweet." The tension between the two women eased, and despite the Alzheimer's disease,
the older woman provides some emotional support to the daughter.

Like other daughters, Mrs. Harris sees the differences in the experiences of married and unmarried caregivers. There are no competing pulls for
her because she is divorced and childless. She also points out the importance
of services, which she, fortunately, is able to purchase.

SEPARATED DAUGHTER

"I'm Caught in a Web That Goes Down Deeper and Deeper"

Mrs. Stern's 95-year-old father has been totally helpless for 22 years.
Her 26-year-old daughter has multiple sclerosis. She is separated from her
husband and in the midst of bitter divorce negotiations. She had cared for
her mother through a long illness. She had helped her mother-in-law who
had Alzheimer's disease.

Plunged in deep   Mrs. Stern says "I've been plunged in deep problems for 22
problems   years." She feels "caught in a web that goes down deeper and
deeper." She is struggling to extricate herself from the web and
from her depression and is intensely anxious about the future. She
describes a long list of symptoms including exhaustion, sadness,
resentment, and feelings of helplessness.

Wanted to work   A suburban housewife from a highly educated and successful
family, Mrs. Stern is verbal and articulate. Her father was a judge,
and her mother a physician. She has no siblings. She holds an
advanced degree in art history. Dr. Stern, her husband, is a
well-known surgeon. As the Stern's children moved toward

adolescence, she wanted to work, but there was no market for her skills. Mrs. Stern, therefore, decided to take another degree—this time in computer science—and started back to school. Things were fairly stable at that time. Her father had been paralyzed from a stroke for many years and was totally aphasic, but was being cared for by her mother and nurses, with help from Mrs. Stern. Then, when her children were in their teens, her mother became ill and went downhill steadily for 2 years before her death. In the meantime, Dr. Stern's father died, and his mother showed signs of Alzheimer's disease. Mrs. Stern had to assume responsibility for her mother-in-law's care as well. Dr. Stern's brother took no responsibility. Immediately after her mother-in-law's death, Mrs. Stern's daughter, then 20 years old, showed the first symptoms of the progressive disease from which she suffers. "What I know best is catastrophic illness," Mrs. Stern says. She dropped out of school. "It got too crazy. Something had to go. My husband and children couldn't go. The parents couldn't go. So school had to go."

"What I know best is cata-strophic illness"

Something had to go

Then Dr. Stern announced that he was leaving his family. He had never been home a lot, not even during his daughter's illness, but his wife had attributed his absences to his busy surgical practice and professional meetings. When he left, she was in shock—"a basket case."

Her husband leaves her

Mrs. Stern is alone in facing all these serious problems. Her income has plummeted as Dr. Stern has now stopped giving her money. She had trusted him and knew nothing of their financial affairs. She is ill-equipped to earn a living. Though she is looking for a job, her father and daughter require considerable time and effort. The divorce negotiations are ugly and stressful. She is extremely worried about finances and does not even know whether she will be able to keep her home. Her disabled father's money is running out as well, and she is frightened about what will happen to him if he outlives his resources.

An uncertain future

Mrs. Stern's daughter is now in remission, but her elderly father is in a continuing decline. There are constant crises, and he often is in a hospital. He lives in an apartment with round-the-clock attendants since he can do absolutely nothing for himself and cannot communicate. Mrs. Stern runs that household and manages her father's financial affairs. Keeping nurses on hand is a major problem. Sometimes they don't show up or quit without notice. She constantly has to "soothe their feathers" and has a sense of desperation about keeping the ball rolling.

Caring for Dad

Despite her problems, Mrs. Stern refuses to consider nursing home placement for her father. She would do so only if his mind goes. "I'd rather go into debt first." The daughter describes her father as a "model of surmounting adversity. He's indomitable."

Dad is indomit-able

*Dignity and
grace*

*"I'm hiding
something"*

*She cares for
and about him*

He deserves it

*A good wife and
mother*

*Dependency a
bottomless pit*

*Laying on the
"guilt trip"*

She is proud of him. He reads, listens to music, and is interested in politics. He bears his terrible situation with dignity, grace, and cheerfulness, and tries to make it as easy as possible for his daughter. "We were always very close," says Mrs. Stern. "He was always a good guy. He taught me to be open and honest, but now I'm deceiving him." She is referring to the fact that she has not told him about Dr. Stern leaving her because she does not want to add to his anxiety or worry about his own care. "I'm hiding something major that affects his welfare, but I'm doing it to protect him." The deception bothers her. She knows that if she told him about her separation, she would feel emotionally supported by him, but "I have to look out for his emotional well-being as much as possible."

There are pluses and minuses about caring for her father, Mrs. Stern says. "The way he has dealt with it makes me proud of him, and I've learned from it, but it is a drain. I don't know whether the pluses and minuses neutralize each other. There's that duality."

Why does she provide care for her father? "Who else is there? And he gave to me so much and so caringly and so completely. There's no way there's too much I could be doing. It's not an exchange. He just deserves it. Sure my mental health has suffered, but in a way it's been enhanced by helping Dad. I'm doing something." She hints of having her own health problems and jokingly says, "If I became disabled, I'd move in and let Daddy take care of me."

Mrs. Stern was close to her mother too. Though her mother was a physician, she always made time for her daughter. When her husband became ill, she cared for him "incredibly well." "The best thing I can do for my mother now," says Mrs. Stern, "is to take good care of Daddy." Unfortunately, during the last year of the mother's life, her brain was affected, and she became so dependent that it was "a bottomless pit." "It wasn't her fault, but our relationship deteriorated. She became the child, and I became the mother in terms of role reversal."

How was it different to care for her mother and mother-in-law? Mrs. Stern replies, "One loved me. The other did not. Guess which was which. One rejected me all the way. It was difficult to be kind and respectful, but she was weak and frail, and I had to try regardless of the past. I didn't want to let my negative feelings take over and take advantage of the fact that she was weak now. I owed her something. She was my husband's mother." The mother-in-law had played her two sons off against each other and made them compete for the "Golden Apple" of who was best to Mom. "She was laying on the guilt trip. Which son was going to be the kindest? Which daughter-in-law?"

Mrs. Stern does not really think taking care of all the parents caused her husband to leave. She understands that there was

Parent care and being separated

much stress, and the tension may have put additional pressure on the marriage, just as their daughter's illness added stress. However, "The stresses should have made us closer rather than driven us apart. His psychopathology would have done this even without the parents."

Surely, parent care and being separated at the same time make things harder. "Now I have to face things alone. I'm alone in the world. I'm without a support network. I have friends, but people turn away from misfortune. Couples turn away. You're a fifth wheel. Your friends don't want to hear it. And there's no longer a couple, so social relationships have fallen by the wayside. One of the hardest things is the financial problems and realizing that my earning capacity is limited. The children wish they could mend the parental relationship. They're hurt and resentful and feel vulnerable. We're trying to be mutually supportive. I guess I haven't set too good an example in how to cope."

I'm without a support network

"I just want to do the things normal people do. Vacations are out of the question. I feel bitter and pessimistic. I don't see light at the end of the tunnel. I guess you have to rise to it."

"I fit into this slot."

Asked why she was willing to be interviewed, Mrs. Stern replied, "I don't fit into many slots in my job hunt. I saw the notice about the research and thought 'I sure fit into this slot'."

Mrs. Stern has indeed had "deep problems" for more than two decades. Still involved in her long caregiving career, she is now experiencing two very serious additional problems—her daughter's illness and the trauma of her husband leaving her. Each of the problems has an impact on the others. The sharp drop in income creates anxiety not only about her own future and that of her children, but also about future care of her father whose money is running out. The father's care creates an additional problem for this beleaguered woman. Being separated has reduced the support network she needs badly. Not only has she lost what support her husband could have given her, but since she is "no longer a couple," her friends are less in evidence.

It is particularly poignant that her father, though unable to move or speak, still represents emotional support for Mrs. Stern. She wishes she could have a full measure of that support, but is denied it because in order to protect him she hasn't told him about her separation from her husband. Her wish is also apparent in her sad little joke: "If I became disabled, I'd move in and let Daddy take care of me."

Mrs. Stern illustrates some of the themes that are common to many other caregivers. She would place her father in a nursing home only "if his mind goes." Helpless as he is and overburdened as she is, she still sees a "plus" in caregiving—she is proud of her "indomitable" father, and by helping him she's "doing something." That is one area in which she can feel good about herself. She feels responsible for her parent's emotional as well as physical well-being. She cares *for* him as well as *about* him.

It is interesting that Mrs. Stern used the phrase "role reversal" in relation to her mother, but not in relation to her father or mother-in-law. The context in which she used that phrase is suggestive. The mother's brain was affected, and the relationship "deteriorated" into role reversal. In so saying, Mrs. Stern implies that "role reversal" is not desirable or healthy.

Mrs. Stern's mental health surely has suffered from the multiple assaults she has experienced. She is in an uncertain limbo because she doesn't know what the divorce settlement will be or what her life will be like "at the end of the tunnel." She may exemplify the anxious transitional state of other separated women who are neither here nor there. It is not only in relation to her search for a job that Mrs. Stern feels she does not "fit into many slots."

NEVER-MARRIED WOMAN

"She'll Be a Comfort to You in Your Old Age"

"My life is on hold"

"My life is on hold," says Ms. Collins. "I'm 32, I'm not married, I have no children. It'll be too late for me." Ms. Collins lives in her 67-year-old mother's home. The mother has severe emphysema, is arthritic, and has some memory problems. She needs some help with grooming, bathing, and toileting. The youngest of three siblings by 12 years, Ms. Collins attributes the fact that she is the main caregiver to being a woman, to being the youngest child, to her sister's mental illness, and to her brother's geographic distance. The brother makes all the decisions, but Ms. Collins feels that's fine. "After all, he's a policeman and has even saved people's lives." Her siblings and her mother put her in the role of a child and tell her what to do. She quit her job when her mother was acutely ill. Now, the brother tells her, "Stay home with Mom." The mother expects her to keep house and take orders. "Wash the windows," she says, and complains about how the housework is done.

Brother makes decisions

Quit her job

Ms. Collins says, "When I was born, my mother was 35. That was old in those days. My Mom thought I was a boy, but the nurse said no. Mom was disappointed. People consoled her and said 'She'll be a comfort to you in your old age.' But she got more than she bargained for. We fight all the time. She does things to make me feel guilty. I take care of her because I owe her. I feel like I was a little spoiled in being the youngest and coming along later."

A baby girl: "a comfort in your old age"

A sympathetic boyfriend

Care is "off time"

Depressed and immobilized

"I need counseling"

Because Ms. Collins is not working, she has no money and cannot be independent. She has a boyfriend who also lives in the same house. Her family does not approve of her life-style but has accepted it. She and her boyfriend would like to take a place together but cannot. A previous relationship with a man ended because the latter did not understand about Ms. Collins' need to take care of her mother. He wanted her to move with him to Pittsburgh. Jim (the current boyfriend) is more understanding. His own mother is taking care of his grandmother. But, Ms. Collins says she's doing things like a 50 year old. The neighbors across the street care for elderly parents, but their own children are in the same age bracket as Ms. Collins.

Ms. Collins is disconsolate. "My self-esteem is down. I should make a list of things to do—a schedule—and save some time for myself. In this hot weather, the beer in the frig looks better and better, and I drink it. My sister gets to go away. I don't. I should put my foot down more. I get Jim off to work. I get breakfast, do the laundry and the dishes. Then I sit down and argue with Mom. I have no energy left. I watch TV. All the things I should do seem overwhelming—paying bills, getting the car fixed. I'm lonely. If I didn't have Jim, I wouldn't have anyone. I feel I'm losing my identity, abandoning my life. No one admits I'm doing it all. I have problems. Do I get married? Do I have children? Do I abandon her? Should I take charge and fight my siblings and Mom? I'd be fighting everyone. I need counselling. But I can't afford it. If I wasn't single, I might be forced to say 'I can't stop my life because of you'."

Clearly, Ms. Collins is depressed and immobilized. Everyone in her life exerts pressure to keep her in the caregiving role. Even her current boyfriend is "understanding." She is not struggling to extricate herself from the virtual isolation in which she lives. She does not look for a job, though her mother can be left alone during the day, and she is beginning to drink. She complains, but she thinks it's right for her brother to make decisions. The question here is how to reach Ms. Collins with the counselling help she knows she needs before, as she puts it, it is too late for her to move in a positive direction and get her life off "hold."

ONLY AND ALONE

Some parent-caring daughters have been only children all their lives, whereas others become "only" children when a sibling (or siblings) dies. The major theme for such women is their intense sense of being alone in caregiving. Those who have always been only children often say they had expected and anticipated eventually being the only caregiver to their parent(s); they wish in advance for someone with whom to share filial care when the time comes. Those who had sibling(s) who died also wish for a sibling who could share and provide emotional support, but, in addition, they experience a sense of desolation and loss.

When women without husbands or children are also without siblings, they are totally alone during their parent-care years. They often have unusually close bonds with the parent for whom they care and are burdened by the sense that it's all up to them. There simply isn't anyone else at all on whom to rely.

Two questions are part of the inner experiences of these women: "What will happen to my parent if something should happen to me?" and "Who will take care of me when I am old?"

"It's an Awesome Responsibility"

It's an awesome responsibility

Ms. Brown, who had never married, has always lived together with her mother, now 84. The mother, a former school teacher, is intact mentally but needs considerable personal care because of severe arthritis. Ms. Brown had a brother who died suddenly of a heart attack 12 years ago and a sister who was killed in an automobile accident 4 years ago. Ms. Brown said, "I never ever thought of sharing my mother's care. My sister and brother just shared. But now I realize I'm alone in caring for my mother. It's an awesome responsibility."

What would happen to mother?

Ms. Brown has stopped working as a secretary because of a back injury. She sings in the church choir and teaches music to the children at the church. She occasionally feels depressed, overwhelmed, or tired, but says it passes and she becomes "normal." She referred often to the loss of her siblings and her feeling of being solely responsible for mother. "It's scary to think what would happen to mother if anything happened to me."

No competing responsibilities

Ms. Brown notes that being single has some advantages when parent care is necessary. "When people are married, they have to take time from their families and children. I don't have those problems. Being single never bothered me. I have a busy and productive life. You don't have five or six people to worry about. My biggest problem is being the only child. And I don't have children to help. I was put into it because my sister was taken. Before that, she would come whenever. It makes a big difference. If there is no one to do it, you have to do it. It's a big responsibility."

As for the problems experienced by parent-caring women of various marital statuses, Ms. Brown says it depends as well on factors other than marital status. "You can't put a label on who has it the hardest. First in importance is how much care is needed. Then marital status. If you're married, it takes away attention if a parent is severely ill. But mental capacity is important. If my mother were senile, that would be different. It also depends on the individual and their capacity and how they look at life. One person is stressed out at something, and another one not. And there are different stages for different people. A woman may have raised her children and planned to go back to work. Freedom, that's it. Are they mentally prepared? You can't pinpoint things and say this is good and this bad."

Life stages and parent

"Nobody Cares About Us"

Unmarried and an only child

Ms. Fox's elderly mother has Alzheimer's disease. Unmarried and an only child, she has lived together with the 86-year-old widowed woman for 4 years. Ms. Fox has a degree from a respected university and works for a large industrial firm as an accountant.

A compliant mother

The elderly mother has two brothers, both of whom also suffer from Alzheimer's disease. One is in a nursing home, and the other is cared for at home by his wife. By contrast with Ms. Fox's mother, those elderly men wander, their behavior is aggressive, and sometimes they are "nasty." Ms. Fox's mother is "sweet; she doesn't complain or argue." The mother enjoys going places, and Ms. Fox takes her every place she goes. At home, the mother wants to help and does so, with instruction. She cleans, dusts, and washes the dishes after dinner. She enjoys going places.

Will I get that way too?

Ms. Fox describes her mother as having been a pleasant, efficient person in earlier life—outgoing, very social, and having lots of friends. Now she can't do anything on her own. "I wonder if I'll get that way too," says Ms. Fox, "but my father was very alert. I don't know which one I'll take after. I have to put her clothes out and tell her what to wear. She can't put her clothes away. She's even lost one shoe. I have to cook everything. I have to buy her clothes. She wants to look nice so she cooperates."

Planning for the future

A companion

As insurance for the future, Ms. Fox has registered her mother at a sectarian nursing home where she is at the top of the waiting list. Ms. Fox says, "I'll keep her as long as I can. Why should I be alone? I even take her on group day trips. She looks fine. I buy her nice clothes. Other people don't even know she has Alzheimer's. She's a companion for me. I have no other family. Even though we can't carry on a conversation, she is a companion. She loves to go out. I say to her, 'Do you want to go out?,' and she says, 'Sure.' I take her to New York all the time. I guess it sounds weird. But I'm not alone."

The elderly woman goes to day care so that Ms. Fox can go to

Day Care   work. The day care center is located at a hospital so the mother gets her medical care there—"doctor, x-rays, even a foot doctor. That's a tremendous load off me. I don't have to take time off from work. Now I only have to take her to the dentist."

Ms. Fox describes crises during which her feelings of being alone were acute. "I had a scare when we had an automobile accident, but she did get better. She doesn't give up and get

I have no one   depressed. She keeps pushing. I get depressed, but she doesn't. I get depressed mostly about being alone. I have no one to call on. I had a mastectomy 3½ years ago, and I have a bad heart. I think 'What would happen to us if I become an invalid?' After the auto accident, I was in the hospital, and I was almost hysterical. However, I've put all my mother's money in trust, and there's a trust officer if anything happens to me. They could even put her in a nursing home. I think I've done very well to do all that. But I still have not taken care of myself. I don't even have anyone to talk

Some counselling   to. I go to a counsellor three or four times a year. My job pays for five sessions a year. But now my firm has been bought out. There are constant lay-offs, and another one is coming up. People over 59 have been asked to take voluntary retirement, but I'd get a very small pension, and at my age I'd have trouble getting another job. So I'll stay as long as they'll keep me. I get depressed and upset, but there are a lot of people worse off."

Ms. Fox says her worst caregiving problem is her inability to go out occasionally in the evening. Teenagers don't want to "baby sit"

No respite   as they get upset. The homemakers charge $11 an hour, and sometimes they come late or leave early. "I can't go to a club meeting or even a retirement party. I can't go away for a weekend. I haven't had a vacation in years."

Ms. Fox compared herself with other caregivers who have family support. "My mother's brother has a wife and children and grandchildren. She's like a general. She tells them all what to do

Nobody cares about us   to help. I don't have anyone. I even went to a support group, but it only made me feel bad. All they talk about is to tell their families to do this and that. Well, I don't have any family. I feel as though nobody cares. Nobody cares about us. It's true. I don't even go to support groups anymore. They don't *know*. There aren't too many people all alone, but they exist. It's best for caregivers who have family. When I had surgery, I had to go to the hospital myself. When I came out of the anesthesia, there was no one there."

Ms. Fox feels very tired. She never gets to bed before 1 or 2 a.m. because she has housekeeping and things to do and gets up at 5 a.m. to get things ready before she goes to work. She loves to

A heavy schedule   cook and spends a lot of time doing that in the evening. She sometimes feels frustrated and angry and is often depressed and worried. She attributes all of those feelings to her situation of being alone in caregiving. Even when she had the accident, she had to take care of everything herself—car repairs, insurance, taking care of her mother, taking care of herself after her hospitalization. On holidays, she and her mother are alone. She thinks people should be more caring and invite them. She wonders if its her own personality. She says in a low voice, "Maybe it's my mother. Maybe they don't want my mother." She's even given up

No friends

inviting people to her home. "They don't come. They don't realize what it's like to be alone. Even at Christmas. We used to do it. When we met people at church and they were alone, we always invited them. I can't understand it. Maybe I take things too seriously. Maybe someone else would handle things better. I guess there's people in worse situations. At least she's not an invalid in bed."

It's my duty

As for why she keeps on caregiving despite her multiple strains, she says "All my life I remember my parents saying that children have to take care of their parents. It's my duty. My parents were very strict. I was brought up that way."

Care for both parents

Ms. Fox had also helped her father, who was practically blind, before he died. He had his own business, and she helped him with the accounting work. At that time, Ms. Fox cared for both parents. She was tied down. But her father was alert even though he got very depressed. He would sit in a chair and cry and get irritable. "But at least I could tell him something, and he would remember. With my mother, it doesn't go through to her brain. She's been getting worse during the last 8 years."

It isn't fair

"If I came from a big family, there would be lots of demands and fights, so maybe this is better. But some families do get along. It isn't fair that I was an only child. But she was always a good mother—caring and thoughtful and understanding. I was brought up to do unto others as they do unto you. But even if she had not been good to me, I would take care of her. In lots of ways, I have no choice."

Work life affected

There are many limits on Ms. Fox's life. Not only can't she go out in evenings, but she can't have people in. Her social network has shrunk. Her work life is affected. Her boss is not understanding. On a couple of occasions, she had to miss work to go home, and he resented it. It affects the ratings he gives her.

"I come last"

Her priorities are clear, Ms. Fox says—"My mother comes first, my job comes second, the house and my three dogs come next, and I come last."

Being alone the most strain

On balance, Ms. Fox says, "My mother does what I tell her to, so I have some control," and the older woman's income covers her expenses. "If I were unhappily married, it would be worse. I have friends who are married, and some of them are unhappy. In some

ways, I'm better off. Nothing is perfect. I will take care of my
mother until I can't do it. Then she'll have to go to a nursing
home. If I had a cooperative husband and children, it might make
it easier. Being alone is the most strain. It really depends on the
situation. Some widowed women are helpless because their husbands did everything. It depends on the relationship."

Trying hard to look at the positives in her life and in her situation,
Ms. Fox says, "When I was young, I always wanted to go around the
world. I did it. I've been in 50 countries and lived in some far-away
places. [She used to work for the State Department.] Its made me a
stronger person." At this point, Ms. Fox wept, then said "Being
stronger makes me able to do the caregiving. I have to take care of
myself, and I might as well take care of her too."

Do your best   As for the future, when her mother is gone, she'll sell her house
and go to a retirement community. She advises others like her,
"Do your best."

The theme expressed by both Mrs. Brown as well as Ms. Fox is, of course,
the feeling of being alone. "I don't have anyone." "I feel as though nobody
cares." "I don't have anyone to help." "What will happen to my parent if
something happens to me?" "What will happen to me when I am old?" "It's
scary."

It is striking that for both women, their elderly mothers provide their
only sense of having someone, having family. Ms. Brown's mother is mentally intact, and the daughter respects and loves her. But Ms. Fox says of her
cognitively impaired parent, "Even though we can't carry on a conversation,
she is a companion. I guess it sounds weird, but I'm not alone."

Ms. Brown, though alone, manages to live an active life. Because her
mother is intact mentally, she can be left alone while the daughter pursues
her outside interests. Mother and daughter get along well. Ms. Brown is
perceptive in assessing the pros and cons of being a not-married caregiver.
She notes the absence of competing demands but also that she has no
children to help her. Overall, the strain Ms. Brown is experiencing at
present is mild, but she worries about the future.

Ms. Fox's life is much more restricted than that of Ms. Brown because
of her mother's Alzheimer's disease. Ms. Fox does go to work, thanks to the
day-care program. But like many other caregivers, she cannot locate satisfactory helpers so that she can have some diversionary activities. Her social
life has been shrinking. She cannot even go to a "retirement party," let alone
take a vacation. She is fortunate that day care is available and that she is able
to purchase it, but respite service is not available in her community. Ms. Fox
has planned as well as she can for her mother's future and for her own by
locating a nursing home and a retirement community, again underlining the
importance of adequate financial resources. But what can be done to alleviate the painful sense of aloneness and loneliness with which people such as
Ms. Brown and Ms. Fox live?

Chapter 11

Daughters-in-Law

When sons are identified as their parents' primary caregivers, it is likely that their wives are the ones who do most of the day-to-day care. Thus, though daughters-in-law are named as principal caregivers much less often than biological children, they probably serve in that role more often and provide more care than is generally known. At the same time, there undoubtedly are many daughters-in-law who do not assume the role of principal caregiver. Existing information hints that daughters-in-law in general may not be as willing as daughters to provide the high levels of personal care needed by extremely disabled older people. For example, old people without daughters enter nursing homes at lower levels of disability (Soldo, 1982b).

Whatever the prevalence of daughters-in-law as principal caregivers at present, their experiences are important to understand not only in their own right, but because the continuing fall in the birth rate means that even fewer daughters will be available for parent care. In turn, fewer daughters results in more daughters-in-law becoming involved in care of their parents-in-law. Moreover, when there are fewer adult children, more couples have more than one older parent between them who may need care. A woman nowadays, therefore, stands an increased chance of becoming a caregiver in both roles—as a daughter and as a daughter-in-law, a pattern that will increase in the future.

Little is known about the qualitative aspects of daughter-in-law care—about such women's inner experiences and how they differ from those of daughters. As noted in Chapter 6, acceptance of caregiving to the elderly as a woman's role is so deeply ingrained that some daughters-in-law simply assume that they should provide the care when their husbands, the sons, become the ones in the family responsible for seeing to it that an elderly parent receives help. Though this usually happens when a daughter is not available, some daughters-in-law become the caregivers even when there is a daughter if such behavior is culturally dictated or there is some special circumstance. Some daughters-in-law accept caregiving as their role so completely that they are grateful for the help their husbands—the elderly parents' own sons—give them in the caregiving enterprise.

There are, of course, similarities in caregiving by daughters and daughters-in-law—particularly in the "externals" of care. Emotional strains are caused by such factors as "heavy" care, the sharing of a household with the dependent older person, the disturbed behavior of Alzheimer's patients or those who are mentally ill, and life-style disruptions. But the subjective experiences of the two groups of women differ in significant ways, and there are some qualitative differences in the nature of their strains.

Some daughters-in-law are relatively uninvolved in providing services either because someone else is the main caregiver and their own help is secondary, or because their husbands provide much of the help the elderly parent(s) needs. Some sons go beyond their traditionally assigned tasks of decision-making, money management, home repairs, and chores to do things like shopping and transportation. It is rare for sons to provide personal care to their mothers, however, although they may do certain personal things for a father such as shaving and bathing. When their mothers need personal care, they enlist the aid of their wives. Daughters-in-law who are relatively uninvolved may experience little emotional strain, though there are exceptions. When a mother-in-law actually lives in the daughter-in-law's household, the stress can be extraordinarily severe, particularly if the older woman requires a good deal of help or the relationship of the two women was poor previously.

Some of the themes and issues that will appear in the cases to be presented are not experienced by all daughters-in-law, of course, but recur often in the caregiving stories they tell. One theme is the clear distinction the women make between the quality of their emotional involvement with parents-in-law and with their own parents. Some report more detachment and less strain in relation to their in-laws. Those who are having or who have had caregiving experience in both roles—that is, as a daughter *and* as a daughter-in-law—describe this well.

> There is less emotional involvement [with a mother-in-law]. One is your mother, and the other isn't. I can deal with it much easier when it's my mother-in-law. I don't get upset as much. Maybe you have less guilt.

***

> You don't carry the emotional baggage into the situation [with a mother-in-law] that you do with your mother.

The sense of responsibility they feel is related to the intensity of their emotional involvement.

I never have the feeling that I have to be "in charge" with my mother-in-law. It's my husband. With my mother, it's *my* responsibility.

***

I don't feel the same sense of responsibility for my mother-in-law that I do for my father.

In a related vein, elderly parents-in-law are sometimes perceived by daughters-in-law as being less demanding of them than their own parents because there is no biological link. The elderly in-laws may be more cautious and feel less entitled to help from daughters-in-law. "My mother-in-law is a 'lady of control.' Her daughters feel it, but as a daughter-in-law, I do not."

Because the sense of obligation to parents is different from that to parents-in-law, daughters-in-law do not say (as daughters do), "She took care of me so now it's my turn to take care of her." They do not have the powerful motivation of reciprocity for the care they received as children, or the feelings of love (albeit ambivalent) and biological connection. They say such things as "Blood is thicker than water," and "One is your mother. The other is not. There is a bond."

A different kind of obligation often exists, however. Some daughters-in-law see care of their parents-in-law as having been an implicit part of the marriage contract: "It's part of the deal," and "I owe her because she's my husband's mother."

Reciprocity with one's husband also plays a role, in that care of a parent-in-law may be viewed as repayment for the husband's help with the caregiver's own parent in the past or even in anticipation of the future.

My husband was patient and understanding when my father was ill and was kind to him.

***

My husband doesn't complain about my mother. I'll have his mother here some day. I know it.

The qualitative relationships between older people and their daughters-in-law are extremely variable, of course. They may be close and warm at one extreme or actively, openly hostile and conflicted at the other extreme. There are instances of extreme devotion to a parent-in-law.

A woman who is divorced from the son of the elderly man for whom she has provided care for 7 years says: "He [the father-in-law] is 92 years old, and he and I always had an excellent relationship. If I didn't take care of him, who would?"

A widowed daughter-in-law continues to tend to the needs of her mother-in-law: "She lives in Senior Housing, but she needs someone to do her laundry and shop for her and take her to the doctor. We always got on well. I see it as my responsibility."

The ultimate example of devotion appears in the biblical story of Ruth and her mother-in-law Naomi. Ruth says to Naomi, "Intreat me not to leave thee, or to return from following after thee: for whither thou goest, I will go; and where thou lodgest, I will lodge" (Book of Ruth).

There also can be extreme conflict, antipathy, hostility, and resentment.

When she [the mother-in-law] is in the room I put my magazine or newspaper high in front of my face so I don't have to see her.

***

She never accepted me. She tries to control our lives completely and criticizes me to my husband.

A major and pervasive issue that is almost invariably present, though it may be barely discernible or overt and dominant, is the competition that sometimes erupts into a bitter struggle between wife and mother-in-law for the man who is husband to the one and son to the other. Conventional wisdom has it that the mother-in-law/daughter-in-law relationship is often characterized by tension and conflict. An elderly mother-in-law's need for care, particularly her presence in the same household, may exacerbate the situation so that the emotional currents are intense. In such instances, there is no respite from the day-to-day contact that provokes those feelings. The shared household becomes like a pressure cooker without an escape valve.

As Chapter 3 indicated, when households are shared, daughters-in-law may experience more strain than any other category of caregiving relatives, and open-ended interviews with daughters-in-law provide some clues to the reasons. The competition between mother-in-law and daughter-in-law and resentment at needing to help someone who is not even their own parent add an extra edge of bitterness to their stories of caregiving. Such feelings are heightened if the mother-in-law had "rejected" them from the outset and there were relationship problems along the way.

All of those inner feelings and others as well appear in the seven case studies that follow. In two of the situations, the daughter-in-law became the caregivers because their husbands were "only" children and in two because their husbands became only children when sibling(s) died. In the fifth case, the husband had no sisters. In the last two cases, the husbands did indeed have sisters, but there were special circumstances.

"She's Sitting in My Chair"

Alzheimer's disease

Mrs. Chase, age 36, lives with her husband, three preschool children, and her 78-year-old mother-in-law who suffers from Alzheimer's disease. Although confused and in need of help with all instrumental and personal care tasks, the older woman is still ambulatory, knows where she is, and recognizes her family members.

Husband an only child

Mr. Chase is an only child. His mother had lived in a rural area in Massachusetts and was widowed 1½ years ago. The elderly woman then had several fainting spells, and became unable to drive, shop, or manage her affairs. She called her lawyer repeatedly about tax reports that had already been done. She had approximately 15 kinds of pills, which she took indiscriminately; her apartment was a mess; and her son found "enough cleaning supplies to open a store." Finally, when the rescue squad took the elderly woman to a hospital, the doctor refused to discharge her to go back to her apartment alone. At that point, the Chases considered various options such as a nursing home and a housekeeper, but decided to bring her to their home because she lived too far away for them to manage her care effectively.

A career woman

Mrs. Chase had been married for 5 years when her mother-in-law joined the household. She holds a master's degree in computer science, had enjoyed a successful career for 10 years, and had continued to work, taking her two children to a babysitter during the day. She had stopped working 8 months prior to the interview. At that time, she was pregnant with her third child, who is now 3 months old.

Quits work

When Mrs. Chase stopped working, she became a full-time caregiver to her own children and to her mother-in-law, who could no longer stay alone in the house. Mrs. Chase is thoughtful and candid about her decision to quit her job. She said, "I would not have quit just to take care of my mother-in-law, but I could do it for my kids. It's not like I turned my back on my career. I'm still doing some consulting, and I'll work again eventually." Another factor determining her decision was that she had been passed over for a promotion she had earned and for which she was well qualified. A man had received the promotion. Mrs. Chase feels that her pregnancies and caregiving responsibilities made the male employee more desirable in the eyes of her employer.

Behavioral symptoms

Mrs. Chase does all the household and child-care tasks. She gives her mother-in-law her medicines, washes her hair, and takes her with her on all errands such as grocery shopping. Mr. Chase manages his mother's money. The mother's behavioral symptoms are getting worse. She put paper on the stove when it was lit and hides her money. Her personal hygiene is poor, and she has an unpleasant odor.

Mrs. Chase has been trying hard. She says she is not normally a nervous person and even now knows how to set priorities. She does what had to be done first. However, the situation is wearing her out mentally; she is often upset and occasionally depressed, feels emotionally drained and overwhelmed. She says, with humor that her mental health is okay, "but it's being challenged." The family privacy has been "invaded," and Mrs. Chase is never alone with her husband and children. The couple cannot do certain things, but at the same time, Mrs. Chase says that the needs of her children and mother-in-law coincide in some ways— that is, in requiring a constant presence in the household. She thinks it might be worse for caregivers whose own children are grown. They would be deprived of the freedom to go out. However, Mrs. Chase says, "She is always with me." The Chases had to buy a larger car and are looking for a more spacious house.

Mental health being challenged

Off-time and on-time

There is no paid help except on occasional sitter. Mr. Chase cuts the grass and cooks Sunday dinner. The caregiver feels he is a great help psychologically. On one occasion, Mr. Chase's cousin took the mother-in-law for a 2-week visit at the same time the latter's sister was visiting. It was "a great rest" for the Chases, but the cousin said, "Never again." Day care is too costly at $40 a day. If the mother-in-law gets to the point of not even recognizing her family members, Mrs. Chase says nursing home placement will be made. Then, "It won't make any difference."

Husband helps

Mrs. Chase attributes her stress to her relationship with her mother-in-law and to the behavioral symptoms of Alzheimer's disease. Despite the many problems, Mrs. Chase feels that the positive side is that they are helping someone. "We're making her happy. That's a good feeling. It's a juggling act, a balancing act—to make everybody happy. You do what has to be done at the moment. It's crisis management, that's what it is." Her role as wife is constantly being "squeezed." It is a constant effort to find time with her husband.

Making everyone happy

Mrs. Chase is well aware of her own inner feelings and is candid in saying she is jealous of the bond between her mother-in-law and her husband. "When he comes in, he hands *her* the newspaper. He's a gentleman, and I was the queen of the house. Now *she's* the queen. At dinner, he serves her first. Even on my child's birthday, she got the first piece of cake. She's taken over. I know it's not rational. All of a sudden it's like the mother/son ties are there again. It makes me feel like he's not really married to me. I know it's not the case. But that's why having her here is so psychologically trying. We bought a new car because she couldn't get into the back seat in a two-door. The front seat was mine, and all of a sudden she was in my seat. I thought 'She's sitting in *my* chair.' I tell my husband 'She is not a full voting member of this

The mother/son ties

Now she's the queen

She's sitting in my chair

family.' Decisions must be between my husband and me. She *cannot* be a third member of this adult family. She is here because she needs care or she wouldn't be here."

Mrs. Chase says: "I do what I should for her. I do for my children because I love them." She and her mother-in-law "got off on the wrong foot" because the older woman did not want her son to marry Mrs. Chase. "A parent should never do that. I think it's a big hurt. It's hard to get over. Maybe I'm beginning to get over it. It's a big struggle in my life. I try not to let her presence affect my relationship with my children. I don't let her discipline them, though she tries. I try not to let my feelings spill over onto the children. Once I was vacuuming the rug and she was sitting in a chair. When I approached the chair, she lifted her feet for the vacuum. I said, 'I'm not your servant.' I do it because I'm a human being and a Christian."

"I do what I should"

Mrs. Chase feels that her relationship with her husband has been strengthened by the caregiving. Her husband appreciates it. He knows that if he hadn't married her, he couldn't do it. "I try to give my mother-in-law respect because she is the mother of my husband. Maybe I could be more patient. I try to do my best. I could do better, and I could do worse." But sometimes she explodes. She understands that it is hard for Mr. Chase to see his mother going downhill. He thinks of her as she used to be. Mrs. Chase says, "It's a stress to see an intelligent parent degenerate."

An appreciative husband

Mrs. Chase is thoughtful about how it is different for a daughter or a daughter-in-law to provide care. In some ways, she says, it's easier for a daughter-in-law. "There is less past baggage." In some ways, it is harder. "How much do you love her? respect her? A daughter-in-law can be more detached, like running a nursing home." Mrs. Chase imitates a nurse's cheery voice saying, "Here's your medicine. Here's your juice." "You wonder why this role is falling on me, I'm a professional woman?" She answers her own question: "When you're growing up, you see your mother doing stuff so you fall into that. Little boys learn from their dads. So that's the way it happens."

It's different for a daughter-in-law

Women's role

Mrs. Chase's plans for the future are to raise her children and go back to her career. "I hope my mother-in-law can live out the rest of her days with us, but I hope it's not 20 years." When asked if she has any advice for other women in her situation, she advises them to go to support group meetings, get whatever help they need, and try to be patient and understanding. "Rely on other people to get whatever you need in the way of emotional support." She tells the interviewer, "Even talking to you today has helped me. I read the article about the research, and I said 'This is me.' A lot of people are facing it. I've learned a good deal and can learn more. If I can help others I want to, and I thought it could help me."

Plans return to work

Mrs. Chase was open in her description of her problems and acutely, even painfully, aware of her own inner feelings—feelings that arise to some degree in most daughters-in-law. She articulated clearly the theme of competition of daughter-in-law and mother-in-law—the underlying struggle between mother and wife for primacy with the son/husband. Such competition often begins early in the relationship. Mrs. Chase also states clearly one of the main differences between caregiving daughters and caregiving daughters-in-law—namely, the quality of the emotional investment and problems but says she does not carry the "emotional baggage" into the situation that a daughter might.

Though she is highly educated and espouses the new views of women's roles with respect to employment, Mrs. Chase does not challenge the notion that she should do the day-to-day care. She states that she became the caregiver because she is a woman and was socialized into the caregiving role. Her husband was an only child, so there were no siblings to step in or to share. She sees it as her role not only to provide the actual care, but (as daughters do) to make her mother-in-law happy.

Like some other working women, Mrs. Chase quit her job due to a combination of circumstances that included the need to care for an elderly person. She and her husband share the parent-care tasks in traditional "gender-appropriate" ways. Mrs. Chase does the actual care, whereas he manages money. She is grateful to her husband for helping. He cuts the grass and cooks Sunday dinner.

The difficulties of caring for an Alzheimer's patient are well described—the distressing behavior, poor hygiene, and the need for constant surveillance. Yet, like many daughters, Mrs. Chase says she will not consider nursing home placement until the older woman no longer recognizes family members.

In caring for an elderly person while there also are preschool children in the family, Mrs. Chase is "off time" (see Chapter 7). She points out, however, that there is an "on-time" aspect to the situation in that the life-style restrictions attendant on caring for the young children are similar to those of caring for the older person.

Mrs. Chase experiences and describes the negative emotional and life-style effects of caregiving that are shared by many caregivers. Nevertheless, like so many women, she sees her role as going beyond caregiving to making people happy. She also expresses the gratification derived from helping someone and living up to one's religious beliefs.

On a practical level, it is apparent that Mrs. Chase could use services such as respite care and case management, particularly since her mother-in-law's condition will inevitably worsen.

"Women Like Me Are Dinosaurs"

Now 48 years old, Mrs. Austin had worked as a young woman, but stopped 25 years ago when she married. She then worked as her husband's unpaid secretary and bookkeeper, putting in more than 40 hours weekly. Her career caring for her parents-in-law had begun 15 years previously. Mrs. Austin stopped working 4 years ago because by then the elderly couple needed so much attention.

Stopped working

Mrs. Austin says it's been a "very long siege." Since Mr. Austin is an only child, there are no siblings to help with parent care. The parents-in-law lived a few minutes away from the Austins until the elderly man died 10 years ago. He had suffered from Alzheimer's disease and was violent. They often were called in the middle of the night to pick him up from various parts of the city. Eventually, he had to be tied to a chair. The family did not put him in a nursing home because they needed to conserve his funds for his wife.

A long siege with two parents-in-law

Mrs. Austin's mother-in-law went to a retirement community after her husband died. The daughter-in-law used to take the elderly woman out several times a week, do her shopping and banking, and take her to the doctor. She spent several hours daily with the older woman. The mother-in-law entered a nursing home 3 months ago at age 87. She had been in the hospital, fell out of bed, suffered multiple fractures, and became mentally disturbed. The elderly woman then caused her son and daughter-in-law much anguish. She was verbally abusive to them, phoned them every few minutes, and also called her bank dozens of times accusing every one of stealing her money. She called her son at work. "She'd have my husband weeping, and he was such a good son. She turned on him."

Difficult behavior

Mrs. Austin feels very angry about caring for her mother-in-law. Her husband is not as involved in helping his mother as he was in helping his father, and it is a terrible strain on the marriage.

Mrs. Austin says, "The woman is in the middle, taking care of old people and children." She describes taking her mother-in-law for routine visits to the doctor and sitting for hours, and "all they do is take her blood pressure." "My life revolves around my mother-in-law," she says. Taking the older woman to the dentist, podiatrist, and physicians consumed considerable time. She has read whole books while waiting in doctors' offices and had to learn to give her mother-in-law enemas. "There was no one else to do it." Mrs. Austin does an imitation of the doctor talking to her as though the older woman was not present. "He treated my mother-in-law like she was a jerk. She never complained, but it's degrading to an older woman. She wasn't deaf or blind. I felt angry. The doctor said to me 'Take her home and give her an enema.' It never occurred to him that I didn't know how and didn't want to. So I did it. The female gets the brunt of it."

"The woman is in the middle"

A doctor's attitude

"My husband's an only child, so what's the alternative?" She says wryly, "My husband would take care of *big* things such as

The dirt work

picking a doctor when she was hospitalized. He'd find the best hip surgeon around. My job was going to the supermarket, buying her stockings—the dirt work, the day-to-day stuff. They presume because you're a woman, there's no reason why you can't do it."

Nothing was good enough

"My mother-in-law was never satisfied. I made sure she had the right shoes, that there were no cords for her to trip over. Nothing was quite good enough no matter how hard we tried. There were days I could strangle her and days when I felt so sorry for her I would weep."

Trapped

"It's part of the deal"

The constant stress caused marital problems. "It wears you down. You get nuts." As for why she did it, she says, "Someone has to do it, and he can't. What are you going to do? I felt trapped. My husband tried a little harder to do things for her, and I tried to stop feeling martyred and to make a positive thing of it. I'd take her out to lunch to make it pleasant when I had to be with her. I made him take her to the doctor sometimes. But there's no way out. It's part of the deal when you get married."

Not like child care

Mrs. Austin's own parents died young. "I don't know how I would have managed four old people." This has been her only experience with old people. "At least with a 2-year old, you put them down for a nap and they wake up better. We probably spent more time caring for them than for our children. Children grow up and become less dependent on you. It's different with children."

"She's my husband's mother"

The two women had always gotten along well on a superficial level. "We were civil. We never had words, but I don't feel toward her like she was my mother. She's my husband's mother. But caring for a mother-in-law is not like caring for a mother. "It's different with your mother just because she's your mother. It's a bond. She's been a very good loving grandmother to my children. They're very attentive to her."

Now the mother-in-law is calmer but living in the past. She wants her mother, who's been dead for 60 years. When told her mother's dead, she weeps and says, "Where was I when it happened?"

"It's been bad," says Mrs. Austin, "but I'm starting to heal. I have no one to take care of for the first time in my life. There's no one sucking at me. I don't even want to take care of a goldfish. I feel liberated."

Hard for older people

"It was hard on me. I'm not the nurse type, but I had to give her enemas." Mrs. Austin empathizes with old people. "It must be awful to have to rely on another person for everything."

"It's my turn"

Mrs. Austin referred to her stage of life and sums things up. "In a way, I'm lucky. It's over. Now it's my turn. Most women are older when they to do this. I did it because it was expected of me.

She is my husband's mother. I like me. I did a good job. I tried. I'm a better person for it. I really did it for him [her husband]. I couldn't have done anything more."

Look for help

She advises other women in her situation to try not to feel martyred by it and to maintain a sense of humor. "Look for help! That's important. There must be something out there to help. Services. Facilities." She and her husband recently had a big conversation. They want to make the most of the years they have left. For the first time ever, Mr. and Mrs. Austin have no one else living in their home. Their children are out of the nest. "It's made us sit back and say, 'Let's change our lives. Our responsibilities are over. Let's not keep the pace up. He's worn out.'"

People don't know

"I think I'm the last generation of women available. Women like me are becoming dinosaurs," said Mrs. Austin. She tells the young interviewer, "Your generation of women won't do it because you're working." She responded to the call for research participants because "I saw the little thing in the paper, and I thought 'My God. There are other people out there like me.' Maybe people can learn from this. People don't know."

In saying that women like herself are dinosaurs, Mrs. Austin is referring to women's changing life-styles, in particular their participation in the labor force and the increased assertiveness associated with the Women's Movement. She is also expressing her deep resentment and anger at how totally her life and her husband's life had been disrupted by care of the elderly in-laws—feelings that are more intense because it is not her own parents for whom the care was provided. She points out that the bond is different when it's your own mother. She did it not because of her own indebtedness to her in-laws but for her husband. "It's part of the deal when you get married."

Like so many other women—daughters *and* daughters-in-law—Mrs. Austin has had a "long siege," a career of caregiving to more than one older person. The disturbed and disturbing behavior of both parents-in-law undoubtedly intensified the stress. Like other caregivers, she advises people like herself to look for help. "There must be something out there."

Mrs. Austin's critique of the doctor's attitude was pointed and caustic. He not only talked about the mother-in-law as though she were not in the room, but was totally insensitive to the caregiver's feelings and needs. Despite her anger, she did what he ordered. She is rebelling against the traditional gender role-assignment, and her anger no doubt is due (at least in part) to her own compliance with injustice.

"It's Like a Cloud Over Our Heads"

At age 62, Mrs. Cohen has an 83-year-old mother and an 89-year-old mother-in-law, both in need of help. Her mother is in a

A mother and a mother-in-law need help

care facility following a hospitalization, and it is not known whether she will be able to return to independent living. The mother-in-law lives in senior housing, and Mrs. Cohen wants her to go to a nursing home, but the mother-in-law refuses. Though she provides very little help to her mother-in-law, Mrs. Cohen defines herself as caregiver because her husband's only brother had died. Thus, there is no other woman in the picture. As for help with caring for her own mother, her two sisters live too far away.

According to Mrs. Cohen, she and her husband agree on issues concerning both mothers, but are now "obsessed" with the problems. "It's all we talk about. It's like a cloud over our heads." The couple's sons are grown and out of the house, but Mrs. Cohen's small business is being neglected.

A rejecting mother-in-law

A heart attack on Mother's Day

Mrs. Cohen describes her mother-in-law as controlling, domineering, unpleasant, and rejecting. She had not wanted her son to marry Mrs. Cohen. Mrs. Cohen's intense dislike of her mother-in-law was readily apparent. She attributes the strains she and her husband are experiencing to her mother-in-law, not to her mother. The mother is appreciates the things done for her, but the mother-in-law does not. The latter had lived with the Cohens for 1 year many years ago, but it was an impossible situation. The day after she moved out, Mr. Cohen had a heart attack. It happened on Mother's Day.

"It has taken my husband away"

A man-in-the-middle

Mrs. Cohen's severe strains do not relate to providing instrumental help to her mother-in-law, since it is Mr. Cohen who helps his mother with shopping and anything else she needs. However, Mrs. Cohen resents the situation. "It has taken my husband away" and "She treats me like I'm an outsider." She attributes her very frequent fatigue and resentment to her mother-in-law (only occasionally do such feelings arise because of her own mother, and they are mild) as well as her frequent feelings of frustration, being emotionally drained, and overwhelmed. Another clue to her feelings is her description of her own mother as being acquescient, whereas her mother-in-law refuses to be controlled in any way. Mr. Cohen has become seriously depressed and appears to be caught in the middle between two strong women.

Like Mrs. Chase and Mrs. Austin, Mrs. Cohen's husband has no sister to assume responsibility, nor is there another daughter-in-law. Because Mrs. Cohen has both a disabled mother and a disabled mother-in-law, she highlights some of the qualitative differences in those relationships. She is actively and openly hostile to her mother-in-law, attributing all problems to the latter's personality and behavior. The "externals" of care are also different for Mrs. Cohen and the daughters-in-law in the first two cases in that Mrs. Cohen is providing virtually no instrumental help or personal care to either mother. Yet Mrs. Cohen reports experiencing much more stress. The theme of competition with her mother-in-law for her husband is strong, and Mrs. Cohen's feelings about her mother-in-law combine with her inability to control the older woman to result in fury and frustration. Mr. Cohen too is showing signs of severe stress. He has become a man in the middle between his wife and his mother.

Empty Nest Refilled

The Empty Nest Refilled with young and old

Mrs. Blum, age 58, works part time as a substitute teacher in a private school. Her husband, a college professor, is semiretired due to three heart attacks and open heart surgery. Mrs. Blum says, "We were an empty nest, and now we're filled." Living in the household are her mother-in-law and two of the Blum's grown daughters. A son has moved out, but both daughters returned home after completing graduate school and are looking for jobs.

Suddenly a new person

Mr. Blum is now the only child. His mother moved in 3 months ago when her other son, in whose home she had lived for 32 years, died after a short illness. The widowed daughter-in-law immediately said she could no longer keep her mother-in-law in her home. With her husband gone, she felt she no longer had an obligation, and the Blums had to make room for the elderly woman. "Suddenly, there's a new person in the household," says Mrs. Blum. She was devastated and is deeply angry. Her own widowed father had died 1 month previously at age 92, but he had been fiercely independent and was still living alone. Mrs. Blum contrasts her father with her very dependent mother-in-law.

Symptoms of mental decline

The elderly woman is extremely depressed due to her son's death, eats very little, is losing weight rapidly, and is "losing her faculties." Mrs. Blum too is depressed. "Our whole life has been disrupted." The mother-in-law hides things, accuses her granddaughters of taking her possessions, is very forgetful, lives in the past, and only gets bits and pieces of what people say to her. She turns night into day, and her personal hygiene is poor. The granddaughters try to give her emotional support.

A difficult adjustment

The change in the mother-in-law has been dramatic since her son's death. She had memory loss before, but in her familiar environment had bustled about doing the cooking and household tasks. Now, the Blum's have to see to it that she eats something.

The mother-in-law had always been a controlling person and still is. She doesn't like Mr. and Mrs. Blum to go out, and if they do she stands at the window and watches for them. She forgets to eat. The Blums have absolutely no privacy and have to make sure there is someone at home at all times. They can't travel or take a short vacation. What makes matters worse is Mr. Blum's attentiveness to his mother. He sits with her even after his wife has gone up to bed.

When the mother-in-law first moved in, she tried to continue the pattern of living developed when she lived with her other son and daughter-in-law. Then, she had done all the shopping and cooking. Here, she wanted to make her son's breakfast, and Mrs. Blum had to make it clear that it was *her* kitchen. At times, Mrs. Blum tries to let her help with cooking, but it doesn't work because the older woman criticizes the daughter-in-law's style of food preparation. She does let her set the table and help with the dishes, but all of these readjustments are very hard.

One kitchen two women

Mrs. Blum has colitis and gets very upset. She tries to "detach" herself from too much involvement with her mother-in-law. She is always worried about her husband and had been hoping for a few peaceful years. She was deeply devoted to her own father, was very proud of him, and is grieving profoundly about his death.

Mrs. Blum thought of day care, but her mother-in-law would not accept it. The older woman's whole life had been housework and family. "She's very old-fashioned and was never involved in activities outside the home. She's a relic," says Mrs. Blum. "Women nowadays are different." She points out that her sister-in-law whose widowhood occurred at the same age as the mother-in-law's, did not move in with her son and try to control the household. Rather, the new widow is trying to make a new life—taking courses, traveling, working part-time, and going to exercise class.

An old-fashioned woman

"I never ever expected this," Mrs. Blum says. "My father would never have moved here. When my mother was ill, we had nurses and my sisters came in from out of town, but most of it fell on me. My parents had cared for their parents, but my parents always said they would never do that to their children."

"I never ex- pected this"

Mrs. Blum gets tired, is depressed and very angry, and doesn't sleep well, but working is a great help to her. So far, the mother-in-law can stay alone for a few hours during the day, but "we are keeping our fingers crossed." Mrs. Blum is resentful because she has her mother-in-law to care for, particularly because her husband had never been very willing to help her parents, who needed very little. Mr. Blum is, however, trying to share his mother's care by taking her to the doctor and supervising her medications. Nursing home placement would be a last resort.

Work as respite

The Blums are again involved in many lives—not only because of the mother-in-law, but also because of the daughters who returned home. Mrs. Blum had thought that once her three children had finished college, it would be a time for herself and her husband. "Women have to be everything to everybody," she says. She adds wistfully that she likes to take courses and learn and had tried very hard to be independent. But women of her generation, she says, were not encouraged to be independent, but rather

Women have to be everything to everybody

to be appendages of their husbands. It has been a struggle for her to achieve some feeling of being her own person.

Different life styles

The life-styles of mother and daughter-in-law are very different. To the older woman, "You're not a woman unless you are married." She was interested only in home and family. Mrs. Blum always went to school, took courses, and wanted to work.

"I'm a woman of the '50s and we're living in the '80s. In my generation, the woman took care of the children, and you were the woman behind the man. You helped your husband in his work. But I got cabin fever. After I had my children, I just had to get out, and I went back to work. I was home when the children got home from school. The money helped to educate the children, to do special things, and to build up my social security. She feels that she and her husband have "paid their dues" by raising their children and so on. "That's life."

Blood is thicker than water

Mrs. Blum had given personal care to her own parents and would do it for her mother-in-law if it became necessary, but says she would be resentful. It would be a struggle. "Blood is thicker than water. We're friends, but we're not deep close buddies. Superficial."

Pulled between wife and mother

The Blums worry about the future, particularly if the mother-in-law should get worse. Mr. Blum feels the pressure, his wife says. It has caused some marital problems. There is a pull between his mother and his wife. Mrs. Blum's work has been affected. She calls home to see if the older woman is all right, but can't get a straight answer about what's going on.

Mrs. Blum says, "I see myself in her. That's what will happen to us if we live long enough." It is very painful to Mr. Blum to see his formerly strong mother age and decline. Mrs. Blum tries to escape the situation by going to her own room to read or by going out for a while. The whole family is trying hard. She hopes taking care of the elderly woman means that her husband will never have to feel guilty.

The story of my life

"Caregiving is the story of my life," Mrs. Blum says. "Maybe women have a nurturing instinct." She advises women in her situation to try to take time out for themselves. "Women of today understand that better than we did. We weren't allowed to have careers." She hopes research will help to do something about the plight of women.

Again, in the Blum situation, the theme of competition between mother-in-law and daughter-in-law is apparent. Mrs. Blum asserts her own control over the kitchen, but her husband stays with his mother after the wife goes to bed. Mr. Blum is another man in the middle.

The daughter-in-law describes the pull of different values in her life very clearly, and she contrasts herself with her mother-in-law. The older woman's whole life was household and children, whereas the younger woman had tried to educate and assert herself. Now 58 years old, Mrs. Blum was in her late 20s and 30s when the Women's Movement was gaining momentum. She is caught between the "old" traditional values and the new values about women's life styles. Though angry about it, she lives her life largely in conformance to the old values.

The Blums' situation also illustrates the predicament of many middle-generation couples nowadays whose nests have been refilled with their young adult children as well as with an elderly person.

Although the daughters-in-law in the situations described so far were articulate in expressing whatever anger, resentment, and upset they felt, the two women whose stories will be told below do not appear to protest their situations. These two women differ from the others, too, in that their husbands have siblings, but they are the main caregivers to their mothers-in-law nonetheless. The reasons for their assumption of that responsibility are very different, however.

"I'm Not Really Passive"

Trays to 3 elderly in-laws

"I've watched trays go up and down the steps to the third floor for 35 years," says Mr. Holden sadly while the interviewer is waiting to see his wife. Mrs. Holden is upstairs bringing a tray to her mother-in-law, age 95. When she comes down, Mrs. Holden describes her caregiving history in a matter of fact way. As a young couple, the Holdens moved into the parents-in-law's home with their 1-year-old baby. Mr. Holden's sister had recently married and moved out. Mr. Holden had been in the Navy during World War II, and when he was discharged he and his wife came home to help care for his disabled grandfather. Before the elderly man died, his grandmother had a bad stroke and needed care and was on the third floor for 3 years until her death. Then, Mrs. Holden's mother-in-law, the current recipient of the trays, became ill. For 2 years, she was in a coma from an undiagnosed illness, and her devoted daughter-in-law worked hard day and night to bring her back. A miracle happened. She had been "really out of it," and then she got her mind back.

A career in care-giving

Into and out of the labor force

During her caregiving career, Mrs. Holden gave birth to a second daughter. (Both are now married.) Over the years, Mrs. Holden moved into and out of the workforce (she is a stenotypist) as the care needs of the various family members dictated. She finally retired 2 years ago when her mother-in-law could not be left alone at all.

"No problems"

Mrs. Holden does not complain. "It all worked out well," she said several times. "We never lacked for a babysitter, and the old people enjoyed the children. No problems." Her mother-in-law is "great fun to be with," she says, though the older woman does get upset and nervous, and she's harder to take care of when she's not feeling well. Mr. Holden, who had been listening to the interview from another room, has another opinion. "She wants to be waited on hand and foot," he says of his mother.

It all works out

Mrs. Holden praised the help her husband gives her. He rigged up buzzers so that his wife could respond whenever his mother needed her. "It's real handy," Mrs. Holden said. She also praises her sister-in-law for keeping her mother supplied with books from the library. "She never ever forgets and brings the same one again," Mrs. Holden said admiringly.

I'm not passive

"I don't mean that I'm passive," Mrs. Holden repeats, "It all works out." She tells of a time when she asserted herself. She wanted to go to her own daughter who was having a baby, so her sister-in-law came to stay temporarily. But "things were a mess" when she returned.

The day after the interview, Mrs. Holden phoned the interviewer to emphasize the fact that she's not really passive.

Mrs. Holden, who is providing total care for her mother-in-law and had done so for two grandparents-in-law as well, is deeply appreciative of her husband's help in caring for his three elderly relatives. She tells herself and others "Its all worked out." Why, then, does she need to reiterate, "I'm not passive"?

The following case differs from the others in that Mrs. Parker is caring for two disabled people of different generations simultaneously—her son and her mother-in-law.

"I Have a 40-Year-Old Retarded Son and a 94-Year-Old Teenage Daughter"

A career of caregiving

Sixty-four-year-old Mrs. Parker has had a long caregiving career. Married for 45 years, she has cared for many people simultaneously and sequentially. For all of his life, she has taken care of her retarded son, who is now 40 years old. The Parkers also have a normal 30-year-old son who is now on his own. The retarded son goes to a day-time "workshop," but he cannot read or write. He requires direction to dress and bathe himself, and needs skin care and supervision of his diet.

A retarded son

Mother-in-law moved in

Twenty years ago, when her father-in-law died, Mrs. Parker's mother-in-law moved into the Parker home. The two grandsons had to share a room in order to accommodate her. In the past few years, the older woman has needed more care because of a variety of chronic and acute ailments. During the same period, Mr. Parker had several bad heart attacks, and his wife quit her job to

Husband has heart attacks

Work was

care for him. "It was too much," she says, "with three people to care for." She misses her job. "I could turn off things that happened in the house when I went to work. Now I can only turn off when I go to market."

A demanding mother-in-law

The elderly mother-in-law is very demanding and critical. "The emotional strain is the worst part of it," says Mrs. Parker. "After all, I married my husband, not my mother-in-law." Her mother-in-law doesn't hesitate to speak her mind. "She has a heart as big as an elephant and a mouth to match." The older woman complains about the house and the neighborhood. The family would like to move, but it would mean a year's waiting list for the son to get into a workshop in the new catchment area. The mother-in-law wants the family to have a fancier car, she complained bitterly because the dress she wore to a family wedding was not the most expensive one there, and her main worry is what to wear and how

A 94 year old teenager

she looks. "I have a 94-year-old teenage daughter," says Mrs. Parker. The older woman refuses all nonfamily services—even transportation. She came from an affluent and sophisticated family. Mrs. Parker stands in awe of that background as she herself came from an immigrant family.

One person does the most

The mother-in-law tries to control everything. "It's competition," says Mrs. Parker. "It's always been that way, but it was better when she could go out by herself and I was working. My husband shares that now that he's retired. His brothers take no responsibility. I guess it's that way in most families. One person does the most." Mrs. Parker says jokingly, "There's not much I can do except run away." She and her husband would like to take a short vacation, even a weekend, she says wistfully, but the

No vacation

mother-in-law would "sabotage" it. "Ten years ago, we had a 2-week vacation. My younger son was here at night, and my brother-in-law during the day. It was wonderful. But my mother-in-law wouldn't let it happen now. I guess I resent it. She has a lot of fears and is afraid to be left alone. She keeps us from going out."

Restricted lives

Mrs. Parker became caregiver to her mother-in-law, she says, because her husband had always assumed responsibility in his family, though he has two older brothers who are now in their 70s. Also, Mrs. Parker's own family was a close one and had a tradition of caring for older people in the home. She thinks her brothers-in-law should help more. The Parkers can't go out at night unless their younger son comes to stay or they take the older son and mother-in-law with them. Their social life is virtually nonexistent and their budget squeezed. As for privacy, Mrs. Parker asks, "What privacy?" She says sadly that her own father went to live in Senior Housing because she had no room for him. He would have been easier to have in the home than her mother-in-law is. "He wouldn't interfere."

Competition   Mr. Parker has always shared equally in caring for their son.
                  There was mutual support. But there are things he can't do for his
                  mother. He is often torn between his wife and mother, but takes
                  his wife's part when his mother is critical. "It's more stressful for
                  him," says his wife.

"It could be   Mrs. Parker tries to be philosophical. She wishes she could have a
worse"   little time for herself. Even a whole day. "I'm getting older, and I
                  have more responsibility than ever. But I know people worse off,"
                  she says, "I know single parents who have retarded children."

What will hap- "It's lucky we have a good marriage. This caregiving. That's my
pen to our son? life. I read. That's my outlet. But what would I do if my husband
                  should die before my mother-in-law? What will happen to our son
                  when we're not here?"

The poignancy of the Parkers' worry about the future of their son need
not be underlined, a worry shared by all such parents. Mrs. Parker's story
illustrates a situation that is growing more and more common as more
developmentally disabled people have been enabled to live longer lives. It is
not unusual nowadays, for example, to see elderly women even in their 80s
still caring for their "children." The prevalence of "double dependency"
situations such as that of the Parkers is not known, but a clue is provided in a
study done by Soldo and Myllyluoma (1983). They found that when an older
couple lived with others in caregiving households, approximately one in nine
of the caregivers provided assistance to two or more disabled persons, one of
whom is an elderly person and the other most often being an impaired adult
child of the older couple.

The Parkers' lives and experiences reflect many of the themes already
described: the caregiving careers many women have, the difficulties of
shared households, employment as respite for caregivers, the struggle for
control between the elderly woman and caregiver, the competition between
daughter-in-law and mother-in-law with the husband/son caught in the
middle, and the family's severe life-style restrictions.

The sadness of the Parkers' story is overwhelming. But surely, it could
be alleviated, if only a little, if they could obtain some respite and if
the mental health system permitted the family to move without having
the retarded son wait for a year in the new catchment areas until he could
attend the "workshop." An overarching question, of course, is why Mrs.
Parker permits her mother-in-law to control her life. The mother-in-law
doesn't let them go out, doesn't let them take a vacation, and refuses Senior Citizen's transportation. Mrs. Parker allows that to happen. Her only
respite is going to market; her only outlet is reading. She jokes about
running away, but continues on without even the day off for which she
longs.

"I Would Like to Be Able to Take a Walk"

"I was here"

At age 48, Mrs. De Lisi provides her 95-year-old mother-in-law with virtually total care. Mrs. De Lisi had moved into her parents-in-law's household as a bride. Her husband had fallen in love with her photograph, shown to him by a cousin, and went to Italy to marry her and bring her to the United States. The elderly woman's other sons and her daughter had already married and moved out of the parental home. The De Lisi's have three sons (young adults) still at home. Asked how it happened that she became the main caregiver, the daughter-in-law replied simply, "I was here."

A good marriage

Though the other siblings do nothing to help with caregiving, Mrs. De Lisi is uncomplaining. "I do not hold it against them." She voices no resentment and appears to accept her role as caregiver. It had never occurred to her to work outside the home. The De Lisis are devoted to one another. Mrs. De Lisi speaks of her husband lovingly and describes with appreciation his willing help around the house and with his mother's care.

This is the way it should be

This daughter-in-law does not make any effort to change her situation. "This is the way it should be. Its just something that you do." In her view, this is the role she should play. When asked directly, she admits to feeling very tired and having some emotional symptoms. She attributes her "nervous stomach" to the caregiving situation and says she gets hurt "real easily" when criticized by her unappreciative mother-in-law. She and her husband can't go out in the evening, but their friends visit them, and she has "a bunch of rain checks." The only time there is any respite is when they get a sitter for a truly important occasion such as when a son was graduated from college.

A nervous stomach

"I'd like to take a walk"

What would Mrs. De Lisi want for herself? She thinks for a minute and then says, "I would like to be able to take a walk once in a while." As for the future, she says wistfully that she'd like to visit her family in Italy.

A critical mother-in-law

Mrs. De Lisi thinks it might be easier to take care of her own mother. The mother-in-law is critical of her at times, and the older woman is very different with her own daughter. Mrs. De Lisi can't feel close to her mother-in-law though she had been close to her father-in-law before he died. "He was more modern." She feels her caregiving is made possible because she and her husband have such a loving relationship.

Mrs. De Lisi advises others in her situation to "have a ton of patience" and to "keep in mind that you'll get old someday, and you'll want someone to do for you what you did for her. They suffer so much to bring you up, you have to repay them. You never really can repay."

In Mrs. De Lisi's culture, sons (therefore, daughters-in-law) are often groomed to take the responsibility for parents. She does not protest. Women like Mrs. De Lisi probably will not disappear from the scene in the near future because of the large immigration into the United States of people from Asia and Hispanic countries who have similar values about women's roles and care of the elderly. Though accepting of her role, Mrs. De Lisi pays for her passivity with her "nervous stomach." Her low expectations of what she herself could do to fulfill her own needs epitomize the low expectations so many women hold: "I would like to be able to take a walk once in a while." The theme of repayment of care from one generation to another appears, but on the collective level—"You have to repay *them*"—rather than on the personal level, as with the daughters who say, "It's my turn to care for *her*."

A COMMENT ON DAUGHTERS-IN-LAW

In some ways, the "internals" of care for daughters-in-law resemble those that daughters experience. The two groups of women react to the pressure with similar emotional symptoms, and many strive to make the older people "happy." The women also have in common their awareness of their stages of life during the parent care years. Daughters-in-law as well as daughters (and their husbands) enact the "traditional" gender assignment of roles. And both groups are grateful to their husbands for any help they receive in caregiving. The daughters-in-law are appreciative even when the older person involved is the *husband's* mother.

The stress on women who care for their mothers-in-law (particularly when they live in the same households) appears to have several unique sources, however. The competition between the two women for the man they share may be minimal or fierce, but has potential for strain. Certainly, as the case studies have shown, the emotional ties to a mother have much deeper roots than the bonds to a mother-in-law, and there is a genetic link to a mother. Although daughters often feel that they should reciprocate the care their mothers gave to them in childhood (see Chapter 6), daughters-in-law have no such histories with their husbands' mothers. Some daughters-in-law, then, are deeply angry at finding themselves in the caregiving situations. And, given the fact that they provide care as a matter of obligation, they may also be harboring resentment against their husbands for expecting it of them. At the same time, some of them do it to earn their husbands' appreciation.

Some of the daughters-in-law whose stories appeared above express their anger, whereas some seem to accept their situations passively as "the way it should be." What is striking is that even the women who are explicitly angry provide care for their parents-in-law. They complain of their own severe problems, of the disruption of their marriages, life-styles, and personal ambitions, and comment that they are "dinosaurs." But they do it nonetheless. The women who responded to the research call for participants are, of course, the ones who did assume the caregiving role. Information is simply not available at present about daughters-in-law (and daughters, for that matter) who do not do so.

There is more than a hint in the stories of the daughters-in-law of the strains their husbands experience even though their wives do most of the parent-care work. The unexplored inner experiences of sons are part of the unfinished business of research about parent care.

Chapter 12

Commentary on the Case Studies

The themes described in Chapters 6, 7, and 8 were played out in the lives of the women who told their stories in the case studies. The full impact of the demographic changes was seen, as many of the daughters and daughters-in-law enacted long careers of caregiving to several older people in their families. Most suffered negative effects on their own well-being and put themselves at the bottom of their priority lists as they tried to meet the needs of all the people in their families. The women often articulated their sense that parent care was "off-time" in the lives—they were too young or too old, or had envisioned their middle years differently. Those whose nests had been emptied found those nests refilled with elderly parents, and sometimes refilled as well with their children who had grown, left the nest, but then came back to the parental home. Also illustrated were nests that contained both "young" and old because the caregiver had a developmentally disabled adult child. The compelling force exerted by the value that care of the elderly is a woman's responsibility often drove out the new values about women's roles. Some of the women, for example, even gave up their own opportunities and jobs that they needed or enjoyed when work and parent care competed. (This is discussed in detail in Chapter 13.)

Those and additional themes in the lives of parent-caring women were delineated by the case studies in Chapters 9, 10, and 11. It was apparent that older people themselves and other people in the family know intuitively and from experience who is accessible for the role of principal caregiver, whatever the reasons may be. (Listening to the inner experiences of those adult children who do *not* become caregivers is another item on the agenda of the unfinished business of parent care.) Potent influences in either producing strain or easing the situation for those caring women are the quality of their long-standing relationships with the dependent older person and the latter's personality. When the older person was appreciative, accepting of her care needs, and considerate of the caregiver and her family, the strains of the daughters and daughters-in-law were eased. But women went on providing the needed help even for parents or parents-in-law who were controlling and critical or with whom relationships were problematic historically. Some caregivers yielded when the older people refused to accept any help from other members of the family or from nonfamily sources. In such cases, the elderly parent or parent-in-law held the psychological "balance of power."

The impact of the caregiving situation on all members of the family was described graphically by the women. Their husbands, children, siblings, and even more distant relations affected and were affected by the caregiving process. Not only were the historical relationships between parent and daughter recapitulated and elaborated, but also those among siblings, and between the daughter and her own family members. The women showed the double pull between their own nuclear families on the one hand and the families of origin from which they had moved developmentally. In this, they were "in the middle" in still another sense of that phrase.

Ambivalence was one of the potent inner experiences of the women. They wanted to provide care for their parents and parents-in-law and to make them "happy," but often had strong negative feelings as well, which, in turn, made them feel guilty. Daughters had long-standing, enduring bonds with their parents, for example, but at the same time may have wished to be free of their crushing burdens. Ties between daughters-in-law and their elderly in-laws began later in the women's lives and the initial attitudes of their parents-in-law towards them when they first entered the family colored their feelings even many years later. Though the nature of the bonds was quite different from mother/daughters ties, positive and negative emotions existed side by side in daughters-in-law too—dislike and compassion, for example, and resentment and a sense of obligation.

The sense of obligation and duty took another form as well—that of reciprocity in parent care between husbands and wives. Some daughters caring for one of their own parents pointed out that they had helped their husbands' mothers in the past or might need to do so in the future. Similarly, some daughters-in-law felt that they were reciprocating for help to their parents that their husbands had given or would be expected to give in the future. Marital partners apparently see helping each other's parents as an unspoken part of the marriage contract.

A central and major theme that emerged clearly is the social support women have or that is lacking during their parent-care years. Some have rich networks of family members—husbands, children, grandchildren, siblings, and other relatives as well. At the other extreme are those who quite literally have no one—who are not married, who are childless, who are "only" children, and who have no other relatives.

Some of the problems and rewards women experience derive from the composition of their families. Those with many relatives often received much emotional and instrumental support; some also may have had a unique source of stress due to family conflict and a sense of inequity in caregiving. Women without husbands and children did not have the feeling that they were being pulled by competing responsibilities, but often felt lonely and alone, feelings that were especially intense when they were also without siblings.

Regardless of the quality of their relationships with siblings, women who do have sisters or brothers seem to have a sense of security about their parents. Such daughters do not ask, "Who will take care of my mother [or father] if something happens to me?" There may be severe problems in sibling relationships, or the siblings may be emotionally or geographically distant from the parent and virtually uninvolved in providing instrumental help, but at some level, the primary caregiver knows that if something should happen to her, her sibling(s) would not abandon the frail elderly parent.

In a similar vein, women who have children know that the latter would not abandon their grandparent(s). Indeed, even other relatives—aunts and uncles (the elderly siblings of the elderly parents), nieces, nephews, and children-in-law—behave with a sense of family responsibility when there is no adult child in the picture. The amount and type of help they would provide in the eventuality that "something" happened to the daughter probably would be much less extensive and intensive than that given by women in the middle, but they would see to it that the older person did not go without care. (The experiences of those relatives in care of the elderly is another item on the unfinished agenda of research into caregiving, however.)

When, in addition to the lack of potential caregivers for the elderly parent, the women are childless and therefore have no potential caregivers for themselves, still another theme appeared, "Who will take care of me when I am old?"

The challenge is to understand the problems unique to each family situation and to design appropriate interventions. The needs of the large, but conflicted family, for example, differ in many ways from the needs of daughters who are all alone.

At the least, the case studies justify two conclusions about family support in caring for the elderly. First, they bear out the implicit assumption daughters make that other family members will come forward to help if need be. The sense of family responsibility is powerful indeed and those relatives constitute a back-up system of care.

Second, there is no question but that parent-caring women *need* and *want* social support. Those who have family support are aware of their need and are deeply appreciative when it is forthcoming. Husbands head the list of those family supports. Those men are the ones closest to their wives' situations and the ones whose lives are most directly affected by the women's care of the elderly people. They are their wives' "stabilizers" or "balancing points," who actually help with care of their in-laws and to whom the women "can say anything." One cannot help but be impressed by the efforts and contributions of so many sons-in-law. (An intriguing side light of that support is the extra help those men are able to supply when they have retired from work.)

Also important are those siblings who understand the primary caregivers' efforts and problems, who phone and visit, provide some instrumental help and respite at times, and share important decisions. Still another source of social support comes from grandchildren who "sit" with their grandparents to let their parents go out occasionally, who take their grandparents to their homes for a weekend once in a while to give the caregiver respite or when there is illness in the family, who help with residential moves, and who are understanding about their mothers' problems.

The family supports of daughters-in-law include *their* husbands—the sons of the elderly people being cared for. The women are even grateful to those husbands for helping with care of the men's own parents. (Such is the depth of women's socialization to the nurturing role and the social, cultural, and religious values that exert powerful pressures in defining and keeping them in that role.)

The most poignant expression of the need for social support comes from the women who do not have it—who do not have anyone to meet that universal human need. Their deprivation is such that even a parent who cannot speak or whose Alzheimer's disease has progressed to the point that she doesn't recognize the daughter becomes a source of support. In the words of Lowenthal and Haven (1968), "the maintenance of closeness with another is the center of existence up to the very end of life" (p. 30).

Support of a different order comes from the "formal" system—the complex of organizations and agencies that provide entitlements for the older people and services designed to help them and their caregiving families. When they are available and are utilized, they ease the women's burdens. Unfortunately, however, as the case studies showed, obtaining entitlements is often confusing, even baffling. Services are not always available, available in timely fashion, or accessible, and not all caregivers know of their existence. Undoubtedly, readers were aware of instances in which supports were indicated—day care, respite service, home care, and others that should be available in a true long-term care system (see Chapter 15).

Even when services are available, there are barriers to utilization such as the caregivers' reluctance to use their own and the older people's financial resources until they "really need it" (perhaps when the time comes for nursing home placement), resistance to accepting "charity," not wanting to disclose income and be subjected to demeaning means testing, and poor quality services (Saperstein, in press). As one daughter noted, they may be too rich to be eligible for subsidized services and at the same time too poor to pay for the services themselves. Some cases illustrated the benefits of adapting the physical environment of the home that is the context of care, but for others there was an economic inability to do so (see Lawton, in press for a discussion of the physical environment.)

There are also psychological barriers to the use of services. In addition to deep-seated relationship problems between them and the parents that shape the ways in which the caregiving role is enacted, other barriers are the women's feelings that it is *their* responsibility alone to provide care (and society's reinforcement of this notion), that only they can provide good care, that people in their ethnic, racial, or religious group "take care of their own," and that the acceptance of help or nursing home placement of the older person is a loss of social status (see Brody et al., in press b; Saperstein, in press). Unfortunately, as the case studies showed, some professionals participate in reinforcing the women's reluctance to accept some relief.

In any case, when psychological barriers exist so that severe strains are incurred by caregivers and other family members, counselling is clearly indicated. There are many forms of such counselling that should be available—social case work, group programs, psychological and psychiatric therapy, and family therapy.

Surely, services must be developed and designed so as to reach and be used by women in the middle who need them regardless of their family status. An additional challenge, more difficult to accomplish, is to be creative in reaching out to caregivers who have no one. Although no bureaucratic orgainzation can sutstitute for the intimacy and comfort of having a close family member, ways must be found to give such women the sense that *somebody does care*. As one of them phrased it, "There aren't many of us, but we exist."

Part III

Special Situations

Chapter 13

Women, Work, and Parent Care

The influential trends that have combined to place so many women in the middle were described in Chapter 1—the demographic changes that vastly increased the need for parent care and changing values that resulted in radical changes in women's life-styles, particularly their large-scale entry into the work force. This chapter examines the reciprocal effects of those trends upon each other—specifically, the effects of women working on the care of their parents and parents-in-law, the differential effects parent-caring women experience when they work outside of the home and when they do not, and the actions women take when work and parent care compete. In addition, the response of the business community and social policy to the situation of parent caring employees will be noted. Though some of the case studies in Part II illustrated these matters, additional case excerpts are included here to sharpen the focus on the dilemmas faced by many working women.

WOMEN IN THE LABOR FORCE

Detailed data about the soaring rates of women's labor force participation appeared in Chapter 1. In brief, the proportion who work rose from 24% in 1930 to 70% in 1985, with the most rapid rate of increase being among middle-aged women. Undoubtedly, the Women's Movement and changes in attitudes about gender-appropriate roles were influential in producing such statistics, but other forces have been operating as well: the rising divorce rate sends many women to work, women have fewer children to keep them at home than did women in previous generations, the creation and accessibility of labor-saving devices for the home result in more free time, and increasing educational levels stimulate career interests. Not least, by any means, inflation and the rising cost of living compel many women to seek paid work, and many couples enjoy the higher standard of living accessible to the double-income family. Though career commitment and self-fulfillment account for many women working, the "pull" of employment for most is that the money is needed. Interestingly, among the factors predicting women's continued presence in the labor force is support of a child or an aged parent (Henretta & O'Rand, 1980). Reinforced by the "new" values about women's roles, work satisfaction and economic need together form a powerful motivational combination.

Whatever the reasons that so many women now work, many of them are also helping disabled parents. Thus, two major new roles—parent care and work—have been added to the multiple roles women play. Not all caregiving daughters and daughters-in-law are in the labor force, of course, and not all of those who work have parents or parents-in-law in need of their help. However, approximately 44% of daughters who are providing considerable help (that is, personal care) to their parent(s) are in the work force (Stone et al., 1987). Recent surveys by business firms estimate that at any given time, between 20% and 30% of all working people are helping a disabled older person, and most of those caregivers are daughters (Travelers, 1985; AARP, 1987). Such cross-sectional data do not reveal the number of working women who have had parent-care responsibilities in the past or who will do so in the future. Nor do they include women who may have left their jobs because of parent care.

Parenthetically, by contrast with the pattern of middle-aged women entering and reentering the workforce and working longer, more men are retiring earlier. The drop in men's labor force participation reflects the increasing availability of pensions and other benefits as well as the increasing acceptability of the idea that retirement is natural and has its own enjoyable life-style. Another factor operating may be that nowadays many women are at earlier points in their working lives when men are ready for retirement.

The relatively little attention that has been paid to the problems of middle-aged working women contrasts sharply with the considerable interest focused on young working women. Though concerns about young women who juggle work and family life are well-founded, middle-aged women also are subject to multiple pressures. The specifics of their situations are different, however. The need to provide parent care may arise when middle-aged and aging women—and their husbands—are experiencing age-related changes such as lower energy levels, the onset of chronic ailments, retirement, and interpersonal losses. Almost as many women age 55–64 as those 65 and over become widows each year, for example, and face the major adaptations entailed by that status (Nye & Berardo, 1973). A congressional report on *Midlife Women* (U.S. House of Representatives, 1979) emphasized the importance of the middle years as preparation for and prevention of severe problems in old age. It discussed problems such as widowhood, being a displaced homemaker, low income, and the need for educational and occupational opportunities for women between the ages of 45 and 64—a group projected to peak at approximately 36 million between 1990 and 2010.

Research interest in the work/parent-care interface began slowly a very few years ago but has been accelerating. Among the questions asked have been the following: Do adult daughters who work provide less parent care than daughters who are not in the labor force? What are the differential strains experienced by working and nonworking daughters? What actions do daughters take when parent care and work compete?

DO PARENTS OF WORKING DAUGHTERS GET LESS CARE?

Given the pivotal role of adult daughters in the informal support system, it was often assumed that women's parent-care activities are necessarily reduced when they are employed. Research findings were sparse, tentative, and sometimes contradictory, however. Overall, scattered reports indicated that working women continue to help their elderly family members while continuing to meet their responsibilities to families and jobs. Such daughters deal with their multiple responsibilities by maintaining rigid schedules, negotiating parent-care tasks around their work schedules, and giving up their own free time (Cantor, 1983; Horowitz et al., 1983; Lang & Brody, 1983). Being employed significantly decreases the hours of assistance provided by sons but does not have a significant impact on the hours of assistance provided by daughters (Stoller, 1983).

Predictors of caregiving involvement found to be more significant than the daughter's employment status are geographic proximity, the level of the parent's impairment, responsibilities other than work (such as being married), and sharing a household with the dependent elderly person (Horowitz, 1982; Lang & Brody, 1983). There are few significant differences between working and nonworking daughters in the types of tasks they perform for the elderly (Horowitz et al., 1983).

Sharing a household with an older person is not only associated with more caregiving (Lang & Brody, 1983) but deters labor-force participation for some people (Soldo & Myllyluoma, 1983). An analysis of a national data set (Soldo & Sharma, 1980) indicated that families with working wives were slightly more likely to purchase care in an institution than to provide it in their own homes. That report was focused on a special subpopulation, however, excluding both the preponderant number of instances of interhousehold caregiving and the 83% of institutionalized older people whose care is not financed by family contributions (U.S. Bureau of the Census, 1978).

In the PGC study* of the attitudes of three generations of women about women's roles and filial care (see Chapter 4), majorities of all generations agreed that it is better for a working woman to pay someone to care for her elderly parent than to leave her job to do so. Most of the women in all three generations stated that adult children should not adjust work schedules for parent care, but were more likely to expect working married daughters rather than working married sons to do so. Although the women were strongly in favor of sons and daughters providing equal amounts of parent care, in practice the daughters were doing virtually all of it. (Details of the study appear in Brody et al., 1983, 1984; Lang & Brody, 1983).

Research designed to compare working and nonworking daughters,** all of whom were helping a disabled mother, showed that older people whose caregiving daughters are employed do not receive fewer hours of service-provision from all sources than those whose daughters do not work (Brody & Schoonover, 1986). Families provided the vast majority of helping services, and the daughters were the ones in the family who provided most of that help even when employed.

In that study, the work status of the daughters was, however, associated with variations in the sources of some kinds of assistance. These variations occurred both in the apportionment of help among the various members of the informal network and in the overall balance between the informal and formal systems. Working daughters provided as much emotional support as their nonworking counterparts and somehow managed to do as much housework, laundry, transportation, grocery shopping, money management, and service arrangement for their mothers. However, when the daughters were in the labor force, the provision of help with personal care and meal preparation was more often shared by other providers. Notably, helpers paid by the family and, to a much lesser extent, the women's husbands and other family members, were more involved. For the most part, the services of the paid helpers offset the reduction in the hours of help provided by the daughters themselves.

It is obvious that daughters who are at the workplace are not at home to provide the kinds of help that require a daytime presence in the household. The fact that the working women in the study described were of higher socioeconomic status than the nonworking women may account in part for the larger amount of purchased care for their mothers. This supposition is supported by other reports to the effect that caregivers of lower socioeconomic status tend to provide more services themselves, whereas those of

*This research was financed by the Administration on Aging grant number 90-AR2174.
**This research was financed by NIMH grant number MH35252, "Women, Work, and Care of the Dependent Elderly." The case excerpts are drawn from qualitative interviews supported by the Frederick and Amelia Schimper Foundation of New York.

higher socioeconomic status tend to purchase more care (Archbold, 1983; Kinnear & Graycar, 1984; Noelker & Poulshock, 1982).

Such findings are consonant with women's personal preferences as to who various providers of services should be in their old age (see Chapter 4) (Brody et al., 1984). Personal care and household help are the kinds of tasks that most say they are willing to accept from nonfamily members. The forms of help that most women prefer their children (rather than other people) to provide are emotional support and financial management. Daughters, whether or not they work, provide the overwhelming majority of services with those very tasks—a level of assistance that is stable regardless of the daughter's work status. When formal services are utilized, most of them are purchased by the older person or family, with very few being subsidized by government or community agencies.

It is a common misconception that nonfamily services play a large role in the care of the disabled aged (Comptroller General, 1977). In fact, in the national 1982 Long-Term Care Survey, only 4.3% of the persons receiving help with ADL (an intense level of caregiving) received subsidized government assistance (Macken, undated). All formal services together accounted for less than 15% of all "helper days of care" in the community (including such services as home health, homemaker/chore services, and adult day-care programs) (Doty et al., 1985).

In short, it is apparent that the dependent elderly are not suffering neglect because of the increased work-force participation of the daughters who are their principal caregivers. Moreover, the concern that has been expressed to the effect that women's employment increases the taxpayer's burden by substituting subsidized community services for the women's own help to their parents is unfounded. Employed daughters continue to provide most of the help received by their dependent mothers. When it is necessary for them to reallocate some of the care to nonfamily providers, services are purchased rather than shifting the economic costs to the community.

STRAINS OF WORKING AND NONWORKING DAUGHTERS

Studies of caregivers that do not differentiate between those who work and those who do not are consistent in reporting that large proportions experience negative effects on their emotional well-being and on their family life-styles, and smaller proportions experience physical and economic strains (see Chapter 3). Workplace surveys identify similar strains and also confirm that the average duration of care is approximately 5–6 years (Travelers, 1985; AARP, 1987). Many families report that they have additional expenses (an average of $117 monthly in the AARP surveys) related to caring for an elderly person.

There are some differences in the patterns of strains that working and nonworking women attribute to parent care, however—differences that suggest somewhat different sources of strain for the two groups. In the PGC study (Kleban et al., 1989), interference with privacy was of relatively greater importance among nonworkers, especially in shared households. Shared living arrangements were associated with depression among non-workers but not among workers, even though the two groups contained equal proportions of families in such households. Severely impaired older people tend to live with families (Brody, S. et al., 1978), and those shared households predict larger amounts of care, as well as more caregiver strain than when the older person lives separately. But the depression of the working daughters in the PGC study did not relate strongly to shared living arrangements or to lack of privacy. This suggests that work itself offers respite from the caregiving situation and that some caregivers may require relief from sustained intrahousehold caregiving efforts. Depression among nonworkers was also associated with their dissatisfaction with the mother/ daughter relationship and to lower family income. Again, this implies a lack of relief from the ongoing caregiving situation as well as an economic inability to purchase help that would provide some respite.

Employed daughters' reports of depression and feelings of being upset related as well to their worries about meeting their mothers' future needs, and with the mothers' cognitive deficits and negative personality traits. It is understandable that cognitive deficits signaling dementia are a special source of concern when the caregiver is not at home to monitor the older person's behavior. For working daughters, such symptoms may be particu-larly distressing in that they augur increased caregiving demands and addi-tional changes in life-style, and raise questions as to the women's future ability to juggle their multiple responsibilities. The working daughters' emotional reactions suggest the uncertainty of being in such potentially transitional states, a supposition supported by their anxiety about the future.

Disagreements between women and their mothers about the amounts of help the latter required also related to the depressions reported by employed daughters. Such disagreements may stem from the fact that work responsibilities impose constraints on daughters' attentiveness to the older people, or create a dissonance between mothers and daughters in their expectations about the nature, extent, and timing of the help given. These factors may also cause the mothers' negative personality traits to appear more prominent in their daughters' perceptions and thus to produce ten-sion.

The findings of the PGC research should not obscure the fact that, whether or not they were in the labor force, a substantial proportion of the women studied did *not* report depression and other strains related to their caregiving roles. Nevertheless, the data offered a glimpse of the unique problems associated with the work status of parent-caring daughters. It is apparent that there must be concern not only about the effects of women's work on parent care, but also about the effects of parent care on women's work-force participation and on their well-being.

One finding in particular was a clue leading to the analysis that will be reported below and that is of major importance to parent-caring women. Specifically, depressions of some nonworking women were related to having given up their jobs to take care of their mothers.

WHEN WORK AND PARENT CARE COMPETE

Though it is well known that many women enter and leave the work force in response to family needs such as child care (Lopata & Norr, 1980), until recently there was virtually no information about such patterns in relation to parent care. The PGC study that compared working and nonworking women providing parent care found that 12% of the entire sample (28% of the nonworking women) had left the labor force in order to take care of their disabled mothers. In addition, 13% of the sample (26% of the working women) were considering quitting or had already reduced their work schedules for the same reason (Brody, 1985b; Brody et al., 1987a).

Results from the caregivers study of 1982 Long-Term Care Survey are consistent with the PGC findings about the effects of parent care on women's work force participation. In that national representative sample, 11.6% of all caregiving daughters had left their jobs to take care of an elderly parent and 23% of working daughters had reduced their working hours (Stone et al., 1987), proportions strikingly similar to those in the small, local PGC sample. In the Long-Term Care Survey, 35% of working daughters had rearranged their work schedules and 25% had taken time off without pay, again confirming the PGC findings.

Similar reports have emerged from British studies showing that the most common reason for women to quit jobs before retirement was to look after a sick relative (Rossiter & Wicks, 1982). Moreover, approximately one-fifth of female part-time workers worked part time for the same reason. Hunt (1978) found that among women between the ages of 40 and 59, the need to look after people other than their husbands was second only to ill health as a reason for giving up work (19% of women between the ages of 40 and 49, and 14% of those 50–59). (Only 1.5% of men aged 64 and under gave up work for that reason.) The same investigator reported that one working woman in eight was responsible for the care of at least one elderly or infirm person (Hunt, 1968). Land (1978) commented that daughters are more vulnerable than sons to potential conflict between work and parent care; sons are less likely to stop working for care for an elderly parent, having been socialized to work as their major role.

The PGC study offers the most complete information to date about the interaction between parent care and daughters' labor force participation. The sample was divided into four groups who were characterized as follows: In the *"quit-work" group* were the women who had left the labor force in order to take care of their mothers. A second group, the other nonworking women in the study, were called the *"traditional" women* because they were not working at the time they were interviewed and had not been working when the need for parent care arose. In the third group, called *"conflicted,"* were the working women who were considering quitting their jobs or who had already reduced their work schedules because of the mothers' needs for help. The fourth group, the *"persevering" women,* were so named because they were working and had not considered reducing their working hours or quitting their jobs.

The strong contrasts that were found among these four groups of women highlighted the differential interaction between socioeconomic trends and situational factors in the lives of daughters and their disabled mothers. They also point to potential conflicts in the values influencing women's decisions about parent-care and work force participation.

The women who had quit work and those who were working but were conflicted had the most severe parent-care problems, problems that resulted from work-related pressures in combination with time-extended processes of caring for a severely disabled parent. The women who had left their jobs had the oldest and the most disabled mothers (four-fifths of the mothers were over 80 and 25% were 90 or over), had been helping the longest, and were the most likely to have their mothers living in their households. Relative to the other two groups, more of the women in the quit-work and conflicted groups reported problems and life-style disruptions, and they were more likely to be their mothers' sole helpers. Similar findings have since been reported by another study (Enright & Friss, 1987) in that caregivers who had quit their jobs and part-time workers experienced the most stress and spent more time giving care to relatives who had the most severe behavioral problems.

Socioeconomic status and values also appeared to play roles in the decisions the women in the PGC study made when parent care and work competed. The women who had left their jobs had less education and lower family incomes (40% under $15,000 a year) than any of the daughters in the other groups, and their mothers received the least paid help. They had held jobs of lower status than the two groups of women who were still in the labor force. In addition, the non-working women more often thought of their previous employment as "just a job" rather than as part of a career and held less egalitarian views of women's roles than did either group of working women.

Although many women in all four groups reported competing demands and difficulties in setting priorities, it was the conflicted working women who allow us to see the competition between parent care and work through their eyes. The pull was strong between their feelings of obligation to take care of their parents and their new views of women's roles (Brody, 1981). For example, they had been helping almost as long and reported strain comparable to that of the women who had quit work; furthermore, they experienced the most interference with time for themselves and with their husbands. They held the highest level jobs, were the most career-oriented, and had the highest family incomes, and their new views about women's roles were similar to those of the persevering working women. Although the mothers of these conflicted workers received the most paid help, these daughters were the ones who most often felt tied down and that they had missed out on something. They also reported more negative effects on their occupational activities than the other working women.

The "persevering" workers and the traditional nonworking women appeared to be faring relatively better. The former reported the best health status, felt more in control of their own lives, and had the most capable mothers. The traditional nonworkers, whose views about women's role were less egalitarian than those of either group of working women, reported the least strain. Nonetheless, those traditional women and the women who had quit (that is, the two groups of nonworking women) had poorer mental health than both groups of working women—again suggesting that being employed offers some beneficial respite from parent care.

Taken together, the findings of the PGC study suggested that many of the women who had quit their jobs had worked because they and their families needed the money they earned. Whatever processes were involved in their decisions to leave the work force, their family incomes were much lower than those of the other groups of women. As one reviewer (Allen, 1983) of British studies has pointed out, women do not work for pin money now. It is obvious that the juggling of multiple responsibilities and role overload are not the exclusive province of career women.

These women describe the pressures of having "two jobs" that precipitated their decisions to leave the work force:

> I didn't want to juggle two jobs anymore. I wanted to pick one job over the other. If mother wasn't living with us I would have picked work. But I really didn't have much choice. I would return to work if I had the means to care for my mother. I would love to return to work.

> * * *

> I began to worry about mother at work when she began to do dangerous things. When she became irrational, I decided to quit. But I had enjoyed my career.

* * *

When we first noticed the change in mother, it was very stressful working full-time and going back and forth. I told my husband I couldn't handle everything, so I went part-time. It was no big deal. I didn't feel I was forced into it. It was the last straw. I was glad to be away from the pressure.

* * *

The job was a lot of fun for me because it was intellectually very demanding. But it got to be a strain because I was torn with the home situation. So I quit.

* * *

When my Mom fell and broke her hip I had trouble coping. I considered quitting. Then she fell and broke her arm. The doctor said don't be shocked if she falls again. At that point, I realized I probably wouldn't be able to work again so I told my boss to find somebody else. But I loved the work and felt great there, and my boss and I had a wonderful relationship. I miss the interplay between people and the stimulation.

* * *

I was working when my mother moved in with us. Then it got to the point where I couldn't handle it, and she couldn't handle it. I had to be here. It was emotional strain and stress. When I quit my job, I missed the people.

* * *

After she lived with me, I would come home and find the water running. It wasn't a hard decision to quit. I don't know how I'd feel if I was making big money.

Some women worked part time rather than full time because of parent care:

Mom started being picked up by the police, and we had to move her in here with us. I went part-time in my job. I couldn't handle everything. If it hadn't been for Mom, I would have stayed full-time. Before I thought of my work as a career. Now it's just a job.

* * *

My boss said I had to work full time if he promoted me, but I couldn't. I had to have the time to take care of Mom.

Other working women left their jobs because they could not afford to purchase services for their mothers:

I hired a girl to come in while I went to work. She ended up with more money than I made.

* * *

There wasn't enough finances to hire people to do the things my husband and I did for Mother.

* * *

I never considered using paid help because I couldn't afford it. It never crossed our minds.

Purchased services or help from other family members often did not help enough:

The nurse's aide was some help but you still have a lot—meals, laundry, etc. But that's only a few days. You still have the rest of the week and the weekend. You begin to wear down.

* * *

My husband took off from work early to pick Mom up at day care. He used his vacation time. But you can't keep that up forever.

The attitudes of the elderly mothers towards paid help also influenced daughters' decisions to leave their jobs:

Mother resents paid help.

* * *

Having paid help would be an admission of dependency to Mother. She would have objected terribly.

* * *

Mother needed someone to live with her, but she was not cooperative.

* * *

My mother wouldn't like paid help. She is used to being catered to and taken care of. When push comes to shove, it's not a thing she will be pleasant about.

Needing the money earned at work is a reason that some daughters work despite the demands of parent care:

I have to work because my husband was killed in an auto accident and I have two children to support.

* * *

I went back to work so my oldest child could go to private school.

* * *

I've considered changing my schedule since my mother's stroke. I don't know if going part-time will affect my retirement benefits. I've also thought of giving up work altogether till mother dies. I don't know if emotionally I could handle that. You have to be a financial wizard to figure out what the best deal is.

* * *

I had to go to work to pay for my mother's insulin and diabetic diet. My husband said I had to or we'd lose the house.

The daughters often spoke to the value of work as respite:

Sometimes my work had really helped me to cope. Other times, it's just been another thing on my mind. But sometimes it has helped me to forget things. You become all absorbed with what you're doing at work and forget the personal things in your life.

* * *

When my mother's condition began to deteriorate, I never considered reducing my hours or quitting my job. I needed to get out—it saved me.

* * *

When I'm at work, I usually blank out what's going on at home.

Work is important to women for other reasons:

I'm not the kind of person who wants a super-career. At the same time, work is important to me. I feel I contribute and make a difference.

* * *

I wanted to be a doctor from the time I was 8 years old. What I do is important to me and to my patients. I'm having trouble juggling things, but fortunately I can afford help at home.

* * *

My mother had a stroke just as I was about to be made a partner in the firm. I never considered quitting. Help is hard to get, and there are always emergencies. I stop in to see her every day and to see to it that she's okay. I'd be too resentful if I quit. And I'm not the nurse type.

Even when women are true "career" women, never consider giving up their work, and can afford to hire as much nonfamily help as is necessary, they say the juggling of priorities is a strain. As one such woman put it, her parent-care responsibility is "a constant presence in my life."

A major theme apparent in the case excerpts is that *work is important to the women*, though it has different meanings for different women. Although some feel relief at resolving the conflict between work and parent care by leaving the workforce or reducing their work time, most of those who did so were regretful. They missed the people and the activity on the jobs they held, were wistful in recalling the gratification they received from working, and felt badly about having to forego promotions and further their personal development. Women derive benefits from feeling they are making a contribution in their jobs and that what they do is important.

Among the compelling factors when women quit their jobs were financial barriers to purchasing nonfamily care or to purchasing enough such help. At the same time, some women entered the work force or held onto their jobs because they need the money they earn. Some daughters acceded to their elderly parents' refusal to accept nonfamily help; accordingly, they left their jobs, putting the elderly person's wishes above their own. Financial worries accompanied decisions to quit in some instances, since those decisions meant they would have lower retirement benefits.

On balance, there appeared to be an undercurrent of sadness among the women who gave up their work. Whatever values or situational factors were operating, many of them had given up something they valued and that was important to their self-esteem. Again, it is apparent that for such women, the old values about parent care being *their* responsibility had not been driven out by "new" values concerning women's roles.

The limitations of cross-sectional studies were illustrated again by the PGC study. Because the women who had quit work were interviewed after they had left their jobs, it is not known whether doing so had relieved, intensified, or otherwise changed the nature of the pressures they experienced. Nor can it be assumed that the women had made their definitive decisions. As the capacities of the mothers decline over time, their daughters may experience more pressure and may choose other options concerning both work status and the care of their mothers. Some of them may decide to stop work, and some may decide to return to work or to redistribute parent-care responsibilities in a different manner. Indeed, within 2 years after they had been interviewed, one-fourth of all the women in the study had changed their work status. Some of the nonworkers had entered or reentered the work force, most because they needed the respite from parent care that work provided or because they needed the money. And some of the working women had increased or decreased their working hours, or were no longer working.

Although studies of the shifts in women's roles generally have been focused on the earlier stages of the life-course, it has become apparent that a process of role change also occurs in response to the needs of disabled elderly people in the family. Obviously, patterns of parent care, work, and other role performance must be viewed as long-term processes about which information can best be gathered by longitudinal studies. As yet, we have no data about this extraordinarily diverse and complex mosaic depicting responses to parent care over the individual and family life-course. Little is known about the processes by which different options are selected— processes that have profound implications for practice approaches and social policy, and for employers as well. And little is known about other options chosen such as nursing home placement of the parent or the redistribution of care in other ways along the informal and formal support systems.

Given the increasing diversity in women's life courses (Lopata & Norr, 1980), we do not know what choices will be made by future cohorts of women as they move into the parent-care years, nor is it known how the old behavioral borders that have been measured by research will respond to life-style changes, to possible changes in family structure and size, to economic changes, or to changes in mobility patterns, for example.

Moreover, it cannot be assumed that differential socialization of men and women will be a constant. In the main, the cohorts of middle-generation daughters studied in the 1980s were socialized to being wife, mother, and homemaker. But as Lopata and Norr (1980) have pointed out, it is no longer accurate to speak of women's "typical" work cycle or life course, given the increasing diversity in the patterns of women's lives. Accordingly, future cohorts of caregivers may make different decisions.

There are hints, however, that women who are more highly educated and more committed to careers will tend more than others to continue in the labor force. A similar pattern is being observed among today's young women in that higher rates of labor-force participation among women with newborn children are reported by more highly educated women. Sixty-three percent of women who had a birth in the last year and who had 4 or more years of college were working in 1987, as compared with 38% of those who had less than 12 years of schooling (U.S. Department of Commerce, 1982b).

A major task that lies ahead is to sort out the various kinds of help needed by different types of families. Not only do different women and families require somewhat different consellations of helping services, but their needs may change at different times in the time-extended process of caregiving. For example, money may be a most useful form of help to families of women who quit their jobs and whose family incomes are low. Their service needs may be quite unlike those of families with better educated and better paid working women who have a strong career commitment (a group that is increasing). Flex-time, job-sharing, and parent-care sabbaticals might be of help to women who opt to adjust their work schedules or to take time off for parent care.

There is ample evidence that many parent-caring daughters need help in the form of services, whether or not they work. Apparently, nonworking women who are providing "heavy" care over long periods of time need respite, whereas help to mitigate the strain of competing demands is more apparent for working women. Services and economic help should be available for those who wish to work or need to do so for economic reasons *and* to help nonworkers so that they are not trapped in unrelieved caregiving and economic deprivation. The multiple responsibilities of both groups are obvious sources of strain. As accompaniments to these situational factors, the mental health symptoms and relationship problems they report point strongly to the need for counselling as well as supportive instrumental services.

Government data estimate that caregivers provide an average of approximately $5,000 in in-kind services (calculated at the rate of the minimum wage) (Doty, 1986). But virtually nothing is known about the opportunity costs incurred by some women. That is, definitive data are lacking about how much income is lost by caregivers who quit their jobs, reduce their working hours, are prevented from taking better jobs, or who retire early as a consequence of elder care. There is some suggestive information, however. In one study, caregivers who were deterred from working because of caregiving estimated their lost earnings at an average of $20,400 annually (Enright & Friss, 1987).

EMPLOYERS AND SOCIAL POLICY

Considerable activity has been generated in the business community as it has become aware of the situation of employed caregivers. An article titled "Elder care: the employee benefit of the 1990s?" (Friedman, 1986) appeared in *Across the Board,* the publication of the influential Conference Board. It called elder care a "bottom-line business concern." Based on surveys of their employees, some companies were reporting problems such as absenteeism, lateness, the use of unscheduled days off, excessive phone use by employees and negative effects on their work, excessive stress and physical complaints, and a decrease in productivity and the quality of work. The article suggested that high-level executives are likely to endorse dependent-care benefits (everything from counseling to subsidies), since senior-level decision makers are more likely to be caring for elderly parents than for preschoolers and that solutions may follow for others throughout the organization.

Although most work-place studies find that approximately one-third of working caregivers are at the professional or managerial level, another group was profiled by Enright and Friss (1987)—the "9 to 5ers", whom they call "the backbone of American enterprise":

> She holds onto her 40-hour-a-week job as long as she can because her family depends on the income. As the patient's condition worsens, she loses time from

work and increases her level of stress as competing demands take their toll. Eventually she has to reduce her hours and her salary. She does not quit until she has to, but may have to change jobs. (p. 3)

Some of the potential "solutions" listed in the Conference Board publication were company programs of information and referral, education of managers to the problem, provision of respite care, grants to local service agencies, flex-time and sabbaticals, and adult day care. Particularly intriguing in terms of public policy was a paragraph headed "Using Business Clout":

If companies were familiar with the shortcoming in Government insurance and entitlement programs, they might consider using the resources of their public-affairs offices to advocate policy changes. Companies might also join coalitions concerned with the aged to secure needed benefits and protection from the Government. "At a minimum," says one executive, "governments could be most helpful to business if they would change their business hours so that employees don't have to make all those phone calls at the office trying to arrange for insurance and the like." (p. 51)

Though the issue of caregiving employees has captured the attention of the business community, it is not likely that its activities to alleviate the situation are widespread. A February 1987 article in a newsletter published by The Center for Corporate Community Relations pointed out that most companies are hardly aware of the problem (*Community Relations Letter,* 1987) and that employees who quit or adjust their work hours are likely to be experienced, well-trained workers who are difficult and expensive to replace. It commented that companies' concern for eldercare speaks both to social responsibility and to good business practice.

Some firms are taking a variety of other steps such as evaluating elder day care as an employee benefit; surveying employees and planning to test support programs (such as a telephone line to the local Center on Aging, on-site support groups, and respite care); caregiving fairs to inform employees about community services; referral services to connect employees with resources; and lunch-time seminars. A few companies are giving grants to local service agencies and to universities and nonprofit agencies for studies, and a few offer flexible benefits programs.

Not all approaches are sympathetic, however. In one published article, the personnel manager of a large firm was interviewed and gave advice to these burdened women on "what to tell your boss." She suggested that they talk to their supervisors and offer to make up for time out of the office ("You can take work home, stay late some evenings, skip lunch, or come in on a weekend"), keep day-time phone calls to a minimum, arrange for a 4-day week, and ask for counselling (Miller, 1987).

There is also an undercurrent of concern because some firms are wondering whether to employ such workers at all. Apart from humanistic considerations, such an approach simply does not seem feasible from a practical standpoint. The problem of working while helping an elderly family member potentially affects virtually the entire work force. It is inevitable that many employees who are not helping an elderly family member today will be doing so tomorrow or next year. The employee helping an older person with shopping right now may need to provide bathing, feeding, and dressing as time goes on. Help to disabled older people is given by their spouses and sons as well as daughters and even by other relatives. In fact, some sons-in-law lose time from work, rearrange their work schedules, and experience strain when their wives are the caregivers (see Chapter 9). And workers at all levels are affected, from office cleaners and maintenance people to corporation presidents and Chairpersons of the Board. Elder care is one more problem that has been added to the list of employees' personal problems that affect their work lives. It has joined child care, care of the developmentally disabled, worries about divorces, mental and physical illnesses, and substance abuse on the inventory of problems to which we all are vulnerable and that are part of the human condition.

Many of the services needed by working caregivers are the same ones needed by all caregivers and that would be provided by a good program of federal long-term care insurance (see Chapter 15). There are also, however, some social policies that could focus specifically on the work/elder care problems to which the United States has made virtually no response. The United States is one of the few industrialized nations that does not provide an attendance allowance. Some countries provide benefits such as social security credits for the years that caregivers remain at home, pensions to those who have taken care of an elderly or disabled person, and shorter working hours for caregiving wage earners (Gibson, 1984).

There has been little activity on the part of those most directly affected—the employees themselves. Although some avail themselves of the referral services and support groups provided by employers, there have been no organized attempts to ask for things similar to those wanted by employees involved in child care—flex-time, sabbaticals, day care, and job-sharing, for example.

Alleviating the problems of caregivers who work, no matter their gender, relationship to the disabled person, or the level of their jobs, requires a multifaceted approach. It requires the collaborative efforts of employers, policy-makers, practitioners, and employees themselves.

Chapter 14

Most Painful Decision of All: Nursing Home Placement

Placing a parent in a nursing home is often described by adult children as the most painful decision they ever had to make, even as the worst moment in their lives. In fact, institutionalization of a parent has been termed "a nadir of life" (Cath, 1972). The harshest realities that make such placement unavoidable do not alleviate children's distressing emotions such as feelings of guilt, depression, worry, sadness, and failure at needing to take that step (Brody, 1977).

As the previous chapters have shown, considerable attention has been paid to the effects on the well-being of families when they care for the noninstitutionalized aged. That interest has not been matched by concern with the effects on families of deciding to move an elderly family member into a long-term care facility and having that person live there. This, despite the fact that the well-being of older people and their family members continues to be interlocked no matter where they reside, each affecting the other in reciprocal fashion (Brody, 1985a; Brody & Contributors, 1974).

The notion that older people are dumped into nursing homes by uncaring family members is the most virulent expression of the myth that children nowadays do not care for their elderly parents as was done in the "good old days." In addition, it is widely assumed that once such placement is made, children turn their backs to their parents and are relieved of responsibility and of the stress they have endured. Indeed, the myth assumes that this is the very reason for the placement. To the contrary, adult children continue to be vitally interested in their parents, behave accordingly, and may experience a whole new set of strains.

This chapter describes the extent of the need for nursing home care, the growth in the number of nursing home beds, and the characteristics of institutionalized older people. Caregiving daughters will then be followed through the process of placement: their feelings about nursing home care prior to the parent's admission, the decision-making process, and the effects they experience during the parent's residence in a nursing home. The literature on these matters is reviewed, and case excerpts illustrate the steps in the journeys. The question will be answered: Does nursing home placement of a parent release daughters from the position of being in the middle of competing demands and reduce the strains they experience?

NEED FOR NURSING HOME CARE

The effects on adult children of having an institutionalized parent is of particular importance in the context of demographic projections. The most rapid increase in the elderly population will continue to be among the very old, who are most vulnerable to the chronic disabling ailments that characterize nursing home residents.

At any given time, less than 5% of all older people are in nursing homes. A longitudinal perspective presents a different picture, however. Approximately 9% of the aged spend some time in a nursing home in the course of a given year, and between 23% and 38% of people 65 and over will spend some time in such a facility before they die (Liu & Palesch, 1981; U.S. Department of Commerce, Bureau of the Census, 1982a).

Though nursing home care is generally thought to be a permanent plan, long-stay residents constitute only one of several different populations in those facilities. Three other groups are those who are admitted for relatively short stays (that is, for less than 90 days): those who are admitted for rehabilitation or convalescence, subsequently returning to the community; those who are admitted for terminal care; and those who are discharged to a general hospital. Those three groups constitute about half of the nursing home population at any given time (NCHSR, 1989). Of those discharged alive, approximately one-third go to their own homes or the homes of relatives and two-thirds go to another health facility (most to a hospital, and some to another nursing home or mental facility).

The overall picture, then, is one of considerable movement of older people, who not only move back and forth between community and hospital, but circulate among institutions of various types. Many moves may be made before they become permanent residents of long-stay facilities and eventually die there or are moved back to a hospital for terminal care.

This constant movement has major implications not only for the repeatedly relocated elderly, but for their families. Family caregivers, too, are subjected to the attendant disruption, disorganization, frustration, and emotional strains that are overlaid on their concern and upset about their older family members. The effects on those family members when the older person is a long-stay nursing home resident should be seen against that background.

There is consensus that the *number* of older people in need of long-term care will continue to increase for at least the next two decades; the *proportion* may not increase, however (Brody, S., 1985; Fries, 1984; Schneider & Brody, 1983). One possible scenario is that the nursing home population is expected to increase 80% to 2.2 million people by the year 2000. Barring major biomedical breakthroughs, it may more than triple (to 5.4 million) over the next 50 years (U.S. Department of Commerce, Bureau of Census, 1982a). In the future, then, growing numbers of adult children may have parents in long-term care facilities. Another possibility is that dramatic scientific discoveries to prevent or cure one or more of the major disabling ailments—Alzheimer's disease, for example—will cause a sharp drop in the nursing home population.

GROWTH IN NURSING HOMES

The existence of a large number of nursing homes, which now contain approximately 4.6% of all older people, is a relatively recent phenomenon. In 1939, the Bureau of the Census estimated 25,000 nursing home beds in the United States in approximately 1,200 homes; by 1954, there were approximately 450,000 beds, and by 1970 almost a million. By 1973, there were 1,075,800 residents (almost 1.2 million beds) in 15,033 nursing homes (U.S. NCHS, 1975), and by 1977 there was an increase to 18,300 nursing homes containing a total of 1,287,400 residents (1,383,600 beds), of whom 1,097,900 were 65 or over (U.S. NCHS, 1978, 1973). It is important to note that between 1973 and 1977, while the aged population was growing older, the *proportion* of the total elderly population remained the same despite the 20% increase in the total *number* of older people in nursing homes. The leveling off process continued so that in 1985 there were approximately 1,315,800 people in nursing homes (U.S. NCHS, 1985), of whom 20% were under 65 years of age.

The major factor accounting for the increase in nursing home beds was, of course, the rapid increase in the number of vulnerable older people who reach advanced old age and, in addition, the use of nursing home beds for retarded persons under 65 years of age. The rise in the number of nursing homes was made possible by developments such as federal programs making funds available to purchase long-term care (Old Age, Survivors, and Disability Insurance; Kerr-Mills; Medicare and Medicaid). Perhaps even more importantly, there were also federal grants and loans enabling sponsors to construct, equip, and rehabilitate facilities [for example, Hill-Burton Act,

Small Business Act and Small Business Investment Act (1958), and National Housing Act (1959)].

Large-scale programs to discharge elderly mental patients from state hospitals to the community, spurred by the Mental Health and Retardation Acts of 1963 and 1965, also played a major role in the growth of the nursing home population. That is, institutional beds were redistributed among facilities that are under different auspices, with the major drop being in state psychiatric facilities and the major rise being in proprietary homes. Voluntary homes for the aged remained relatively stable in the proportion of all beds they contain.

CHARACTERISTICS OF OLDER PEOPLE IN NURSING HOMES

The characteristics of older people in nursing homes indicate some of the reasons they have entered those facilities. Comparing them with noninstitutionalized elderly reveals that the two populations are very different:

- Aged people in nursing homes are in advanced old age. They have a median age of 81, in contrast to approximately 72 for the total 65 and over population. The chances of being in a nursing home rise steadily with age from approximately 1% of those who are 65–74, to 6% of those 75–79, and to approximately 22% of people 85 and over (U.S. NCHS, 1985). More than four out of five residents are 75 or over, compared with approximately 36% of nonresidents.
- Most nursing home residents do not have a spouse. Only 16.4% are married, compared with 53% of all older people. Most are widowed (64%), and some had never married (about 13%), or are divorced or separated (6%) (U.S. NCHS, 1985).
- Women predominate in nursing homes. Almost three-fourths of residents are women, compared with approximately three out of five of all older people. One factor contributing to the overrepresentation of women is their longer life-span, which makes them more vulnerable to the social, physical, and mental disabilities associated with advanced old age. Another factor is the tendency of men to marry women younger than themselves. Thus, a disabled elderly man is more likely to have a "young" wife to provide care for him, whereas a disabled elderly woman is likely to be widowed. The net result is that the ratio of women to men is 283 per 100 in nursing homes compared with, 140 to 100 in the total aged population.
- Nursing home residents are markedly more disabled mentally and

physically than older people in general. The salient fact about their multiple problems is that they are chronic and result in *functional disability*, leading to dependence on others to help them in day-to-day living. Half are severely disabled, having five or six deficiences in ADL such as bathing, dressing, toileting, eating and transferring; another 25% have three or four such deficiences. These proportions are immense when residents are compared with the noninstitutionalized older people. Most residents have some kind of mental problem; a minimum of 62% have Alzheimer's disease or a related disorder, compared with approximately 7% of the total elderly population (U.S. NCHS, 1985). Depression is also a prevalent problem among long-stay residents. One recent careful study found that approximately 17% of residents of a large facility suffered from major depression and another 40% from minor depression (some of both groups were cognitively impaired as well, but those whose impairment precluded responses were excluded from the study) (Parmelee et al., 1989).

Most relevant to the concerns of this book is the family status of elderly nursing home residents. As indicated above, the vast majority do not have a spouse to care for them. Approximately 63% of all residents have living children, compared with approximately four out of five of all older people, and more of those in institutions have only one child rather than two or more. Childless women at any age have higher rates of institutionalization than their counterparts with children; women with the largest families have about half the rate of institutionalization of childless women of the same age (Soldo & Myers, 1976). The analysis of Soldo and Myers (1976) found that each additional child decreases the probability of being institutionalized in one's old age. In fact, one of the contributants to the increase of the number of residents in recent years has been the smaller number of children available to older people because of the falling birth rate (Crystal, 1982). The absence of at least one daughter in the family may indicate a greater risk of institutionalization at a lower level of disability, underlining the role of daughters (Soldo, 1982b).

Thus, social support in the form of family is a critical factor in avoiding nursing home placement. The sheer existence of family does not invariably preclude such placement, of course. Other considerations operate as well, such as the characteristics of the family members themselves. People in advanced old age are likely to have children who themselves are approaching or already in the aging phase of life. Institutionalization of a parent is often precipitated by deaths or incapacities among the caregiving adult children (Brody, 1966a). Thus, that proportion of increased institutionalization that is attributed to the increase in the very old is due not only to the functional incapacities that accompany advanced old age but to the absence of said supports and social losses that are age-related. In that light, the trends described in Chapter 1 hold the potential for increasing rates of nursing home placement—specifically, the continuing fall in the birth rate and increasing geographic mobility.

HOW CAREGIVERS VIEW NURSING HOME PLACEMENT

Though most adult children want to continue home care for their parents, their capacities to provide help to severely disabled people are qualified by their own age-related problems such as the appearance of chronic disabilities, lowered energy levels, interpersonal losses, retirement, and lowered income. They and children who are younger may have other limitations such as competing responsibilities to other family members and employment. In the overwhelming majority of cases, however, nursing home placement occurs only after caregivers have endured prolonged, unrelenting strain (often for years) and can no longer continue their efforts.

More subtle factors also are at work. There often is an accumulation or clustering of stresses. The older person's personality, the quality of family relationships, the capacity of individual and family to tolerate stress and their coping abilities, and socioeconomic factors play their roles (Brody, 1969; Brody & Gummer, 1967). Geographic distance of children makes the older person more vulnerable to institutionalization (Townsend, 1965).

In short, there is no one "reason" for institutionalization; it is multiply determined. But the accumulated evidence is definitive: admissions are due to varied social/health problems, and nursing home care is a social/health solution for which in most instances there is no other option.

Caregivers who are providing home care for their parents or parents-in-law almost invariably express deep aversion to nursing home placement, even when they are far along the path and are experiencing severe strains. They say "I can't throw her away," "I can't warehouse her," and "I don't want to give her away." Subjectively, surrendering the parent's care to others is experienced as a total abdication of their own responsibility. They see admission as a dreaded, ultimate solution to be used only if they no longer have the capacity to provide the care needed. When the parent has Alzheimer's disease or a related disorder, most caregiving daughters and other relatives indicate that they would place the parent only when the latter no longer recognizes them—when, in effect, the person they knew and with whom they had a relationship is no longer there.

The following excerpts from interviews with caregiving daughters illustrates their feelings about the prospect of nursing home placement. Their mothers' attitudes and those of other family members are also apparent.

It's a rule of the house, we don't talk about going into nursing homes. My feelings are based on her [the mother's] feelings. This is the one thing in her life that she's been terrified of. All of her life. Her condition would have to deteriorate or have to be pretty bad.

* * *

I hope I never have to do that [nursing home placement]. I really do. If it was absolutely to the point where she became totally senile then and it was a danger then it would have to be done. I'd do almost anything before that. Unless there was a danger somewhere—if I worried about her wandering the streets. I would have her move in here if her situation deteriorated.

* * *

My mother is with me, and this is her home. I felt like I was taking her out of her home. I think if my mother had been living in her own apartment, I would have told her that she couldn't live alone anymore and she should go into a home. But she was with me so to her there was no reason why. Mother wavered in those conflicting emotional feelings that she is hemming me in, that she's done this to me and my husband. But at the same time, she couldn't face going into a home. I don't know about the future; who knows how much longer I can take it.

* * *

I would only consider putting my mother into an institution if she became a vegetable and I couldn't physically take care of her. Otherwise, I would never put her into an institution, I couldn't do that. My father was very sick and I cared for him in my home till he died. My emotions wouldn't let me put them in an institution.

* * *

I visited one home with my mother. She got very upset. I felt such a crunch.

* * *

My mother is depressed and angry about the possibility of going into a nursing home.

Some daughters recognize that the need for placement may be inevitable and try to face that prospect.

I've always told her that I'll keep her as long as I can. I never promised we'd keep her forever. She knows that if she needs 24-hour care and we can't provide it, that she may have to. It's no big secret. We discuss it all with her.

* * *

I have told my brothers that if it comes down to it, if having my mother here affects our health or our marriage, which it could, then she would have to go into a home.

DECISION-MAKING PROCESS

When placement of an older person becomes an imminent reality, it is a critical psychological experience for the elderly individual and all family members. Families rarely are prepared psychologically, and the prospect may precipitate an emotional crisis for all concerned (Brody & Contributers, 1974; Brody & Spark, 1966). Feelings of guilt, conflict, and shame may coexist with the conscious or unconscious but very human desire of caregivers to be relieved of the severe and unrelenting burdens they have carried.

Studies of the paths leading to institutional care have shown that placing an elderly relative is the last rather than the first resort of families and that in general they have exhausted all other alternatives, enduring severe personal, social, and economic stress in the process; the final decision is made with the utmost reluctance (Brody, 1977; Brody & Spark, 1966; Lowenthal, 1964; Tobin & Lieberman, 1976; Townsend, 1965). Some of the case studies in Part II of this book illustrated the long road some caregiving families travelled that ultimately led to placement.

When institutional care is being considered, the degree or intensity of stress may vary, but family relationship patterns are revealed vividly. Although the historical quality of the interpersonal relations between the generations and among adult siblings is a most important component in the complex of psychological reactions, it would be unrealistic to suggest a simplistic model of "good" relationships in which there is no residuum of unresolved conflict.

The elderly person may be in a state of intense anxiety and fear. Even if family relations are basically warm and the necessity of placement is recognized on a reality level, some feelings of abandonment and rejection are still experienced. The feelings of all family members are communicated to each other, and the distress of each increases that of the others. The placement in psychological terms is a separation that stimulates the reactions associated with all separations from those in whom there is an emotional investment. Coming at this phase of life, when the total family is confronted with the fact that this may be the final plan for the old person, it carries overtones of the ultimate separation. Moreover, there still exist strong, deeply internalized, guilt-inducing cultural injunctions against placing an elderly parent regardless of the most reality-based determinants of that placement. Exacerbating the reactions of all concerned is the perception that nursing homes are cold, dehumanizing environments.

Family behavior during the placement process reflects and is part of the natural continuity of past relationships from which it flows. In some families, family members—husbands, wives, adult siblings, and the older person concerned—are mutually supportive and cooperative. This enables them to move forward constructively in the placement process. When there is a history of unresolved relationship problems, however, they are often reactivated, intensified, and acted out at this time. Bitter sibling rivalries may flare up that focus on financial planning or opposing attitudes towards what constitutes the best plan for the parent. Powerful ties between the elderly parent and adult child may intensify the suffering at placement, or even sabotage it entirely.

At best, the decision-making process is never easy. As the following case excerpts will show, there are several major themes in the caregivers' feelings and experiences. They feel guilty, they are careful about selecting a nursing home, and they worry about the quality of care the parent will receive. Some sets of siblings agree about what to do and help each other. Or, the daughter who has been the principal caregiver may receive mixed messages from other family members when some of them support the decision and others oppose it.

This daughter describes her mixed feelings and struggle to make the right decision:

> I don't think I could, from the perspective of my personality or looking at it from her perspective, put her in a nursing home. If I had four kids, I don't think I would want to end up in a nursing home or retirement home if that need not be the case. During one of her illnesses, they told me I might have to consider putting her into a nursing home. That was a hard decision once they are with you and under your care. I had mixed emotions. In one way, you think it would be a big relief, it would be an easier burden if she was elsewhere. I also had to come to terms with the fact that from a medical aspect, if she was as bad as we thought, then I really couldn't care for her. In another way, I wasn't too thrilled from what I knew about nursing homes. As far as that goes, some of it was guilt, in letting her go from here to there. There is something about having to let go and put her into something like that. My siblings were encouraging me that that would be the probable step. My husband agreed with them. They agreed that from a physical, emotional, and medical aspect, we couldn't take care of her at that point. They have also said recently that if mother gets worse and with me and the newborn, that there may come a time when we can no longer care for her here. So that is still in the back of my mind.

Daughters are acutely aware of the parent's feelings:

> When my sister and I picked a place for mother, we looked at it from her perspective. Originally, we never told mother that her placement in the nursing home was a permanent thing. Now, I've had to tell her. She realizes that that's where she should be. My sister and I didn't know how to approach mother about the nursing home. If this is what she had to do, she would do it. It was hard for me because it was such a negative thing. My mother wanted to die rather than go into a nursing home. A nursing home is like the last stop. We didn't want her to go. It's so impersonal. You give up everything; you have to rely on people for everything. It's scary.

Sometimes an inexorable progression of events goes beyond the caregivers' control:

> I feel I didn't make the decision because somehow events fell into place. From the hospital, yes, she should be in rehabilitation. From hospital, yes, she should be in the nursing home for a while.

* * *

> We really didn't consider a nursing home. We thought she would die here. When she got the bladder infection, she became so disoriented, confused, combative in the hospital. I couldn't bring somebody like that home.

Efforts may be made to postpone placement in the hope that things will improve:

> We didn't want to put her in a nursing home, but unfortunately there really weren't any alternatives because she needed 24-hour-a-day care. We were hoping she would come around. For a long time, we kept her apartment. We were hoping she would come out. But she just got worse and worse.

Caregivers often involve their siblings in making this important decision:

> My sister and I made the decision about where to place mother. I wasn't going to make that decision on my own. No way was I going to carry that load.

Family members may have different views:

> My husband thinks it's time for a nursing home. My son said when she began to go downhill to put her in a nursing home. My daughter says I can't put her in a nursing home. She said it would be better if she fell over dead at home.

* * *

> My brother was all for putting mother in a nursing home. My cousins told me I would kill her if I sent her to a home. You know how that makes you feel.

* * *

> My husband was torn about the nursing home decision because then we wouldn't be doing what was expected of us. Two of my sisters were relieved because mother wouldn't be coming to them. Then one of them said we couldn't do it. All of a sudden she was concerned.

When professionals are looked to for advice, their recommendations may be received with relief by the family as permission to make the placement and as in the older person's best interest. Contrast two different professional approaches. One is exemplified by the doctor who told the exhausted daughter of an elderly Alzheimer's patient, "Don't put her in a nursing home. They don't last long there." Another is the doctor who wrote, "it quickly became evident that institutionalization was necessary . . . but feelings of deep affection and nagging guilt had made a realistic decision . . . difficult. My role, as I saw it, was to assuage guilt sufficiently so that the son or daughter could pursue the course that he or she had finally come to recognize as appropriate. . . . The physician's 'orders' can alleviate guilt and resolve the . . . relative's problems regarding difficult decisions in institutionalization" (Hollender, 1988, pp. 105–106).

These daughters describe the role of professionals in the decision-making process:

> Both my parents were in the hospital, and the doctors said they should be transferred to a nursing home. The doctors made this decision.

* * *

> After mother's third stroke, the doctor said to put her in a nursing home because she was ready for that. I called my sister and told her what the doctor recommended. I told her I needed her to come help me find a nursing home for mother. At first she said she wouldn't come. She finally decided to come for 2 weeks. The doctor felt mother might not recover and might need constant care.

* * *

> My sister and I went to a caretakers meeting [a support group]. The speaker was a woman who for a fee helps families decide how to care for parents. We hired this woman to help us. We had been debating about whether a live-in companion or a nursing home situation would be best for mother. The woman told mother she couldn't afford a live-in companion. She gave us guidelines when looking for nursing homes. It took somebody from the outside. We feel the Lord led us down the path. It wasn't coincidence. It all just worked out. She was going to have to go cause she needed what they offered.

Counseling and referral is often helpful:

> After my mother was in the hospital for 3 months, the nurses told us they had to release her. Thank God in a hospital like that, two social workers became involved. They had to make sure we had a placement for her. That was very helpful.

* * *

> A geriatric consultant has given me some leads and advice. In other words, you are thinking of a nursing home type of situation. I don't think she could come back. I don't think she could live in anybody's home or our family's. I think

that our family has bent out lives around enough, and I think that we, with the help of my brother and sister, have given her the best care that we could, and I don't think we have to try to extend it in anyway.

Considerations such as quality and range of services, costs, proximity, the physical environment, and sheer availability determine the choice of a nursing home:

The things we considered were proximity to our homes, the quality of the physical therapy department, physical attractiveness, the staff, and the type of funding they required. We had to look for a facility that accepted Medicaid.

* * *

My sister and I went to a number of nursing homes and checked things out. We would talk about the pros and cons of each one afterwards. Towards the end, it came down to a gut feeling. I don't know if we made the right decision.

* * *

First, I considered the cost. I wanted a simple place that was kept well. I had to feel right about the place. These were the things that helped me decide: simplicity, cleanliness. I try not to think about the food.

* * *

I would want to know that there was good care and that the place was reasonably well run. I would want to be sure the attendants would give her as tender and as good care as possible. I would want it to be somewhere I could visit routinely.

* * *

While she was in the hospital, I tried to get her into a decent facility, but there were no beds. So a social worker called this convalescent home, and I took her there. It was a brand new home, but the food and the care she got was bad. It was like she was there to die. They were robbing me blind. Mother was combative at the time. She didn't know who I was and who my brother was. Finally, there was a bed available at another place. She came around beautifully.

In some instances, the older person and daughter adapt well to nursing home placement and are satisfied with the care.

It took mother a long time to relax and enjoy the nursing home. She kept thinking back to her bad experience in the temporary placement where she fell and fractured her hip the first night. I had to help her with that. It took her 6 months to adjust. Now she feels she is there for a purpose. The staff at the nursing home are wonderful.

Some daughters, however, have severe negative reactions to placement:

> I'm 75 years old. I took care of Mom for 10 years. My husband had an operation, a stroke, and a heart attack. He kept saying we should put mother in a nursing home. I said I didn't think she was ready yet, that it would be worse on me. If she was senile then maybe it would help out. I told him I couldn't force someone in there. . . . A year ago I put an application to a nursing home. I was very desperate. I was sick and lost a lot of weight. I hated to do what I did. I tried to prepare her as best I could. But it was a disgrace as far as the neighbors were concerned. Mom said, "All right. You don't want me anymore." She said she wouldn't forget. She was really sarcastic. The day after I put mother in a nursing home I was sick. I couldn't eat or sleep. I did a terrible thing.

DURING THE PARENT'S RESIDENCE IN A NURSING HOME

Family concern, interest, and contacts do not stop suddenly after institutionalization of the older person. Ties between the elderly parents and their adult children remain strong and viable, and most of the caregiving children continue their caring efforts, though some of the specifics of their activities may be different (Brody, 1985a; Brody & Contributers, 1974a; Kahana, Kahana, & Young, 1985). Theories of family breakdown (Bengtson, 1978) and beliefs that children abandon their parents to the institution remain unsupported (Simos, 1970; York & Calsyn, 1977).

Most elderly nursing home residents have a "next-of-kin," who most often is an adult child. As with community care of the aged, daughters outnumber sons more than three to one in being the one to take most responsibility for and to do more for the parent after placement (Brody, Pruchno, & Dempsey, in preparation, 1989). The individual who was principal caregiver prior to placement almost invariably continues in that role afterwards as well.

A major consideration in selecting a particular facility is its geographic proximity to the relative's home. As might be expected, having family means having more visitors. More than half of nursing home residents with a next-of-kin receive visitors at least weekly, compared with 27% of those without kin. The vast majority of spouses visit at least weekly, as do about three-fourths of the adult children and almost as large a proportion of the grandchildren named, and one-third of residents' siblings who were named as next of kin visit as frequently. [These data are from the national Survey of Institutionalized Persons (U.S. Bureau of the Census, 1978).]

Though family members continue to be involved and to visit regularly, when the elderly person has Alzheimer's disease, visits are progressively shorter and less enjoyable as the impairment is deeper (Moss & Kurland, 1979; York & Caslyn, 1977). Relatives provide many services such as grooming, bringing things (food, clothes, spending money, flowers), straightening bureau drawers, taking care of laundry, taking the resident for a walk, cheering her up, making special visits on the resident's birthday, managing the resident's money, and talking to staff about the older person's care and needs.

Such data do not tell us about the qualitative aspects of family members' activities, however—about the content of their visits to the older people or their contacts with staff, the effects they experience from having institutionalized relatives and from visiting them, or how they perceive their roles.

The continuity of family relationships with elderly nursing home residents and their emotional strains have been described by numerous clinical reports (e.g., Brody, 1977; Lewis, 1980). Adult children may experience guilt and even shame about having made the placement, sadness and worry about the parent's decline, depression, and frustration. Anxiety about their own aging processes is stimulated. Some have negative emotional reactions to visiting the older person, and some continue to experience competing demands on their time and energy. When interpersonal conflicts among adult siblings have existed, they may continue to focus on the now institutionalized older person.

Although some strains family members experienced prior to placement continue, others are different. Families attribute some of their strains to what they perceive as poor care of the parent in the nursing home, negative staff attitudes towards the elderly person and the family, the physical environment, the presence of other deteriorated patients, reluctance to "complain" about care or staff because they fear retaliation on the helpless parent, and ambiguity about their own roles vis-à-vis staff. When the older person is on Medicaid, their families often fear that the nursing home will not continue to keep them because the reimbursement rate is low.

The characteristics and adjustment of the older person also affect family members. When the parent is complaining or unhappy about being in the nursing home, for example, or evidences the same kinds of disordered behavior as prior to placement, there often are negative emotional effects on their family caregivers.

Nevertheless, relationships of the institutionalized elderly and their family members have potential for positive change even at this late stage of the family life cycle. Some relationships improve and close family ties continue following institutionalization, perhaps because the care needs of the parent were stressful and there is now some relief (Smith & Bengtson, 1979). In an intervention study focused on cognitively impaired older people in an institution, the family relationships of the treatment group improved significantly as compared with those of the control group (Brody et al., 1971).

Even severely impaired residents can continue to serve a positive role for family members. In one study, for example, more than one-fifth of the relatives of old people with Alzheimer's disease reported that the residents were helpful to them when they visited—cheering them up at times, giving them advice (e.g., "to take it easy"), telling them about the family's past history, and sharing recipes (Moss & Kurland, 1979). The residents often initiated conversations about family events, the past, and the institutional milieu. Interestingly, they were more likely than their family visitors to bring up disturbing topics (such as family ill-health or deaths, relationship problems, or financial difficulties). For their part, many family members were protective and had not told the residents about most of such problems or events that had occurred during the past year. Most family members said they frequently talked about the resident with other relatives and worried about her, primarily because of her poor health and deterioration.

The well-being of residents in nursing and old-age homes is vitally and beneficially affected by their receiving attention and assistance from preferred members of the family or devoted friends (Harel & Noelker, 1978). The elderly people's emotional bonds with family members often become relatively more important to them than during their middle years, perhaps because of the reduction in their other roles and associations that occurred as they aged and were institutionalized (Kleban, Brody, & Lawton, 1971).

The importance of the physical environment of the facility in encouraging family visiting was underlined in a study that found an increase in visiting when older people with brain impairment were moved from a traditional old building to a new, experimentally designed facility (Lawton, 1978). The expert opinion of most professionals to the effect that demented residents should be segregated from those who are cognitively intact was reflected in the opinions of family members. They overwhelmingly prefer separate living quarters for the two groups (Liebowitz, Lawton, & Waldman, 1979).

FAMILY ROLE CHANGES

Some family roles change dramatically when the old person enters a nursing home. Family members no longer share their homes with the older people, lift and turn the bedfast, bathe and dress the disabled, shop, cook, and clean for those who cannot do so, nor protect the confused from setting fires or wandering away from home. Some roles continue, however, and some new ones are added.

The provision of affective support is a major family role that continues and that is critical to the well-being of older people. Though families have been relieved of many arduous personal care and instrumental tasks, the emotional support and socialization they provide may become even more important to the old people. They care, visit, phone, are present during illness, and provide linkage to the larger family and the outside world. The family continues to be "the someone who cares," to meet the needs for affection and concern that are shared by all human beings.

This does not mean, however, that the expression of this role is free of problems. Family behavior, like the behavior of the older people, may be maladaptive to the nursing home situation. Moreover, the past relationships of older people and their families are carried into the nursing home. All institutional personnel are familiar with family members who make a multi-tude of angry complaints and unrealistic demands, as well as with those who are fearful of "bothering" staff. Some "visit" by arriving daily at the nursing home at dawn and staying until the resident goes to bed (no one else can take proper care of the old person). At the other extreme, some family members distance themselves ("I can't bear to see the way my mother is now"). Anecdotal reports (Brody, 1977; Locker, 1976, 1981) suggest that individual and group counselling/therapy can improve such situations and provide an opportunity to resolve some of the psychological problems.

Family members also continue to play a major role that is accepted as legitimate when an elderly relative is not in an institution, but is ambiguous when nursing home admission has taken place—the role of advocate and mediator with the "formal" system. Now, however, the formal system is the microsystem of the nursing home rather than the social/health macrosystem in the community.

But families are uncertain about how to enact the role of mediator/ advocate in the nursing home. They often are reluctant to complain about the resident's care, fearing that staff will retaliate to the disadvantage of the resident who is "in their power." The uncertainty of family members about their roles is compounded by differing perceptions and attitudes on the part of the facilities' personnel who may send mixed messages. On the one hand, some staff assume that the family has no legitimate role once the care of the old person becomes the responsibility of the nursing home and they have "taken over." Family involvement—that is, asking questions about the elder-ly nursing home resident's condition, "complaints" about various aspects of care, and so on—may be viewed as "interference" and criticism. But if family members are not visible and articulate in expressing their concerns, their behavior is indicted as evidence of "dumping"; they may be considered to be hard-hearted and to have abdicated their responsibility. Thus, family mem-bers are caught in a classic "Catch-22" bind.

Another role—participation in decision-making—is equally ambiguous. A multitude of decisions are constantly being made about the lives of the residents. Some are necessarily the prerogative of nursing home staff—

when, for example, a room change is necessary because the resident's changed condition indicates a move to a different level of care. But when the resident does not have the capacity to make certain decisions for herself, who has the right to make those decisions? Who decides, for example, whether the Alzheimer's patient who is unsteady on her feet should be restrained or permitted to walk and risk falling?

Not only the differing perceptions of staff and family about the latter's roles, but the different perceptions of family and the residents themselves may be a source of difficulties. For example, are the expectations and wishes of the old people with respect to family visiting congruent with the family's perceptions of what constitutes appropriate frequency of visits?

EMOTIONAL EFFECTS ON FAMILY CAREGIVERS

When an older person has been placed in a nursing home, it would seem that family caregivers should experience considerable relief from strains. They no longer need to provide the most arduous instrumental and personal caregiving tasks, no longer are giving up privacy and space in their homes, and no longer witness any disturbed behavior the older person may exhibit on a minute-to-minute basis.

The belief that nursing home placement of an aging parent eases the family caregiver's burden is not borne out by clinical observation or by research, however. In one study (George, 1984), there were no significant differences in mental health, stress symptoms, and physical health between caregivers whose patients resided in long-term care facilities and those whose patients lived with them. Families of nursing home residents spent almost as much time with the patient as if they were caring for the patient at home. The researcher observed that the emotional stress of watching the deterioration of a loved one continues regardless of living arrangement and that while nursing home placement may solve some problems it causes new ones. It was concluded that institutionalization brings only limited relief from caregiver burden.

Other studies cast additional light on the problems of families. In one investigation, the patients' behaviors were identified as the most salient factor predicting the relatives' well-being—even more salient than interactions between caregiver and staff, and the practical/logistical aspects of the caregiving role (Stephens & Townsend, 1988). The most frequent sources of stress affecting three-fifths of adult children were dealing with the older person's mental state and problems relating to balancing time for the resident with other commitments (Townsend et al., 1988). Significant proportions of the children (roughly between one-third and one-half) were concerned about the cost of care, problems such as getting parents to eat properly and their complaints about food and other people in the nursing home, and staff not listening to them.

There were some particularly cogent findings in the Townsend et al., 1988 study about adult children's strains. First, the children who reported greater difficulty coping with the parent's placement were the ones who perceived their parents as having more trouble adjusting. This serves as a reminder of the impact on the entire family when one member experiences a problem. It is reminiscent of Gurland's (1978) concept of the "contagion of depression" between depressed older people and the family members in whose homes the depressed people live. A similar phenomenon was revealed in another study in that relatives of depressed older people in nursing homes and senior housing were found to be more depressed than relatives of nondepressed relatives (Brody, Hoffman, & Winter, 1987). Relatives of depressed residents felt more burdened, worried more, had the poorest relationships with the elderly people, and had the poorest mental health. Nevertheless, the depressed residents' relatives visited them regularly. Apparently, depression is not only "contagious" (Gurland et al., 1978) when caregiver and an older person share a household in the community. The "contagion" appears to operate even when the elderly and their relatives are separated by the walls of congregate facilities.

Among other problems experienced by family members in the Townsend study was getting other family members to visit the nursing home. Adult children who had greater difficulty coping with the placement had significantly more trouble with the institutional environment—different expectations than staff and uncertainty about their new roles. Cost and quality of care also created difficulties. Finally, it was found that children's sources of stress were significantly correlated with their mental health. The investigator commented that children need "to feel that their parent is *happy* there" (italics added). Guilt loomed large, characterizing nearly three-fifths of the adult children. The researchers wrote:

> . . . greater guilt was significantly associated with nearly all the sources of stress, including greater difficulties coping, balancing multiple demands, the parent reportedly not adjusting well to placement, dealing with the parent's mental state, getting family to visit, and the facility's environment . . .

The Townsend et al. (1988) study compared adult children with spouses. Significantly greater proportions of children than of spouses experienced stress due to dealing with the older person's mental state (Alzheimer's disease), not being able to visit enough or having time to devote to the elderly resident, and being torn between and competing demands. (Elderly spouses, of course, usually have fewer competing demands on their time and energy.) Though the study did not differentiate between adult sons and daughters, the majority of the children were daughters. Obviously, daughters continue to feel pulled in multiple directions even after a parent is placed.

Another large study of adult children whose parents were in nursing homes confirmed the continuing negative emotional effects on adult children, with large proportions of them feeling frustrated, angry, guilty, upset, worried, sad, overwhelmed, or emotionally drained as a result of having the parent in a nursing home. Particularly relevant in the context of this book is the finding that daughters experienced all of those symptoms to a significant extent more than sons, and daughters were also more depressed (Brody, Pruchno, & Dempsey, 1989).

To underline, *just as with caregivers providing home care, daughters of nursing home residents experience more stress than sons*. Apparently, daughters continue to be women in the middle even after the parent is in a nursing home. Like daughters providing home care, they may feel that "somehow" they have failed to meet their responsibility to provide care. Such feelings are present, even though on a reality level they had recognized that nursing home care was inevitable.

The daughters' guilt may be exacerbated by the parent's feeling of having been rejected, a feeling experienced even when the older person, too, knows there was no other option. The parent may intensify the child's guilt by complaining of the care received in the nursing home ("They don't take care of me the way you did"), by being dissatisfied with the amount of visiting or by simply looking reproachful.

The sadness and worry of family members about the parent's decline is not relieved by nursing home placement. Since a downward trajectory in the health and functioning of the old person usually continues, the adult child continues to experience such painful feelings and to witness the parent's emotional reactions. In addition, the child may be asking the silent question, "Will this happen to me?"

The quality of care in a particular nursing home also affects the emotional well-being of family members. Although there are, of course, many good nursing homes, there are also many in which the quality of care is questionable or poor. Children want their parents to receive good care and to be treated well by the staff. When the parent has Alzheimer's or a related disorder, their concern about such matters is intensified. The older person cannot even communicate her wishes and needs, and staff is not as intimately familiar with her preferences. One daughter, for example, asked, "Will they know to give her the apple she loves everyday?" Moreover, the nature of the disease is such that the patient cannot report instances of neglect or maltreatment.

The daughters speak:

> When we visited her in the nursing home, we could tell she was angry with us. She was among strangers. It was our fault.

* * *

. . . when I come home after visiting, I often have to sleep to forget. In the 2 years I've been going, I see the different ages and stages of aging and what illness can do.

* * *

I felt very guilty.

* * *

It still upsets me. I can't handle it.

* * *

I got a horrendous bill from the nursing home and looked for another place.

* * *

It's a lot of money for someone to be unhappy.

* * *

We thought we were covered for expenses for Mom in the nursing home, but they said she was not covered. We didn't leave her there. The reason was financial.

* * *

So there she is, and we have to make the best of it. When we realized she would have to stay in, I felt horrible. I don't know if we made the right decisions. Sometimes I think we did, sometimes I don't.

Sometimes the placement works well:

She came around beautifully. It was better than the first place. They keep a good check on her and they do take care of her but not like I would. I don't know if they'll keep her. I don't know yet if she will have to leave. I think that as long as they know we are waiting for a bed for mother at the same place where my aunt is that they will let her stay [a facility that will accept Medicaid].

In summary, research and clinical practice are consistent in confirming the continuity of family bonds after nursing home placement as well as before. Although such placement is often unavoidable, it is most often the last option to be explored and is regarded with dread. Placement often is "successful," and the well-being of the older person and family members is enhanced. In other instances, however, family members suffer negative emotional effects that are similar to those of families providing home care, in both cases deriving from the parent's symptoms of Alzheimer's disease, competing demands on their time and energy, life-style disruptions, family conflict, and the parents' complaints and declining capacities. New strains may emerge, however, that are specific to the placement—dissatisfaction with the quality of care, staff attitudes and behavior, the physical environment of the institution, role ambiguity, fear of exhausting the older person's assets, and economic strains when the family is contributing toward the cost of care. Guilt is a pervasive feature of the caregivers' subjective experience.

The daughters who predominate as the "significant" relatives of nursing home residents continue to feel that it's up to them to do whatever they can, to see to it that good care is provided, and to make the parent happy (see Chapter 6). More than prior to placement, however, matters are out of the daughters' control. Perhaps the gap between what they feel they should do and what they actually do is even wider now, and that discrepancy reinforces the guilt they feel at having surrendered care to others.

Though total alleviation of the suffering of these family members is an unrealistic goal, much can be done. The most do-able actions relate to reimbursement of care coupled with strict regulations regarding quality considerations and oversight. Even if financial contributions are voluntary, family members should not have to be under economic stress to pay for the old person (most of the adult children are approaching old age or are already there). Nor should they have to feel that they have consigned their relative to a "warehouse" or to outright mistreatment.

Attention to the socioemotional and mental health problems of the elderly residents is important in its own right, of course. Special treatments for and ways of managing Alzheimer's patients stand out in this regard. Since the well-being of family and resident is interlocked, it is obvious that such attention will pay dividends for their family caregivers as well. Programs that focus on family members (individual and group counseling, for example) could help them deal with their painful feelings. Family group counseling could improve or resolve family conflicts that focus on the older person. The residents themselves can only benefit from such efforts. Role ambiguity of staff *and* family also requires attention to clarify for the different actors on the scene what each expects of the others, and the problems each group experiences.

Finally, different categories of relatives may experience different sources and amounts of strain, and all are deserving of attention. It is reiterated, however, that most family caregivers of nursing home residents are adult children, and three-fourths of those adult children are daughters— the women in the middle who continue to be in the middle.

Part IV

Unfinished Business

Chapter 15

Unfinished Business on the Parent-Care Agenda

There is much unfinished business on the parent-care agenda. The importance of that business goes beyond the need to attend to the plight of women in the middle, since older people themselves and all members of the family feel the repercussions as well. Moreover, unless solutions are sought and found, reverberations will be felt down through the generations by the women in the middle of the future and their families. It is the purpose of this book not only to present information currently available, but to generate further exploration and to stimulate activities that could contribute to the well-being of all concerned.

It cannot be assumed, however, that a neat list of agenda items can be drawn up and checked off in turn as each is accomplished. There will always be unfinished business because change is a constant in addressing issues concerning parent care. The number and proportion of older people in the population inevitably continues to change. Their characteristics and needs change in unpredictable ways as each new cohort enters the aging phase of life and as new scientific and social developments occur. The health status, values, life-styles, preferences, and personal resources of the elderly change. So too do changes occur in lives of their family caregivers. Changes also occur in the environment in which caregiving takes place—in the social and economic climate, and in social policies that create, eliminate, or reduce services, entitlements, and facilities. Nor are values immutable, though they change slowly and unevenly.

Despite all of the potential changes and those that are already occurring, there are clear indications of some directions to be taken now.

PERSPECTIVE

It is important to recall that the increase in the elderly population is a most positive development. Each new cohort of older people in past decades has

been progressively healthier, better educated, and has enjoyed higher incomes and more leisure. Most of the aged are not sick and dependent and
are able to enjoy the gift of longer life. People who have worked for many
years can look forward to a retirement in which to rest from their labors or
become involved in new activities, and enjoy their children, grandchildren,
and great-grandchildren. At any given time, most do not need any more help
than the normal, garden-variety of reciprocal services that family members
of all ages exchange on a day-to-day basis and at times of emergency or
temporary need.

The younger generations, too, benefit from the demographic developments and scientific advances that have resulted in a large aging population.
Many more babies and children nowadays can expect to have both of their
parents survive while they are growing up. Many more young parents can
raise their children without fearing that smallpox, poliomyelitis, dyptheria,
or other epidemic diseases will carry those children off. Today's young
children are fortunate in that they can learn to know many more grandparents and great-grandparents than earlier cohorts of children. Older people
are often a resource to the younger generations in the family, giving them
emotional support and financial aid, caring for young grandchildren, and
providing other services. In fact, the proportions of old people who *give* help
to their children exceed the proportions who *receive* help from their children (Kingson, Hirshorn, & Cornman, 1986).

There are few people who would wish those opportunities away in order
to return to the "good old days" of family life that weren't as good in those
ways as nowadays.

It is undeniable, however, that one result of the vast increase in the
number of very old and disabled people in the population is that parent care
is now a normative experience. Although the burden falls differently on
different population groups, most people need to help an elderly family
member at some time during their lives. Adult children nowadays provide
much more care and more arduous care to more older people for longer
periods of time than ever before in history. Their capacity to supply all the
help needed has been exceeded. The daughters and daughters-in-law who
provide most of the needed help, therefore, often experience the severe
strains documented in this book.

What the elderly want most from their children is caring, affection, and
continuing warm relationships and contacts. Above all, they do not want to
be dependent on anyone. In one research study after another, older people
consistently express their fear of dependency and emphasize their wish not
to be "a burden." The last thing they want is to become a source of worry and
strain to their children. They do expect, however, that when they become
disabled and need help, their children will see to it that they are cared for.
But most do not demand that their children's love be demonstrated by

cleaning, cooking, personal care, or financial help when these can be obtained from nonfamily sources.

For their part, adult children who are privileged to have surviving parents want them to live on and to do so in a state of well-being. They want to provide care when it is needed. These attitudes reflect strong family values and bonds of affection forged over many decades. Their commitment is a potent and constructive force, and they feel rewarded when they honor that commitment.

Against that background, women's profound and compelling conviction that care of the elderly is *their* responsibility has been demonstrated. These women feel and behave as though it's up to them to provide all the help older people need and to make their parents and parents-in-law happy as well. Indeed, they try to make everyone in their families happy.

Women set high standards for themselves in enacting all of the roles they play and in meeting what they perceive as their responsibilities to their parents, to other members of their families, and to their jobs or volunteer work. They put themselves at the bottom of their priority lists, giving up their own free time and chances to socialize and take vacations when need be. Many women are deprived of opportunities to meet their own needs; they even forego opportunities for their own development in the form of employment and education when they cannot manage to juggle all of the things they are called upon to do. Yet they often feel that somehow they are not doing enough.

Some of the values held by women have remained constant, and some have changed. Despite the pressures exerted by the demographic changes, the women's "old" values about family care of the elderly and about their responsibility to be the caregivers have not changed. Changes in other of their values have, however, been expressed by their large-scale entry into the labor force in recent years. When the new and old values compete and the women's actual behavior in caring for parents is scrutinized, in the main it is the old values that are controlling. It is thus clear that the new values have not driven out the deeply rooted old values.

Unquestionably, daughters and daughters-in-law are in an uncomfortable middle position in many ways. In the middle generationally, in their middle years, in the middle of competing responsibilities to various people in their families and to their jobs, and in the middle of values that compete, they often ignore their responsibilities to themselves.

As the data and the women's narratives showed, parent-caring women are at various stages of life. It is not unusual for them to have caregiving careers that overlay several life stages as they take care of several older people simultaneously or sequentially. As a result, many of them experience negative effects on their emotional, physical, and economic well-being and on their own and their families' life-styles. If things do not go well, they often think that somehow they have failed.

Among the reasons some women push themselves so hard is the feeling that they must return in kind the total care they were given by the parent in childhood—a goal that is unachievable. They confuse *providing care* with *caring*—as though they must give all the care the older person needs themselves, and if they do not, they don't *care* enough. They are subject to pressures to continue, not only from their own inner processes, but also from societal values that intensify their internal pressures. Whatever the reasons, and there are many, some women refuse even those services that are available and that could give them some relief during their parent-care years.

All indications are that the problem will increase. If help is to be offered to women in the middle and their families, several paths must be taken in the search for solutions. The various tasks to be accomplished require different approaches—separate, but interrelated and interdependent activities that have implications for each other. Since knowledge is incomplete and broad trends continue while new ones emerge, it is urgent that the problems be explored further and that the trends be monitored by research. Social policy must see to it that community services that can help are in place and that long-term care facilities are available when placement of the older people is necessary. Service organizations and agencies and their workers must see to it that those in need know of the existence of those services and can gain access to them. Those women who do not use available services even when their need is great, require help to do so. And the agenda for all of us is to see to it that we move in a positive direction toward those goals.

RESEARCH AGENDA

Social and economic trends are susceptible to change and are not always predictable. Moreover, new trends constantly emerge. Continuing and newly emerging trends require constant and systematic tracking and study to determine their effects on patterns of parent care and on the recipients and providers of care. Some of the trends described in the book are continuing— demographic changes, for example, that are further reducing the supply of filial caregivers and increasing the pressures on women to care for several older people. At the same time, there is no sign that the increase in women's labor force participation will change direction. The Bureau of Labor Statistics estimates that women will account for almost two-thirds of the labor force growth between now and the end of the century (Otten, 1989).

Multiple caring responsibilities may also increase because older people who have no children on whom to depend will be more numerous. At present, about one-fifth of all older people are in that group not only because they have always been childless, but because being in advanced old age increases the possibility of outliving one or more of their children. Though they probably do not do as much as children, nieces and nephews (as well as elderly siblings) rise to the occasion to help the childless even when they are caring for their own parent(s). Caring for the childless elderly presents a special challenge to society and professionals.

Particular attention should be given to certain other changing patterns. Because of high rates of divorce and lower marriage rates, more women will not have husbands during their parent-care years. Developmentally disabled people are living longer, so that more caregivers will experience "double dependency" as they care for their elderly parents and disabled children at the same time (often well into the latter's adulthood). Another increasing form of double dependency derives from the later ages at which women are electing to have their first child. More of them, then, will be in the parent-care years while they still have young children at home. The nests of some middle generation people are not only remaining filled with their offspring for longer periods of time, but are being refilled to a greater extent with young adults who return home. A Census Bureau survey found that 18 million single adults 18–34 years old were living with parents, an increase of about one-third since 1974 (Cowan, 1989). The nests of more families, then, are filled with young adult children as well as with disabled elderly parent(s). Still another trend is the increase in geographic mobility, which (combined with fewer children) creates special problems when distance separates parents and children.

Although there has been a groundswell of research attention to primary caregivers such as elderly spouses and adult children, such work is just a beginning. The findings about the inner experiences of daughters and daughters-in-law reported in these pages should be tested, modified, and expanded, as should the early information about the experiences of their siblings, husbands, and children (the caregivers of the future).

The focus of this book on caregiving women is not meant to ignore or exclude the disabled elderly themselves. The inner experiences of the older people stand out as requiring exploration. How do they feel, what are their reactions and their perspectives, when they are dependent on adult children? They are the ones who fear becoming "a burden" on their children. What effects do they experience when their fears become reality? Nor have we heard the accounts of those of their children who do *not* become the main caregivers and how it happened that they are "secondary," rather than primary caregivers. Their perspectives are a major gap in knowledge about parent care that remains to be filled in.

Though adult daughters and daughters-in-law predominate as filial caregivers for elderly people, there are other patterns of care of the old by the younger generations that have barely been addressed. The differences between care of mothers and fathers and in-laws of both genders have not been fully studied, for example. Nor has there been investigation of sons who care for their mothers and fathers. Some adult children of both genders help elderly caregiving spouses, and some care for both parents at the same time. And some grandchildren become primary caregivers when deaths in the middle generation leave a caregiving gap. Indeed, some grandchildren find themselves responsible for two generations of older people—their parent(s) and grandparent(s). Even when not in primary caregiving roles, those grandchildren and other members of the caregivers' nuclear and extended families as well, constitute the heretofore invisible back-up system, making important appearances at times of emergency or special need. Study of the operation of that system—its composition, how it is mobilized, and how it functions—is a fascinating and potentially fertile area for investigation.

Although quantitative studies of all of those patterns of care and of the other actors on the parent-care scene are indicated, qualitative studies from the unique perspectives of clinicians and ethnographers are vitally important. Such studies permit a view of the processes at work within individuals and families. They inform quantitative studies, aid in interpreting findings, point the way to methods of helping, and would present a more rounded picture of matters we now know about primarily from the vantage point of "principal caregivers." Underresearched areas that emerge as important in open-ended interviews, for example, are the roles of personality (of caregiver and care-recipient) and interpersonal relationships in affecting the care patterns and the strains experienced.

There is a particular need for longitudinal studies to supplement cross-sectional surveys. People's situations change over time, and it is the trajectory of change that informs us of their needs. Moreover, parent care is not an event that is isolated from the continuum of life experience; the patterns have their roots in early childhood. We know little of the meaning of the parent-care years as they shape the contours of people's entire lives. What changes occur in the wake of the parent-care years? What are the sequelae even long after the parents' deaths? And how does the parent-care experience influence the lives of all concerned when the caregivers themselves grow old?

PUBLIC POLICY AGENDA

It is not within the purpose of this book to set a comprehensive policy agenda; policy options are explored in detail elsewhere (e.g., Abel, 1987; Brody, S., 1987; Select Committee on Aging, 1988). Delineating what has been done and what remains to be done with the broadest of brush strokes, however, it is apparent that policy has moved forward primarily in the areas of income maintenance and acute medical services for the elderly. Little progress has been made in the direction to which the trends described have pointed—that is, the area of supportive health/social services. There is an urgent need to create the continuum of acute, transitory, and long-term care services and facilities dictated by chronicity.

Income maintenance and payment of acute medical costs for older people have been of direct benefit to their families as well as to older people themselves. As was indicated, prior to Social Security (1935), SSI (1972), and Medicare (1965), to be old virtually meant to be poor. Although there are still some poor older people (and that should not be), poverty no longer characterizes most of the elderly. Only a very small proportion (1.5%) are now totally dependent on their children for day-to-day living expenses, in contrast to the more than half who were dependent before Social Security. Similarly, because of Medicare, the elderly and their children do not have to worry about being wiped out financially because of acute catastrophic illnesses of the old (for a detailed discussion, see Brody & Brody, 1987 and Brody, S., 1987). The well-documented care needs of mentally ill old people (and therefore the needs of their families) have been grossly neglected, however; reimbursement for care under Medicare is much more limited than for physical ailments, for example (Lebowitz, in press).

Modest progress has been made in the provision of housing. Both the research data and the case studies show how important living arrangements are. They figure in the emotional well-being of the old and their adult children, with separate housing clearly preferred by both generations and in their best interests. Thirty-five years ago, subsidized housing for older people that includes services such as meals, housekeeping, and health care simply did not exist. Such housing remains scarce, but in the main, the increase in senior housing and more importantly the improved income position of older people have enabled them to live as they wish—close to their children but in separate households (Shanas, 1979a). Although retirement and life-care communities now offer more options for the elderly, such arrangements are not subsidized by government and are, therefore, available only to those who can afford them.

The major unfinished business on the social policy agenda is long-term care insurance. Such insurance should create a broad array of the kinds of day-to-day sustained services needed by functionally disabled older people and caregiving family members—respite care, day care, in-home services such as personal care and homemaker services and transportation, for example. These could relieve some of the strains that family caregivers experience. At present, such services are in very short supply and are uneven regionally. The notion that nonfamily services would cause families to shirk their responsibilities has proved to be unfounded. Services improve the quality of care given to the elderly but do not substitute for family care or undermine family efforts.

At present, community health and social services are limited and disproportionately underfinanced as compared to acute medical care services for the aged (Brody, S., 1979). Enormous inequities exist among the various states in their expenditures for Medicaid services, both for nursing home care and community-based services (see U.S. General Accounting Office, 1983). At this writing, there are a number of proposals for long-term care insurance before Congress that address the unfinished business of long-term care. Such insurance should be oriented to functional status rather than medical needs alone and should also cover both short-term and long-term nursing home residence.

Nursing homes are appropriate long-term living arrangements for the severely disabled older people who need them. At present, the major public provision of nursing home care is for Skilled Nursing Facilities (SNF) under the Medicaid program. It has been known for years that, in many parts of the country, government reimbursement rates are too low and standards are either inadequate or not enforced. Although some facilities provide high-quality care, poor and even dangerous conditions continue in too many. In most states, elderly spouses have to impoverish themselves by "spending down" so that the disabled older person becomes eligible for nursing home care under Medicaid (although the new Catastrophic Medical Care Act provides a minimum floor). The destitute "intact" spouse then is at risk of economic dependency on children. Some adult children purchase nursing home care for their parent(s) when Medicaid beds are unavailable and experience financial strain as a result. Among the remedies needed are adequate reimbursement, strict oversight and monitoring of facilities, and an emphasis on quality that includes attention to the social as well as medical aspects of care. These would not only elevate the quality of care, but could alleviate to some extent the intense fear so many people have of nursing home placement.

The policy trend in recent years has been to embrace community care as an "alternative" to nursing home care and to create barriers to institutional placement. The "either/or" approach that places nursing homes in competition with community care has been proven to be inappropriate; different populations are served, and community care is not cheaper for the severely disabled. Yet at the same time that the so-called alternative of community care is encouraged, health and social services have been systematically reduced, and housing subsidies have been virtually eliminated, reinforcing the burden on caregiving families by closing avenues that might relieve them.

To emphasize, the financing of long-term care, in the community and in nursing homes, must come from the federal government. The cost of public insurance would not be "a bottomless pit," but its development depends on the value judgment made by society (Brody, S., 1987). In a major report, The Brookings Institution strongly endorses public long-term care insurance; it states that private insurance should be encouraged but could not be afforded by most people (Rivlin & Wiener, 1988). The issue is not our ability to take this step, but our willingness.

A question being debated by policy-makers and professionals is the "mix" of services that should be provided by the "informal" or "natural" support system of family and friends and by the "formal" support system of voluntary and governmental agencies. Experts agree that the mix must be altered, that the informal support system itself is in need of support. There is consensus that government must lead by encouraging and reimbursing services that help caregiving families.

At present, social policy does little beyond cheering the family on. Concrete actions have not backed up the lip service given to the need for a "family policy." The focus of what little service delivery is available is on the needs of the old people alone rather than on the needs of the entire family. Services are needed that would help the family continue to do what it has always done and is committed to doing.

Part of the problem is the confusion about the meaning of words such as "dependency," and family "reliability" and "responsibility." As this book has shown, there are different kinds of dependency—financial, physical, and emotional—that have quite different meanings to those involved. The elderly wish to depend on different people for different needs and services. Thus, their expectations for filial support vary when anchored to specific tasks.

No one pretends that bureaucratic organizations can substitute for the emotional support (expressed in closeness, concern, continuing contacts, and help in emergencies) that families provide to older people. But family reliability does not necessarily mean giving ongoing personal and nursing care or performing household tasks. As many gerontologists have pointed out, some functions are appropriate for families and others for the "formal" support system. Unless such blurred distinctions are clarified, inappropriate value judgments will continue to hamper the development of social policy.

Money would also help. In the United States, financial assistance to caregiving families is virtually nonexistent except for a token program that permits a tax deduction for the adult child purchasing care for an economically dependent parent and a Veterans Administration allowance for caring for a spouse disabled from wartime injury. In fact, there is actually a dollar penalty when an older person lives with his or her family because the amount of the old person's SSI is reduced. By contrast, economic supplements to caregiving families (such as attendance allowances or social security credits for caregivers remaining at home) are much more prevalent in other industrialized nations (Gibson, 1984). Some policy options that have been proposed are financial compensation for caregivers such as direct payments for caregiving, social security benefits for those who leave jobs for caregiving, and tax relief.

Among other economic considerations is the opportunity costs incurred by caregivers (and their families) when parent care interferes with their vocational lives. Virtually no information is available about that important matter or about the financial costs of health care (mental and physical) for those caregivers who are negatively affected by the help they provide to the old.

There is a long way to go in inventing flexible ways to buttress and complement family efforts. But enough information is at hand to enable policy-makers to mount a vigorous attack on the problems. Scapegoating the elderly by encouraging intergenerational competition and the allocation of resources belies understandings about the linkages in the well-being of the generations. This is an aging society made up of aging families in which women in the middle play a key role. Yet attitudes are often sanctimoniously judgmental when it comes to providing services to help families care for the old. "Filial responsibility" is seen in all-or-nothing terms as involving *total*, round-the-clock responsibility. The question is, *when does the public's expectation of filial responsibility mean abdication of social responsibility?*

AN ORGANIZATIONAL AGENDA

Even if public policy should permit the creation of all of the services needed, it would be an exercise in futility unless those services were actually accessible to the families in need. The sheer existence of an array of services is not equivalent to their actual utilization.

The stories that parent-caring women told in these pages illustrated not only the effects they and their parents experienced as a result of the absence of a coherent program of long-term care, but also the access problems that exist. Obtaining even those services that exist is often a frustrating, defeating enterprise.

> Health services for the aged are multiple, parallel, overlapping, non-continuous and at the very least confusing. . . . Rarely do they meet the collective criteria of availability, accessibility, affordability or offer continuity of care in a holistically organized system. Planning for health services for the aged is similarly confused. Parallel systems of service have their own planning mechanisms. As a result, the various planning efforts overlap, contradict and are unrelated one to the other.
>
> Virtually all the services are funded by differing public money streams and have varied administrative arrangements, widely ranging eligibility requirements and different benefits for the same or similar services (Brody, S., 1979, p. 18).

The major public effort since 1972 in the social service arena has been the mounting of demonstration projects to rationalize these intermittent efforts and establish a pattern of continuous care (for example, through Medicaid and Medicare waivers and "channeling" demonstrations; these have been shown *not* to reduce institutionalization.)

If existing services are to reach those who need them, one of the major tasks is organizational and individual case management. This involves arranging the varied planning and service-delivery agencies so that they constitute a system in each community. Such a system would articulate the formal and informal medical and social/health services and relate the acute care services to what have been called the short-term long-term care (STLTC) and long-term care (LTLTC) subsystems (Brody, S. & Magel, in press) so they can respond in a coordinated manner to each individual and family in need. Separating out these three systems is no longer relevant; continuity of care should follow the trajectory of chronic illness (Brody, S., 1989, in press). Organizational arrangements should respond to the values and resources of each locality and each family; there can be no single, universally applicable prescription for organization and delivery. The underlying objective should be to provide a continuum of appropriate levels of care as the older person's needs change in kind, level, and intensity.

The problem at the level of organizational systems inevitably is reflected at the level of the individual and family, for whom it is a baffling problem to mobilize and coordinate the needed services. Among the barriers to obtaining services are the lack of administrative linkages from one to the other. Other barriers include the clients' lack of knowledge about the service, inability to connect with it, unpalatable eligibility criteria or humiliating procedures, the tendency of service agencies to perceive need only in terms of the services they offer, the complexities of entitlements, and bewildering regulations. Interventions designed to deal with such issues are variously called information and referral service, service management, outreach, case management, matrix management, or channeling.

Though case management is usually thought of as a professional role, basically it is enacted by the family—most often by caregiving women. They need help in doing so, however. And where there is no available family, the need for professional help is obvious. There should be ways to supplement or substitute for the family role of case management—that is, act as a combination of advocate, mediator, and mobilizer to obtain, arrange, and monitor the complex entitlements and services provided by the formal system.

More subtle issues also impede service utilization and speak to the need for counselling or casework. As the case studies in this book showed, there are psychological barriers that inhibit some women's use of needed services. In addition, the acceptability of services differs among older people with different socioeconomic and ethnic backgrounds and among individuals and families with diverse personalities and expectations. Therefore, whatever the label given to the process now most commonly referred to as case management, it must include the enabling process called counselling or casework.

Because of the complex nature of the problems with which case managers deal, effective case management is a highly skilled, knowledge- and values-based activity. It should not be seen solely as the mechanical manipulation or arrangement of services, but should include the offering of sensitive help with psychosocial issues. The blending of these activities cannot be carried out by untrained people, no matter how well-meaning they may be.

The need for training extends to the workers who actually deliver the direct "hands-on" care. Women who try to use nonfamily help in caring for parents are often discouraged by problems such as high turnover rates, unreliability, lack of skill, and inappropriate attitudes. Whether they are to be employed for in-home services or in nursing facilities, the recruitment and training of a sufficient cadre of such workers is an urgent item on the agenda.

PRACTICE AGENDA

The emotional strains of parent care would not be eliminated even in the best of all possible worlds in which all needed services existed and were available, accessible, and affordable. Though understanding of the dynamic processes at work is by no means complete, the information already at hand has not been fully integrated into the curricula of professional schools or applied in practice. There is growing awareness among professionals of the needs (medical, psychological, and social) of older people themselves, but that interest has not been matched by interest in the intra- and interpersonal problems of family caregivers. It is difficult to shift from tunnel vision focus on the individual to a wide-angle lens view that includes other members of the family. That should be done, however, not only in the interest of the caregivers, but for the sake of the elderly recipients of care.

The nonuse and underuse of services by some of the neediest caregivers is a constant frustration to service workers. Reports about subsidized respite services, for example, including those for caregivers of Alzheimer's patients, consistently report that they are grossly underutilized by caregivers and when used, are used very modestly. This, despite concerted efforts to educate and counsel them. (Brody et al., in press; George, 1988; Lawton et al., in press; Lawton et al., 1989; Montgomery, 1988; Saperstein & Brody, in press.) Surely, the therapeutic professions must turn their attention to the profound subjective problems some caregivers experience that prevent them from using help to ease their distressing (even health-threatening) situations.

AGENDA FOR ALL OF US

Recently there has been a flow of books of advice on parent care. Women are being instructed in techniques of nursing care for older people and what symptoms to look for, the importance of assessment and treatment of the elderly, and so on. They are being told about methods of reducing the stress they experience from parent care (relaxation techniques, for example). They are being advised how to manage older people who present personality or behavior problems. Women are being told not to feel guilt or other of the symptoms they experience. Support groups have proliferated, and some women do indeed feel supported, though others need more or different forms of help than support groups can offer. All of those things are important and undoubtedly help some women in some ways.

But one of the most disturbing aspects of the caregiving drama is the resignation of some daughters and daughters-in-law—their acceptance that this is the way it has to be. That acceptance is given such sanction in our society—even powerful, crushing, reinforcement—that relatively few women can resist as individuals.

Women in the middle are victimized by the intense pressure to which they are subjected in being told to embrace caregiving as their lot exclusively no matter the effects on their lives. As a result, some not only have low expectations of help from others, but tend to belittle the value of such help. The expectations of others reinforce the women's expectations of themselves and loom large in producing the strains and symptoms to which daughters and daughters-in-law are so vulnerable.

The studies reviewed in this book have shown that *daughters consistently experience more strain than sons when in comparable parent-caring positions.* Daughters who are the main caregivers experience more strain than do sons who are in comparable positions. The same holds true for sons and daughters who are local siblings of the principal caregiver and for sons and daughters who live at a geographic distance. It holds true even when the parent is in a nursing home. It may be that the underlying anger and feelings of helplessness these women experience (whether or not they are aware of those feelings) are components of the depression, anxiety, and other mental health symptoms so often reported as consequences of parent care.

That is not to say, of course, that women should not help their elderly family members. No one would disagree with the value we all hold that older people *should* receive care. No one would disagree with the proposition that it is the responsibility of the family and society to provide that care. In helping their elderly, however, some women go *beyond* what appear to be the limits of endurance and do so at the cost of severe deprivation and suffering to their own families and their own mental and physical health. Not all women do so, of course. In some instances, care is not unduly stressful. In some instances, help from other family members and nonfamily sources is obtained and utilized. But there are some women who do not seek or accept even the help that is available to them. Although there are those who have special, individual problems, they share with all of their counterparts the pressures of societal values about women's roles in parent care.

A major imponderable in the unfinished business of parent care is how the tension between changing and constant values will be resolved. Values determine not only what is done by society and professionals, but interact with socioeconomic conditions and people's inner processes to determine behavior on the level of the individual and family.

When the Women's Movement began, some people assumed that the goal of women was to gain equality by broadening the scope of their activities in the world of men. But, as psychologist Corinne Weithorn (1975) has pointed out, that notion yielded to the realization that change must occur not only in women's roles but in men's roles as well. Realignment of male/female relationships in the division of labor, she argued, should use the concept of *equitable* rather than *equal*—that is, not equal sharing of identical tasks, but a fair sharing of the total load. Looking at womens' roles in historical and cross-cultural perspective, Weithorn (1975) wrote, "now that strength is no longer a requisite for survival, pregnancy no longer a consequence of sexual activity, and the infant no longer dependent on the mother's breast, women are demanding a revised contract, one more adaptive to survival in contemporary society." (p. 292)

A revised contract between men and women has by no means been drawn up and ratified. The new values about gender roles have taken hold unevenly. Many men have supported the Women's Movement, many accept their wives' working as an economic necessity, and some have made genuine efforts at a radical change in their own life-styles. But all available evidence indicates that real change in the sharing of household and child-care responsibilities is not widespread. Nor do working women enjoy significantly increased assistance from husbands in domestic tasks.

Betty Friedan has called for the "second feminist agenda," that would include the restructuring of the institutions of home and work (*New York Times Magazine*, 1979). She says that social policy and society in general (business and schools, for example) must provide new options such as "flex-time" and individualized, family-oriented flexible benefit packages, as well as child-care facilities both at and separate from the workplace.

Though policies and services to help young women are inadequate, the need for them is becoming more widely recognized and acceptable. Furthermore, many forms of help with young children have always had matter-of-fact acceptance by families and our social institutions. One has only to think of nursery schools, baby sitters, or leaving baby with a friend or relative (usually a grandmother) so that the mother can have an afternoon off or take a vacation.

But the Women's Movement has not offered strong advocacy to middle generation women. It has emphasized the interests of young women and has also paid some attention to elderly women. But somehow, the problems of women between the young and old have received only minimal attention. Today's young women should remember that they are destined to be the women in the middle of the future.

On balance, the socialization of women to the role as caregiver is powerful, and the behavior of today's adult children tells us that most women and men continue to accept the proposition that it is women's role to provide the day-to-day care of the old. The imponderable is whether the resignation some women in the middle exhibit is a cohort phenomenon and whether today's young men will be readier to share nurturing roles.

If young men have not become full partners with their working wives in caring for their children and homes, will middle-aged and aging men be willing to share parent care? Those older men, after all, were socialized to "gender appropriate roles" before values about those roles began to change. And many of today's young children are being socialized in the same way. This mitigates against full sharing between men and women in caregiving to the old in the near future. (An additional constraint on achieving gender symmetry in parent care is that most older people who need personal care are women; in the main, women do not want their sons to help them with intimate personal tasks.) At the same time, however, today's young people and those in early middle age were socialized in the climate of the Women's Movement and values are amenable to change. Will today's young people feel and behave differently when they reach the parent-care years?

An important (and not fully realized) fact is that, no matter the degree to which men share responsibilities, *parent care and women's employment add to the total package of family responsibilities to be shared*. Equity between men and women, then, is not a total solution. Additional help must come from other sources such as the "formal" system as discussed above and from the business community as well (see Chapter 13). Such help serves men as well as women—indeed, it helps older people themselves and the entire family.

There is a growing awareness among bewildered and beleaguered women in the middle that they are not alone in their predicament and that help in various forms can be obtained. It remains to be seen whether that awareness can be channelled into a force for effecting change. Again, it is emphasized that *it is too much of a demand on individual women to deal with the pressures exerted by societal values and expectations*. Perhaps attention to the problem requires a massive sea change of the magnitude of the women's movement itself. Women need the collaboration of all of society—professionals, researchers, policy-makers, and men.

Women will continue to pursue diverse life-styles, and they should have the freedom to do so. Undoubtedly, in the future some women will prefer to work continuously at full-time occupations and some will adhere to "traditional" roles as wives, mothers, and homemakers. Others will move in and out of the work force as the needs of their families dictate. Each woman has to decide for herself what she wants the shape of her life to be.

It is now axiomatic, however, that women's changing roles inevitably affect men as well. In the workplace or in the home, willingly or unwillingly, and no matter what the nature of the changes they experience or their responses to those changes, men cannot avoid having their lives deeply influenced (see *Kramer vs. Kramer*). Though most men undoubtedly feel the repercussions of parent care as husbands, brothers, and sons of women in the middle, some may be finding themselves "men in the middle" when they must become the principal "responsible" family member in helping the old. The demographic trends indicate that more of them will be in that position in the future.

We do not know whether women and men will join with each other to form lobby groups in order to press social policy-makers for the services they need, to demand flexibility and benefits from their employers, and to urge the women's movement to make their cause its own.

We cannot do it all, of course. Women will continue to care for and about the elderly people in their families, to be concerned and sad at the declines of those old people, to provide affection and support, to do what they are able, and to arrange for the needed services that they cannot supply. (Perhaps those are the only appropriate "norms" for filial behavior.) The strains so many parent-caring women experience are not completely preventable or remediable. But those women deserve and *should expect* to receive the help they need to keep them from exceeding the limits of endurance, a point that so many reach now.

The well-being of all generations and both genders is linked inextricably in common cause. Dr. Weithorn's "revised contract" cannot be worked out solely between men and women. All of us, as individuals, as families, and collectively as a society, must be involved in negotiating that contract.

References

AARP (American Association of Retired Persons). (1987). *Caregivers in the workplace. Survey results. Overall summary.* Washington, DC, February.

Abel, E. K. (1987). *Love is not enough: Family care of the frail elderly.* Washington, DC: American Public Health Association.

Abrecht, S., Bahr, H., & Chadwick, B. (1979). Changing family and sex roles: An assessment of aging differences. *Journal of Marriage and the Family, 41,* 41–50.

Allen, I., with collaboration from Levin, E., Sidell, M., & Vetter, N. (1983). The elderly and their informal carers. In Department of Health and Social Security, *Research Contributions to the Development of Policy and Practice,* London, HMSO, 69–92.

Archbold, P. G. (1983). The impact of parent-caring on women. *Family Relations, 32,* 39–45.

Archbold, P. G. (1978). *Impact of caring for an ill elderly parent of the middle-aged or elderly offspring caregiver.* Paper presented at the 31st Annual Meeting of the Gerontological Society, Dallas, TX.

Barusch, A. S. (1987). Power dynamics in the aging family: A preliminary statement. *Journal of Gerontological Social Work, 11,* 43–56.

Bell, R. R. (1981). *Worlds of friendship.* London: Sage Publications.

Bengtson, V. L. (1978). You and your aging parent: Research perspectives on intergenerational interaction. In P. K. Ragan (Ed.), *You and your aging parent.* Los Angeles, CA: University of Southern California Press.

Bengtson, V. L. (1975). Generation and family effects in value socialization. *American Sociological Review, 40,* 358–371.

Bengtson, V. L., & DeTerre, E. (1980). Aging and family relations. *Marriage and Family Review, 3,* 51–76.

Bengtson, V. L., & Robertson, J. F. (Eds.). (1985). *Grandparenthood.* Beverly Hills, CA: Sage Publications.

Bengtson, V. L., & Treas, J. (1980). The changing context of mental health and aging. In J. E. Birren & R. B. Sloane (Eds.), *Handbook of mental health and aging.* Englewood Cliffs, NJ: Prentice-Hall, Inc., 400–428.

Blenkner, M. (1965). Social work and family relationships in later life with some thoughts on filial maturity. In E. Shanas & G. Streib (Eds.), *Social structure and the family: Generational relations.* Englewood Cliffs, NJ: Prentice-Hall.

Brody, E. M. (1988). *Marital status, parent care, and mental health*. (Project 1 of Caregiving and Mental Health: A Multifaceted Approach, NIMH grant number MH43371.)

Brody, E. M. (1985a) The role of the family in nursing homes: Implications for research and public policy. In M. S. Harper & B. Lebowitz (Eds.), *Mental illness in nursing homes: Agenda for research*. NIMH. Washington, DC: U.S. GPO, 234–264.

Brody, E. M. (1985b). Parent care as a normative family stress. The Donald P. Kent Memorial Lecture. *The Gerontologist, 25*, 19–29.

Brody, E. M. (1986). Informal support systems in the rehabilitation of the handicapped elderly. In Brody, S. J. and Ruff, G. E. (Eds.), *Aging and Rehabilitation* Springer Publishing Co., N.Y., 1986, pp. 87–108.

Brody, E. M. (1981). "Women in the middle" and family help to older people. *The Gerontologist, 21*, 471–480.

Brody, E. M. (1979). Aging parents and aging children. In P. K. Ragan (Ed.), *Aging parents*. Los Angeles, CA: University of Southern California Press, 267–287.

Brody, E. M. (1978). The aging of the family. *Annals of the American Academy of Political and Social Science, 438*, 13–27.

Brody, E. M. (1977). *Long-term care of older people: A practical guide*. New York, NY: Human Sciences Press.

Brody, E. M. (1974). Aging and family personality: A developmental view. *Family Process, 13*, 23–37.

Brody, E. M. (1970). The etiquette of filial behavior. *Aging and Human Development, 1*, 87–94. [Also in F. G. Scott & R. M. Brewer (Eds.), *Perspectives in aging*. Corvallis, OR: Continuing Educations Publication, 1971.]

Brody, E. M. (1969). Follow-up study of applicants and non-applicants to a voluntary home. *The Gerontologist, 9*, 187–196.

Brody, E. M. (1966a). The impaired aged: A follow-up study of applicants rejected by a voluntary home. *Journal of American Geriatrics Society, 14*, 414–420.

Brody, E. M. (1966b). The aging family. *The Gerontologist, 6*, 201–206.

Brody, E. M., & Brody, S. J. (1987). Service system for the aged. In *Encyclopedia of Social Work, Vol. 1*, (18th ed.). Silver Spring, MD: National Association of Social Workers, 106–126.

Brody, E. M., & Contributors. (1974). *A social work guide for long-term care facilities*. Washington, DC: U.S. GPO.

Brody, E. M., & Gummer, B. (1967) Aged applicants and non-applicants to a voluntary home: An exploratory comparison. *The Gerontologist, 7*, 234–243.

Brody, E. M., Hoffman, C., Kleban, M. H., & Schoonover, C. B. (1989). Caregiving daughters and their local siblings: Perceptions, strains, and interactions. *The Gerontologist, 29*(4),

Brody, E. M., Hoffman, C., & Winter, R. (1987b). *Family relationships of depressed, dysphoric, and nondepressed residents of nursing homes and senior housing*. Presented at 40th Annual Meeting of The Gerontological Society of America, Washington, DC.

Brody, E. M., Johnsen, P. T., & Fulcomer, M. C. (1984). What should adult children do for elderly parents? Opinions and preferences of three generations of women. *Journal of Gerontology, 39*, 736–746.

Brody, E. M., Johnsen, P. T., & Fulcomer, M. C. (1982b). *"Women in the middle" and care of the dependent elderly*. Final report on AoA grant number 90-AR-2174.

Brody, E. M., Johnsen, P. T., Fulcomer, M. C., & Lang, A. M. (1983). Women's changing roles and help to the elderly: Attitudes of three generations of women. *Journal of Gerontology, 38*, 597–607.

Brody, E. M., Johnsen, P. T., Fulcomer, M. C., & Lang, A. M. (1982a). *The dependent elderly and women's changing roles*. Final report on AoA grant number 90-A-1277.

Brody, E. M., Kleban, M. H., Hoffman, C., & Schoonover, C. B. (1988). Adult daughters and parent care: A comparison of one- two- and three-generation households. *Home Health Care Services Quarterly, 9*, 19–45.

Brody, E. M., Kleban, M. H., Johnsen, P. T., Hoffman, C., & Schoonover, C. B. (1987a). Work status and parent care: A comparison of four groups of women. *The Gerontologist, 27*, 201–208.

Brody, E. M., Kleban, M. H., Lawton, M. P., & Silverman, H. (1971). Excess disabilities of mentally impaired aged: Impact of individualized treatment. *The Gerontologist, 11*, 124–133.

Brody, E. M., Kleban, M. H., Schoonover, C. B., & Hoffman, C. (1988). *Women, work, and care of the aged: mental health effects*. Final Report on NIMH grant number MH35252.

Brody, E. M., Pruchno, R., & Dempsey, N. (1989). Differential strains of sons and daughters of the institutionalized aged. Accepted for presentation at the Annual Scientific Meeting of The Gerontological Society, Minneapolis, Nov. 1989.

Brody, E. M., Saperstein, A. R., & Lawton, M. P. (in press b). A multiservice respite program for caregivers of Alzheimer's patients. *Journal of Gerontological Social Work*.

Brody, E. M., & Schoonover, C. B. (1986). Patterns of parent-care when adult daughters work and when they do not. *The Gerontologist, 26*, 372–381.

Brody, E. M., & Spark, G. (1966). Institutionalization of the aged: A family crisis. *Family Process, 5*, 76–90.

Brody, S. J. (in press). Geriatrics and rehabilitation: Common ground and conflicts. In S. J. Brody & L. G. Pawlson (Eds.), *Aging and Rehabilitation II*. NY: Springer Publishing Co.

Brody, S. J. (1987). Strategic planning: The catastrophic approach. The Donald P. Kent Memorial Lecture. *The Gerontologist, 27*, 131–138.

Brody, S. J. (1985). The future of nursing homes. *Rehabilitation Psychology, 30*, 109–120.

Brody, S. J. (1979). The thirty-to-one paradox: Health needs and medical solutions. In *Aging: Agenda for the eighties. National Journal Issues Book*. Washington, DC.

Brody, S. J. & Magel, J. S. (1989). LTC: The long and short of it. In C. Eisdorfer and Kessler, D. (Ed.), *Caring for the elderly: Reshaping health policy*. Baltimore, MD: Johns Hopkins University Press.

Brody, S. J., Poulshock, S. W., & Masciocchi, C. F. (1978). The family caring unit: A major consideration in the long-term support system. *The Gerontologist, 18*, 556–561.

Brotman, H. B. (1980). Every ninth American. In U.S. Senate Special Committee on Aging. *Developments in aging: 1979, part I*. Washington, DC: U.S. GPO, vx–xxxvii.

Burros, M. (1988). Women: Out of the house but not out of the kitchen. *New York Times*, February 24, p. A1, C10.

Butler, R. N., & Lewis, M. (1973). *Aging and mental health: Positive psychosocial approaches*. St. Louis, MO: C. V. Mosby Co.

Callahan, J. J. (1988). Elder abuse: Some questions for policy-makers. *The Gerontologist, 28*, 453–458.

Campbell, R., & Brody, E. M. (1985). Women's changing roles and help to the elderly: Attitudes of women in the United States and Japan. *The Gerontologist, 25*, 584–592.

Cantor, M. H. (1983). Strain among caregivers: A study of experience in the United States. *The Gerontologist, 23*, 597–604.

Cantor, M. H. (1980). *Caring for the frail elderly: Impact on family, friends and neighbors*. Presented at 33rd Annual Meeting of The Gerontological Society of America, San Diego, CA.

Cantor, M. H. (1978). *The informal support system of the "familyless" elderly—Who takes over?* Paper presented at 31st Annual Meeting of the Gerontological Society, Dallas, TX.

Cath, S. M. (1972). The geriatric patient and his family. *Journal of Geriatric Psychiatry, 5*, 25–46.

Cherlin, A. (1983). Remarriage as an incomplete institution. In A. Skolnick & J. Skolnick (Eds.), *Family in Transition*, Canada: Little Brown and Co., 388–402.

Cherlin, A., & Furstenberg, F. F. (1985). Styles and strategies of grandparenting. In V. L. Bengtson & J. F. Robertson (Eds.), *Grandparenthood*. Beverly Hills, CA: Sage Publications, 97–116.

Cicirelli, V. G. (1982). Sibling influence throughout the lifespan. In M. E. Lamb & B. Sutton-Smith (Eds.), *Sibling relationships: Their nature and significance across the lifespan*. Hillsdale, NJ: Lawrence Erlbaum Associates, 267–284.

Cicirelli, V. G. (1981). *Helping elderly parents: The role of adult children*. Boston, MA: Auburn Housing Publishing. Co.

Cicirelli, V. G. (1980). Relationship of family background variables to locus of control in the elderly. *Journal of Gerontology, 35*, 108–114.

Cohler, B. J. (1983). Autonomy and interdependence in the family of adulthood: A psychological perspective. *The Gerontologist, 23*, 33–39.

Cohler, B. J., & Grunebaum, H. U. (1981). *Mothers, grandmothers, and daughters: Personality and childcare in three-generation families*. New York: John Wiley and Sons, Inc.

Collins, G. (1983). Long-distance care of elderly relatives. *New York Times*, December 29.

Community Relations Letter. (1987). The Center for Corporate Community Relations, Vol. 1, No. 7, February.

Comptroller General of the United States. (1977). Report to Congress on Home Health—*The need for a national policy to better provide for the elderly*. U.S. General Accounting Office, HRD-78-19, Washington, DC, December 30.

Corson, W., Grannemann, T., Holden, N., & Thornton, C. (1986). Channeling effects on formal community-based services and housing. Technical report 86B-10. Princeton, NJ: Mathematica Policy Research.

Cowan, A. L. (1989). Parenthood II: The nest won't stay empty. *New York Times*, March 12, pp. 1 and 30.

Crystal, S. (1982). *America's old age crisis: Public policy and the two worlds of aging*. New York: Basic Books.

Daniels, N. (1988). *Am I my parents' keeper?* New York: Oxford University Press, Inc.

Danis, B. G. (1978). *Stress in individuals caring for ill elderly relatives*. Paper presented at 31st Annual Meeting of the Gerontological Society, Dallas, TX.

Deimling, G. T., & Bass, D. M. (1986). Symptoms of mental impairment among elderly adults and their effects on family caregivers. *Journal of Gerontology, 41*, 778–784.

Deutscher, I. (1966). Words and deeds: Social science and social policy. *Social Problems, 13*, 235–254.

Doty, P. (1986). Family care of the elderly: The role of public policy. *The Milbank Quarterly, 64*, No. 1.

Doty, P., Liu, K., & Wiener, J. (1985). An overview of long-term care. *Health Care Financing Review, 6*, 69–78.

English, O. S., & Pearson, G. H. J. (1937). *Common neuroses of children and adults*. New York: W. W. Norton and Company.

Enright, R. B., & Friss, L. (1987). *Employed caregivers of brain-impaired adults*. San Francisco, CA: Family Survival Project.

Erikson, E. (1950). *Childhood and society*. New York: W. W. Norton and Company.

Fogarty, M. (1975). *Forty to sixty: How we waste the middle aged*. London: Bedford Square Press.

Frankfather, D., Smith, M. J., & Caro, F. G. (1981). *Family care of the elderly: Public initiatives and private obligations*. Lexington, MA: Lexington Books.

Friedan, B. (1963). *The feminine mystique*. New York: W. W. Norton and Company, Inc.

Friedman, D. E. (1986). Elder care: The employee benefit of the 1990s? In *Across the Board*, June, 46–51. New York: The Conference Board.

Fries, J. F. (1984). The compression of morbidity: Miscellaneous comments about a theme. *The Gerontologist, 24*, 354–359.

GAP (Group for the Advancement of Psychiatry). (1965). *Psychiatry and the aged: An introductory approach, vol. 5*. Report number 59.

George, L. K. (1988). *Why won't caregivers use community services? Unexpected findings from a respite care demonstration/evaluation*. Presented at 41st Annual Meeting of The Gerontological Society of America, San Francisco, CA.

George, L. K. (1986). Caregiver burden: Conflict between norms of reciprocity and solidarity. In K. Pillemar & R. Wolf (Eds.), *Elder abuse: Conflict in the family*. Boston, MA: Auburn House, 67–92.

George, L. K. (1984). The burden of caregiving: How much? What kinds? for whom? In *Advances in Research, 8*, No. 2. Durham, NC: Duke University, Center for the Study of Aging and Human Development.

George, L. K. (1984a). *The dynamics of caregiver burden*. Final report submitted to the AARP Andrus Foundation, December.

George, L. K. (1980). *Role transitions in late life*. Monterey, CA: Brooks/Cole Publishing Company.

Gibson, M. J. (1984). *Women and aging*. Paper presented at International Symposium on Aging, Georgian Court College, Lakewood, NJ.

Gilligan, C. (1982). *In a different voice*. Cambridge, MA: Harvard University Press.

Gold, D. T. (undated). *Siblings in old age: Their roles and relationships. (Issues in Aging, No. 1)*. Chicago, IL: The Center for Applied Gerontology.

Gold, D. T. (1987). Siblings in old age: Something special. *Canadian Journal on Aging, 6*, 199–215.

Goldfarb, A. I. (1965). Psychodynamics and the three-generation family. In E. Shanas & G. F. Streib (Eds.), *Social structure and the family: Generational relations*. Englewood Cliffs, NJ: Prentice-Hall, 10–45.

Grad, J., & Sainsbury, P. (1966). Evaluating the community psychiatric services in Chichester: Results. *Milbank Memorial Fund Quarterly, 44*, 246–278.

Gray, R., & Smith, T. (1960). Effect of employment on sex differences in attitudes toward the parental family. *Marriage and Family Living, 22*, 36–38.

Greenberg, B. (1984). The sources speak. In *The Jewish woman in the middle*. Hadassah Study Series, The Women's Zionist Organization of America, 16–22.

Gurenberg, E. M. (1977). The failures of success. *Milbank Memorial Fund Quarterly, Health and Society*, Winter, 3–24.

Gubrium, J. (1975). Being single in old age. *Aging and Human Development, 6*, 29–41.

Gubrium, J. (1974). Marital desolation and the evaluation of everyday life in old age. *Journal of Marriage and the Family, 36*, 107–113.

Gurland, B., Dean, L., Gurland, R., & Cook, D. (1978). Personal time dependency in the elderly of New York City: Findings from the U.S.-U.K. cross-national geriatric community study. In *Dependency in the Elderly of New York City*. New York: Community Council of Greater New York, 9–45.

Gwyther, L. & Blazer, D. (1984). Family therapy and the dementia patient. *American Family Physician*, May, 149–156.

Harel, Z., & Noelker, L. (1978). *The impact of social integration on the well-being and survival of institutionalized aged*. Presented at the Annual Meeting of the Gerontological Society, Dallas TX.

Henretta, J. C., & O'Rand, A. M. (1980). Labor-force participation of older married women. *Social Security Bulletin, 43*, 10–13.

Heuser, R. L. (1976). Fertility tables for birth cohorts by color: United States, 1917–73, Table 7A. Rockville, MD: U.S. DHEW, PHS, Pub. No. (HRA)76-1152, NCHS.

Hill, R., Foote, N., Aldous, J., Carlson, R., & MacDonald, R. (1970). *Family development in three generations*. Cambridge, MA: Schenkman, Publishing Co.

Hoenig, J., & Hamilton, M. (1966). Elderly patients and the burden on the household. *Psychiata et Neurologia, 152*, 281–293.

Hollender, M. H. (1988). House calls on housebound patients. In J. A. Talbott & A. Z. A. Manevitz (Eds.), *Psychiatric house calls*. Washington, DC: American Psychiatric Press, Inc., 105–106.

Horowitz, A. (1985a). Family caregiving to the frail elderly. In C. Eisodrfer, M. P.

Lawton, & G. L. Maddox (Eds.), *Annual review of gerontology and geriatrics, vol. 5.* New York: Springer Publishing Company, 194–246.

Horowitz, A. (1985b). Sons and daughters as caregivers to older parents: Differences in role performance and consequences. *The Gerontologist, 25,* 612–617.

Horowitz, A. (1982). *Predictors of caregiving involvement among adult children of the frail elderly.* Paper presented at Annual Meeting of The Gerontological Society of America, Boston, MA.

Horowitz, A., & Dobrof, R. (1982). *The role of families in providing long-term care to the frail and chronically ill elderly living in the community.* Final report submitted to the Health Care Financing Administration, DHHS, May.

Horowitz, A., Sherman, R. H., & Durmaskin, S. C. (1983). *Employment and daughter caregivers: A working partnership for older people?* Paper presented at 36th Annual Meeting of The Gerontological Society of American, San Francisco, CA.

Horowitz, A., & Shindelman, L. W. (1981). *Reciprocity and affection: Past influences on current caregiving.* Paper presented at 34th Annual Meeting of The Gerontological Society of America, Toronto, Canada.

Hunt, A. (1978). *The elderly at home.* London: Office of Population Censuses and Surveys, Her Majesty's Stationer Office.

Hunt, A. (1968). *A survey of women's employment, vol. 1.* London: Her Majesty's Stationery Office.

Ikels, C. (1983). The process of caretaker selection. *Research on Aging, 5,* 491–509.

Isaacs, B. (1971). Geriatric patients: Do their families care? *British Medical Journal, 4,* 282–286.

Johnson, C. L. (1983). Dyadic family relations and social support. *The Gerontologist, 23,* 377–383.

Johnson, C. L. (1982). Sibling solidarity: Its origin and functioning in Italian-American families. *Journal of Marriage and the Family, 44,* 155–167.

Kane, R. A., & Kane, R. L. (1981). *Assessing the elderly: A practical guide to measurement.* Lexington, MA: Lexington Books.

Katz, S., Ford, A. B., Moskowitz, R. W., Jackson, B. A., & Jaffee, M. W. (1963). Studies of illness in the aged. The index of ADL: A standardized measure of biological and psychosocial function. *Journal of the American Medical Association, 185,* 914–919.

Kemper, P. & Associates. (1986). *The evaluation of the National Long-Term Care Demonstration: Final report.* Princeton, NJ: Mathematica Policy Research.

Kent, D. P. (1965). Aging—fact or fancy. *The Gerontologist, 5.* 51–56.

Kingson, E. R., Hirshorn, B. A., & Cornman, J. M. (Eds.). (1986). *Ties that bind: The interdependence of generations.* Washington, DC: Seven Locks Press.

Kinnear, D., & Graycar, A. (1984). Aging and family dependency. *Australian Journal of Social Issues, 19,* 13–25.

Kinnear, D., & Graycar, A. (1982). *Family care of elderly people: Australian perspectives.* Social Welfare Research Centre, University of New South Wales, SWRC Reports and Proceedings, No. 23.

Kleban, M. H., Brody, E. M., & Lawton, M. P. (1971). Personality traits in the mentally impaired aged and their relationship to improvements in current functioning. *The Gerontologist, 11,* 134–140.

Kleban, M. H., Brody, E. M., Schoonover, C. B., & Hoffman, C. (1989). Family help to the elderly: Sons'-in-law perceptions of parent care. *Journal of Marriage and the Family, 51,* May.

Kleban, M. H., Brody, E. M., Schoonover, C. B., & Hoffman, C. (1984). *Some effects of parent care: Patterns of strain for working and nonworking adult daughters.* Revised version of paper given at 37th Annual Meeting of The Gerontological Society of America, San Antonio, TX.

Kovar, M. G. (1986). Aging in the eighties, age 65 years and over and living alone, contacts with family, friends, and neighbors. In *Advance Data From Vital and Health Statistics.* No. 116. DHHS Pub. No. (PHS)86-1250. NCHS, PHS, Hyattsville, MD, May 9.

Lamb, M. E., & Sutton-Smith, B. (1982). *Sibling relationships: Their nature and significance across the lifespan.* Hillsdale, NJ: Lawrence Erlbaum Associates.

Land, H. (1978). Who care for the family? *Journal of Social Policy, 7,* 257–284.

Lang, A., & Brody, E. M. (1983). Characteristics of middle-aged daughters and help to their elderly mothers. *Journal of Marriage and the Family, 45,* 193–202.

Larson, R. (1978). Thirty years of research on the subjective well-being of older Americans. *Journal of Gerontology, 33,* 109–125.

Laslett, P. (1976). Societal development and aging. In R. H. Binstock & E. Shanas (Eds.), *Handbook of aging and the social sciences.* New York: Van Nostrand Reinhold, 87–116.

Laurie, W. F. (1978). Employing the Duke OARS methodology in cost comparisons: Home services and institutionalization. In *Advances in Research, vol. 2.* No. 2. Durham, NC: Duke University, Center for the Study of Aging and Human Development.

Lawton, M. P. (in press). Social, behavioral, and environmental issues. In S. J. Brody & L. G. Pawlson (Eds.), *Aging and rehabilitation: II.* New York: Springer Publishing Co.

Lawton, M. P. (1989). Personal communication.

Lawton, M. P. (1983). Environment and other determinants of well-being in older people. The Robert W. Kleemeier Memorial Lecture, *The Gerontologist, 23,* 349–357.

Lawton, M. P. (1978). Institutions and alternatives for older people. *Health and Social Work, 3,* 109–134.

Lawton, M. P. (1971). The functional assessment of elderly people. *Journal of the American Geriatrics Society, 19,* 465–481.

Lawton, M. P., & Brody, E. M. (1969). Assessment of older people: Self-maintaining and instrumental activities of daily living. *The Gerontologist, 9,* 179–186.

Lawton, M. P., Brody, E. M., & Saperstein, A. R. (1989). A controlled study of respite service for caregivers of Alzheimer's patients. *The Gerontologist, 29,* 8–16.

Lawton, M. P., Brody, E. M., Saperstein, A. R., & Grimes, M. (in press). Respite services for caregivers: Research findings for service planning. *Home Health Services Quarterly.*

Lawton, M. P., Moss, M., Fulcomer, M. C., & Kleban, M. H. (1982). A research- and science-oriented multilevel assessment instrument. *Journal of Gerontology, 37,* 91–99.

Lebowitz, B. D. (in press) Rehabilitation and geriatric education: Mental health perspectives. In S. J. Brody & G. Pawlson (Eds.), *Rehabilitation and the Elderly II*. New York: Springer Publishing Company, Inc.

Lewis, K. (1980). Services for families of the institutionalized aged. *Aging*, DHEW, Fall, 15–19.

Liebowitz, B., Lawton, M. P., & Waldman, A. (1979). Designing for confused elderly people: Lessons from the Weiss Institute. *American Institute of Architects Journal, 68*, 59–61.

Lingg, B. A. (1975). Women Social Security beneficiaries aged 62 and older, 1960–1974. *Research and Statistics Notes*, No. 13, 9/29.

Litwak, E., & Silverstein, M. (1987). *Changes in caregiving over distance with disability*. Presented at 40th Annual Meeting of The Gerontological Society of America, Washington, DC.

Liu, K., Manton, K. G., & Liu, B. M. (1985). Home care expenses for the disabled elderly. *Health Care Financing Review, 7*, 51–58.

Liu, K. & Palesch, Y. (1981). The nursing home population: Different perspectives and implications for policy. *Health Care Financing Review, 3*, 15–23.

Locker, R. (1981). Institutionalized elderly: Understanding and helping couples. *Journal of Gerontological Social Work, 3*, 37–49.

Locker, R. (1976). Elderly couples and the institution. *Social Work, 21*, 149–150.

Longino, C. F., Biggar, J. C., Flynn, C. B., & Wiseman, R. F. (1984). *The Retirement Migration Project: A final report to the National Institute on Aging*. Coral Gables, FL: Center for Social Research on Aging, University of Miami.

Lopata, H. Z. (1973). *Widowhood in an American city*. Cambridge, MA: Schenkman Publishing Co.

Lopata, H. Z., & Brehm, H. P. (1985). *Widows and dependent wives*. New York: Praeger Publishers.

Lopata, H. Z., & Norr, K. F. (1980). Changing commitments of American women to work and family roles. *Social Security Bulletin, 43*, 3–14.

Lowenthal, M. F. (1964). *Lives in distress*. New York: Basic Books.

Lowenthal, M. F., & Haven, C. (1968). Interaction and adaptation: Intimacy as a critical variable. *American Sociological Review, 33*, 20–30.

Macken, C. L. (undated). *1982 Long-Term Care Survey: National estimates of the number and degree of functional impairments and sources of support among elderly Medicare beneficiaries living in the community*. Washington, D.C.: Health Care Financing Administration.

Manney, J. D. (1975). *Aging in American society*. Ann Arbor, MI: Institute of Gerontology.

Manton, K. G. (1988). Planning long-term care for heterogeneous older populations. In G. L. Maddox & M. P. Lawton (Eds.), *Varieties of aging. Annual review of gerontology and geriatrics, vol. 8*, New York: Springer Publishing Co.

Marshall, V. W., & Rosenthal, C. J. (1985). *The relevance of geographical proximity in intergenerational relations*. Presented at 38th Annual Meeting of The Gerontological Society of America, New Orleans, LA.

Mason, K. O., Czajka, J. L., & Arber, S. (1976). Change in U.S. women's sex-role attitudes, 1964–1974. *American Sociological Review, 41*, 573–596.

Matthews, S. H. (1987). Provision of care to old parents: Division of responsibility among adult children. *Research on Aging, 9*, 45–60.

Mercier, J. M., Paulson, L., & Morris, E. W. (1987). *The effect of proximity on the aging parent/child relationship.* Presented at 40th Annual Meeting of The Gerontological Society of America, Washington, DC.

Miller, J. A. (1987). The sandwich generation. *Working Mother.* January.

Mindel, C. H. (1979). Multigenerational family households: Recent trends and implications for the future. *The Gerontologist, 19*, 456–463.

Montgomery R. J. V. (1988). *Respite services: Correlates and consequences of use.* Presented at 41st Annual Meeting of The Gerontological Society of America, San Francisco, CA.

Moss, M., & Kurland, P. (1979). Family visiting with institutionalized mentally impaired aged. *Journal of Gerontological Social Work, 1*, 271–278.

Murray, J. (1973). Family structure in the preretirement years. *Social Security Bulletin, 36*, 25–45.

Myllyluoma, J., & Soldo, B. J. (1980). *Family caregivers to the elderly: Who are they?* Presented at 33rd Annual Meeting of the Gerontological Society, San Diego, CA.

NCHSR (National Center for Health Services Research). (1989). Unpublished Advance Data based on 1985 Nursing Home Survey.

National Institute on Aging. (1982). *Population Aging.* Report of a Conference sponsored by the American Council of Life Insurance and Health Insurance Association of America, May.

Neugarten, B. L. (1973). Personality changes in later life: A developmental perspective. In C. Eisdorfer & M. P. Lawton (Eds.), *Psychological processes in aging.* Washington, DC: American Psychological Association, 311–335.

Neugarten, B. L. (1968). *Middle age and aging.* Chicago, IL: University of Chicago Press.

Neugarten, B. L. (1968a). Adult personality: Toward a psychology of life cycle. In B. L. Neugarten (Ed.), *Middle age and aging.* Chicago, IL: University of Chicago Press, 137–147.

Neugarten, B. L., & Hagestad, G. O. (1976). Age and the life course. In R. H. Binstock & E. Shanas (Eds.), *Handbook of aging and the social sciences.* New York: Van Nostrand Reinhold, Co., 35–57.

New York Times Magazine. (1979). Betty Friedan, "Feminism takes a new turn." Section 6, 11/18.

Noelker, L. S., & Poulshock, S. W. (1982). *The effects on families of caring for impaired elderly in residence.* Final report of AoA grant number 90-AR-2112. Cleveland, OH: Benjamin Rose Institute.

NRTA-AARP (National Retired Teachers Association-American Association of Retired Persons). (1981). *National survey of older Americans.* Washington, DC, July.

Nye, F. I., & Berardo, F. (1973). *The family: Its structure and interaction.* New York: Macmillan Publishing Co., Inc.

Otten, A. L. (1989). Women's growing role in the work force. *The Wall Street Journal,* March 7, p. B1.

Parmelee, P. A., Katz, I. R., & Lawton, M. P. (1989). Depression among institutionalized aged: Assessment and prevalence estimation. *Journal of Gerontology*, *44*(1), 22–29.

Parsons, T., & Bales, R. (1955). *Family, socialization, and interaction process*. Glencoe, IL: Free Press.

Peck, R. C. (1968). Psychological developments in the second half of life. In B. L. Neugarten (Ed.), *Middle age and aging: A reader in social psychology*. Chicago, IL: University of Chicago Press, 88–92.

Pillimer, K., & Finkelhor, D. (1988). The prevalence of elder abuse: A random sample survey. *The Gerontologist, 28*, 51–57.

Posner, W. (1961). Basic issues in casework with older people. *Social Casework, 42*, 234–240.

Cartoon. *Punch*, October 21, 1988, p. 16.

Quinn, M. J., & Tomita, S. K. (1986). *Elder abuse and neglect*. New York: Springer Publishing Company, Inc.

Reece, D., Walz, T., & Hageboech, H. (1983). Intergenerational care providers of non-institutionalized frail elderly: Characteristics and consequences. *Journal of Gerontological Social Work, 5*, 21–34.

Reid, O. M. (1966). Aging Americans. A review of cooperative research projects. *Welfare in Review, 4*, U.S. DHEW, 1–2.

Rivlin, A. M., & Wiener, J. M. (1988). *Caring for the disabled elderly: Who will pay?* Washington, DC: Brookings Institution.

Robinson, B., & Thurnher, M. (1979). Taking care of aged parents: A family cycle transition. *The Gerontologist, 19*, 586–593.

Rosenheim, M. K. (1965). Social welfare and its implications for family planning. In E. Shanas & G. F. Streib (Eds.), *Social structure and the family: Generational relations*. Englewood Cliffs, NJ: Prentice-Hall, Inc.

Rosenmayhr, L., & Kockeis, E. (1963). Propositions for a sociological theory of aging and the family. *International Social Science Journal, 15*, 410–426.

Rosow, I. (1965). Intergenerational relationships: Problems and proposals. In E. Shanas & G. F. Streib (Eds.), *Social Structure and the family: Generational relations*. Englewood Cliffs, NJ: Prentice-Hall, Inc., 341–378.

Ross, H. G., & Milgram, J. J. (1982). Important variables in adult sibling relationships: A qualitative study. In M. E. Lamb & B. Sutton-Smith (Eds.), *Sibling relationships: Their nature and significance across the lifespan*. Hillsdale, NJ: Lawrence Erlbaum Associates, 225–250.

Rossiter, C., & Wicks, M. (1982). *Crisis or challenge? Family care, elderly people, and social policy*. Occasional Paper No. 8. London: Study Commission on the Family.

Sainsbury, P., & Grad de Alercon, J. (1970). The effects of community care in the family of the geriatric patient. *Journal of Geriatric Psychiatry, 4*, 23–41.

Sainsbury, P., & Grad, J. (1966). Evaluating the community psychiatric services in Chichester: Aims and methods of research. *Milbank Memorial Fund Quarterly, XLIV*, 231–242.

Sanford, J. R. A. (1975). Tolerance of debility in elderly dependents by supporters at home: Its significance for hospital practice. *British Medical Journal, 3*, 471–473.

Saperstein, A. R. (in press). Increasing families' use of formal services. In S. J. Brody

& L. G. Pawlson (Eds.), *Aging and Rehabilitation: II*. New York: Springer Publishing Co.

Saperstein, A. R., & Brody, E. M. (in press). What types of respite services do family caregivers of Alzheimer's patients want? *Aging Magazine*.

Schneider, E. L., & Brody, J. A. (1983). Aging, natural death, and the compression of morbidity: Another view. *The New England Journal of Medicine, 309*, 854–856.

Schoen, R. (1985). Marriage and divorce in twentieth century American cohorts. *Demography, 22*, 101–114.

Schoonover, C. B., Brody, E. M., Hoffman, C., & Kleban, M. H. (1988). Parent care and geographically distant children. *Research on Aging, 10*, 472–492.

Schorr, A. L. (1980). "*. . . they father and they mother . . .": A second look at filial responsibility and family policy*. U.S. Department of Health and Human Services, Social Security Administration, SSA Publication No. 13-11953, July.

Schorr, A. L. (1960). *Filial responsibility in the modern American family*. Washington, DC: U.S. DHEW, Social Security Administration, GPO, June.

Schwartz, A. N. (1979). Psychological dependency: An emphasis on the later years. In P. K. Ragan (Ed.), *Aging parents* (pp. 116–125). Los Angeles: Ethel Andrus Gerontology Center, University of Southern California Press.

Seelback, W. C. (1977). Gender differences in expectations for filial responsibility. *The Gerontologist, 17*, 421–425.

Select Committee on Aging, House of Representatives. (1988). Subcommittee on Human Services, Comm. Pub. No. 100-665. Washington, DC: U.S. Government Printing Office.

Shanas, E. (1979a). Social myth as hypothesis: The case of the family relations of old people. *The Gerontologist, 19*, 3–9.

Shanas, E. (1979b). The family as a social support system in old age. *The Gerontologist, 19*, 169–174.

Shanas, E. (1973). Family-kin networks and aging in cross-cultural perspective. *Journal of Marriage and the Family*, August, 505–511.

Shanas, E. (1967). Family help patterns and social class in three countries. *Journal of Marriage and the Family, 29*, 257–266.

Shanas, E. (1963). *The unmarried old person in the United States: Living arrangements and care in illness, myth and fact*. Paper presented at International Social Science Research Seminar in Gerontology, Makaryd, Sweden.

Shanas, E. (1961). *Family relationships of older people*. Health Information Foundation, Research Series 20. Chicago, IL: University of Chicago.

Shanas, E. (1960). Family responsibility and the health of older people. *Journal of Gerontology, 15*, 408–411.

Shanas, E., & Streib, G. F. (1965). *Social structure and the family: Generational relations*. Englewood Cliffs, NJ: Prentice-Hall, Inc.

Shanas, E., Townsend, P., Wedderburn, D., Friis, H., Milhog, P., & Stehouwer, J. (1968). *Old people in three industrial societies*. New York: Atherton Press.

Simos, B. G. (1973). Adult children and their aging parents. *Social Work, 18*, 78–84.

Simos, B. G. (1970). Relations of adults with aging parents. *The Gerontologist, 10*, 135–139.

Smith, K. F., & Bengtson, V. L. (1979). Positive consequences of institutionalization: Solidarity between elderly parents and their middle-aged children. *The Gerontologist, 19,* 438–447.

Soldo, B. J. (1982a). *Supply of informal care services: Variations and effects on services utilization patterns.* Report for contract number HHS-100-80-0158, DHHS. Washington, DC: Center for Population Research, Georgetown University.

Soldo, B. J. (1982b). *Effects of number and sex of adult children on LTC service use patterns.* Presented at 1982 Annual Meeting of Social Security Administration, Boston, MA.

Soldo, B. J. (1980). *Family caregivers to the elderly: Who are they?* Paper presented at 33rd Annual Meeting of The Gerontological Society of America, San Diego, CA.

Soldo, B. J., & Myers, G. C. (1976). *The effects of life-time fertility on the living arrangements of older women.* Presented at the Annual Meeting of the Gerontological Society, New York.

Soldo, B. J., & Myllyluoma, J. (1983). Caregivers who live with dependent elderly. *The Gerontologist, 23,* 605–611.

Soldo, B. J., & Sharma, M. (1980). *Families who purchase vs. families who provide care services to elderly relatives.* Presented at 33rd Annual Meeting of the Gerontological Society, San Diego, CA.

Spark, G., & Brody, E. M. (1970). The aged are family members. *Family Process, 9,* 195–210.

Stafford, R., Backman, E., & Dibona, P. (1977). The division of labor among cohabitating and married couples. *Journal of Marriage and the Family, 39,* 43–58.

Stehouwer, J. (1968). The household and family relations of old people. In E. Shanas, P. Townsend, D. Wedderburn, H. Friis, P. Milhoj, & J. Stehouwer (Eds.), *Old people in three industrial societies.* New York: Atherton Press, 177–226.

Stephens, M. P., & Townsend, A. (1988). *Daily stressors for family caregivers to institutionalized AD patients.* Presented at 41st Annual Meeting of The Gerontological Society of America, San Francisco, CA.

Stoller, E. P. (1983). Parental caregiving by adult children. *Journal of Marriage and the Family, 45,* 851–858.

Stoller, E. P., & Earl, L. (1983). Help with activities of everyday life: Sources of support for the noninstitutionalized elderly. *The Gerontologist, 23,* 64–70.

Stone, R. (1986). Personal communication.

Stone, R., Cafferata, G. L., & Sangl, J. (1987). Caregivers of the frail elderly: A national profile. *The Gerontologist, 27,* 616–626.

Streib, G. F. (1958). Family patterns in retirement. *Journal of Social Issues, 14,* No. 2.

Streib, G. F., & Shanas, E. (1965). An introduction. In E. Shanas & G. F. Streib (Eds.), *Social structure and the family: Generational relations.* Englewood Cliffs, NJ: Prentice-Hall, Inc.

Sundstrom, G. (1986). Intergenerational mobility and the relationship between adults and their aging parents in Sweden. *The Gerontologist, 26,* 367–371.

Sussman, M. (1979). *Social and economic supports and family environment for the elderly*. Final report to the Administration on Aging, grant number 90-A-316.

Sussman, M. (1965). Relationships of adult children with their parents in the United States. In E. Shanas & G. F. Shanas (Eds.), *Social structure and the family: Generational relations*. Englewood Cliffs, NJ: Prentice-Hall, Inc., 62–92.

Sutton-Smith, B., & Rosenberg, B. (1970). *The sibling*. New York: Holt, Rinehart and Winston.

Taeuber, C. M. (1983). *America in transition: An aging society*. U.S. Bureau of the Census, Current Population Reports, Special Studies Series P-23, No. 128. Washington, DC: GPO.

Thornton, A., & Freedman, D. (1979). Changes in the sex role attitudes of women, 1962–1977: Evidence from a panel study. *American Sociological Review, 44*, 831–842.

Tobin, S. S., & Kulys, R. (1980). The family and services. In C. Eisdorfer (Ed.), *Annual review of gerontology and geriatrics, vol. 1*. New York: Springer Publishing Co., 370–399.

Tobin, S. S., & Lieberman, M. A. (1976). *Last home for the aged: Critical implications of institutionalization*. San Francisco, CA: Jossey-Bass.

Townsend, A., Deimling, G., & Noelker, L. (1988). *Transition to nursing home care: Sources of stress and family members mental health*. Presented at 41st Annual Meeting of The Gerontological Society of America, San Francisco, CA.

Townsend, P. (1968). The household and family relations of old people. In E. Shanas, P. Townsend, D. Wedderburn, D. Friis, P. Milhoj, & J. Stehouwer (Eds.), *Old people in three industrial societies*. New York: Atherton Press, p. 178.

Townsend, P. (1965). The effects of family structure on the likelihood of admission to an institution in old age: The application of a general theory. In E. Shanas & G. F. Streib (Eds.), *Social structure and the family: Generational relations*. Englewood Cliffs, NJ: Prentice-Hall, Inc., 163–187.

The Travelers Companies. (1985). *The Travelers employee caregiver survey*. Hartford, CT, June.

Treas, J., & Bengtson, V. L. (1982). The demography of middle and late-life transitions. *Annals of the American Academy of Political and Social Science, 464*, 11–21.

Troll, L. E. (1971). The family of later life: A decade review. *Journal of Marriage and the Family, 33*, 263–290.

Troll, L. E., & Bengtson, V. L. (1979). Generations in the family. In W. Burr, R. Hill, F. I. Nye, & I. Reiss (Eds.), *Contemporary theories about the family: Research-based theories. Vol. I*. New York: Free Press, 127–161.

Troll, L. E., & Stapley, J. (1985). Elders and extended family system: Health, family salience, and affect. In J. M. A. Munnich (Ed.), *Life span and change in a gerontological perspective*. New York: Academic Press, p. 211.

Turnbull, A. P., Summers, J. A., & Brotherson, M. J. (1984). *Manual 5, working with families with disabled members: A family systems approach*. Salinas, KS: University of Kansas.

Uhlenberg, P. (1980). Death and the family. *Journal of Family History, 5*, 313–320.

Uhlenberg, P. (1974). Cohort variations in family life cycle experiences of U.S. females. *Journal of Marriage and the Family, 36*, 284–292.

United Kingdom Statistical Service. (1979). *Social trends no. 9.* ISBN No. 0-11-630176-7. London: HMSO.

U.S. Bureau of the Census. (1988). Current Population Reports. Series P-20, No. 427. *Fertility of American women: June 1987.* Washington, DC: U.S. Government Printing Office.

U.S. Bureau of the Census. (1986). *Statistical brief: Age structure of the U.S. population in the 21st century.* SB-1-86. Washington, DC: GPO, December.

U.S. Bureau of the Census. (1984). *Projects of the population of the United States, by age, sex, and race: 1983–2080.* Publication P-25, No. 952. Washington, DC: GPO.

U.S. Bureau of the Census. (1978). *1976 survey of institutionalized persons.* Current Population Reports, Special Studies, Series P-23, No. 69, June.

U.S. Department of Commerce, Bureau of the Census. (1988). Who's helping out? Support networks among American families. *Current Population Reports,* Household Economic Studies, Series P-70, No. 13, October.

U.S. Department of Commerce, Bureau of the Census. (1982a). Decennial census of population, 1900–1980 and projections of the population of the United States: 1982–2050 (Advance report). *Current Population Reports.* Series P-25, No. 922, October.

U.S. Department of Commerce, Bureau of the Census. (1982b). Fertility of American Women: June 1981 (Advance Report). *Current Population Reports,* Series P-20, No. 369, March.

U.S. DHEW (Department of Health, Education and Welfare, PHS). (1972). *Home care for persons aged 55 and over in the U.S.* July 1966–June 1968, Vital and Health Statistics, Series 10, No. 73, July.

U.S. DHHS (Department of Health and Human Services, PHS). (1985). *Women's health: Report of the Public Health Service Task Force on Women's Health, Vol. II.*

U.S. DHHS (Department of Health and Human Services) Social Security Administration. (1980). *Women Social Security beneficiaries age 62 and older, 1960–79.* Research and Statistics Note No. 8. Washington, DC: Office of Research and Statistics, 7/21.

U.S. Department of Labor, Women's Bureau. (1986). *Facts on U.S. working women.* Caring for Elderly Family Members, Fact Sheet No. 86-4, Washington, DC, October.

U.S. Department of Labor, Bureau of Labor Statistics. (1980). *Employment and earnings.* August 1980, 27, No. 8. Washington, DC: U.S. GPO.

U.S. Department of Labor. (1979). Bureau of Labor Statistics, unpublished data, October.

U.S. General Accounting Office. (1983). *Medicaid and nursing home care: Cost increases and the need for services are creating problems for the states and the elderly.* October 21.

U.S. General Accounting Office, Comptroller General of the United States. (1977). *The Well-Being of Older People in Cleveland, Ohio.* Number RD-77-70, Washington, DC, April 19.

U.S. House of Representatives Select Committee on Aging. (1979). *Mid-life women: Policy proposals on their problems.* U.S. GPO, Washington, DC.

U.S. House of Representatives Select Committee on Aging. (1981). *Elder abuse: An examination of a hidden problem.* 97th Congress Comm. Pub. No. 97-277. Washington, DC: Government Printing Office.

U.S. NCHS (National Center for Health Statistics). (1986). *Advance Report of Final Marriage Statistics, 1983.* Vol. 35, No. 1, Supplement, DHHS, PHS, May 2.

U.S. NCHS (National Center for Health Statistics). (1985). *Preliminary data from the 1985 National Nursing Home Survey.* Division of Health Care Statistics.

U.S. NCHS (National Center for Health Statistics). (1985). DHHS publication number PHS86-1232, Table 10, p. 38, December.

U.S. NCHS (National Center for Health Statistics). (1978). *Advance date. An overview of nursing home characteristics: Provisional data from the 1977 National Nursing Home Survey.* U.S. DHEW, No. 35, September 6.

U.S. NCHS (National Center for Health Statistics). (1975). *Preliminary data from the 1973–1974 National Nursing Home Survey.*

U.S. NCHS (National Center for Health Statistics). (1973). National Health Survey. *Characteristics of residents in nursing home and personal care homes. U.S. June–August 1969.* Series 121, No. 19, HSMHA.

U.S. National Committee on Vital and Health Statistics. (1978). *Long-term health care: Minimum data set.* Preliminary Report of the Technical Consultant Panel on the Long-Term Health Care Data Set, PHS, NCHS, September 8.

Upp, M. (1982). A look at the economic status of the aged then and now. *Social Security Bulletin, 45,* No. 3, 16–22.

Vincent, C. (1972). An open letter to the "caught" generation. *Family Coordinator, 21,* 143–150.

Walker, K. (1970). Time spent by husbands in household work. *Family Economics Review,* June, 8–11.

Walsh, F. (1980). The family in later life. In E. Carter & M. C. McGoldrick (Eds.), *The family life cycle: A framework for family therapy.* New York: Gardner Press, Inc., 198–220.

Walum, L. R. (1977). *The Dynamics of sex and gender.* Chicago, IL: Rand McNally College Publishing.

Weed, J. A. (1981). *National estimates of marital dissolution and survivorship, vital and health statistics: Series III, analytic studies.* No. 19. DHHS publication number (PHS)81-1403.

Weinberg, J. (1976). On adding insight to injury. *The Gerontologist, 16,* 4–10.

Weithorn, C. J. (1975). Women's role in cross-cultural perspective. In R. K. Unger & F. L. Denmark (Eds.), *Woman: Dependent or independent variable?* New York: Psychological Dimensions, Inc., 276–292.

Wolf, D. A., & Soldo, B. J. (1986). *The households of older unmarried: Microdecision model of shared living arrangements.* Presented at Annual Meeting of the Population Association of America, San Francisco, CA.

Wood, V., & Robertson, J. F. (1978). Friendship and kinship interaction: Differential effect on the morale of the elderly. *Journal of Marriage and the Family,* May, 367–375.

York, J. L., & Calsyn, R. J. (1977). Family involvement in nursing homes. *The Gerontologist, 17,* 500–505.

Zarit, S. H., Reever, K. E., & Bach-Peterson, J. (1980). Relatives of the impaired aged: Correlates of feelings of burden. *The Gerontologist, 20,* 649–655.

Zimmer, A. H., & Sainer, J. S. (1978). *Strengthening the family as an informal support for their aged: Implications for social policy and planning.* Presented at 31st Annual Meeting.of the Gerontological Society, Dallas, TX.

Index